The Shooting Gallery

The Shooting Gallery

GAZ HUNTER

VICTOR GOLLANCZ

LONDON

First published in Great Britain 1998
by Victor Gollancz
An imprint of the Cassell Group
Wellington House, 125 Strand, London WC2R 0BB

© Gaz Hunter 1998

The right of Gaz Hunter to be identified as author of
this work has been asserted by him in accordance with
the Copyright, Designs and Patents Act, 1988.

All photographs are reproduced by courtesy of the author.

A catalogue record for this book is
available from the British Library.

ISBN 0 575 06731 4

Printed in Australia by Griffin Press Pty Ltd

98 99 5 4 3 2 1

To Ginger Meredith

Author's note

Some events detailed in this book have been altered to protect the security of individuals and organizations concerned.

Acronyms

14 Int & SY	Intelligence and Security
AFV	Armoured Fighting Vehicle
AIFV	Airborne Infantry Fighting Vehicles
APC	Armoured Patrol Car
ASEAN	Association of South-East Asian Nations
ATF	Alcohol, Tobacco and Firearms
BG	Bodyguard
BTR	Nato code for Russian Armoured Car type
CLF	Commander Land Forces
CO	Commanding Officer
CPO	Close Protection Officer
CRW	Counter-revolutionary Warfare
CT	Counter-terrorism
CTR	Close Target Reconnaissance
DF	Direction Finder
DshK	12.7 mm Triple-A Gun
DMSU	Divisional Mobile Support Units
DPM	Disruptive Pattern Material
DRA	Democratic Republic of Afghanistan
DS	Directing Staff
DSF	Directorate of Special Forces
EMOE	Explosive Methods of Entry
EXFIL	Exfiltration
FCO	Foreign and Commonwealth Office
GPMG	General Purpose Machine-gun
GRU	Soviet Military Intelligence
HAHO	High Altitude High Opening
HALO	High Altitude Low Opening
HE	High Explosive
HEAP	High-explosive Armour Piercing

HF	Height-finder
HMSU	Headquarters Mobile Support Units
HRT	Hostage Rescue Team
ICRC	International Committee for the Red Cross
INFIL	Infiltration
IR	Infra-red
LUP	Laying Up Point
LWB	Long Wheel Base
MILO	Military Liaison Officer
MLRS	Multiple-Launch Rocket System
MRF	Military Reaction Force
MSR	Main Supply Route
NITAT	Northern Ireland Training Advisory Team
OC	Officer Commanding
OP	Observation Post
Pinkies	LWB Land Rovers
QRF	Quick Reaction Force
RPD	7.62 mm Machine-gun
RUF	Revolutionary United Front
SD	Special Duties
SF	Special Forces
SIS	Secret Intelligence Service (MI6)
SLR	Self-loading Rifles
SOP	Standard Operating Procedures
SSM	Squadron sergeant-major
SSU	Special Support Units
SWAT	Special Weapons Assault Team
TAP	Old-style round parachute
TCG	Tasking and Co-ordination Group
TEL	Scud Transporter, Erector, Launcher
UGS	Undisturbed Ground Sensors
VCP	Vehicle Checkpoint
VOPO	East German Police
WO	Warrant Officer
XMG	Crossmaglen

Prologue: *Afghanistan, July 1985*

It was quiet that day. We'd been lying around dozing in the sun, waiting for the Soviet convoy expected through at last light. Most of the Mujahideen were wrapped in their blankets, fast asleep.

The noise came first, a slow thudding on the air. I leaped up, staring. Only one thing made that sound: *whop, whop, whop, whop*. All around me the Mujahideen were scattering, going to ground. Something glinted in the harsh light. It was a Hind D, nose down and coming fast, smudge-brown against the blue sky. A second gunship reared up alongside the first. They had climbed vertically up behind the high ground to our right, catching us completely unawares. It was no more than a kilometre to the edge of the plateau. Already, they were close enough to open fire.

My brain raced while I stood like stone.

There were culverts and holes at the back of the plateau, natural trenches cut over the years by the spring melt-waters. These were my only chance. I turned, and ran as I'd never run before. There was a hollow rushing sound in the air. Looking back, I saw flashes from beneath the wings of the lead Hind. Immediately, the rockets smashed down into the dry ground, flinging great lumps of rock and earth high into the air.

I'd been resting about fifty metres back from the mortar emplacements. Maybe they'd go for the weapons first. Still running, I glanced back again. Rockets were snaking down from the gunships in wave after wave, each salvo leaving long trails of white smoke. A mortar cartwheeled high up into the air, hung for a moment, then crashed back down to earth, bits of a man mingled with it. My feet pounded in time with my heart. Ground strikes were skipping across the surface of the plateau, coming straight at me. I felt the fear of God. In a second that would be me, scattered bone and sinew, with my limbs blown off. I saw a cutting in the ground ahead, and dived headlong for it.

I knew all about the Hinds. As an airborne artillery platform, the Hind D gunship was second to none. It had a four-barrelled 12.7 mm rotary cannon in its bulbous chin turret, remotely operated by a gunner who sat up safely, like the pilot, behind a thick layer of armoured glass. Four rocket-pods hung under its sawn-off wings, each holding thirty-two fat 57 mm rockets. Apart from their awesome firepower the Hinds *looked* terrifying, their double-decker cockpits like the bulging eyes of some gigantic killer bug. They hovered there above us, sure of themselves, contemptuous, not even bothering to weave.

Their rotary cannon opened up now, firing HEAP (High-explosive Armour Piercing) rounds. They made a hideous *Zzzzp! Zzzzp!* noise as they fired, like a massive piece of cloth tearing. I knew the HEAP would cut straight through the soft ground I was hiding in; I could already feel the shuddering impact of the huge shells, feel my bones splintering. I crawled forward. A sharp bend in the culvert ahead led me back in towards the rock face. I burrowed frantically into this pocket of earth and stone, trying to bury myself alive, anything to get out of view. The noise was fantastic, a continuous explosion of sound from the rockets and guns, the slow, arrogant thump of the gigantic five-bladed rotors, the cannon shells ripping and thudding into the earth.

And into the Mujahideen.

Through the continual roar, I could hear people screaming. Then the ground started shaking all around me, the shells thwacking through the earth at my feet as they came my way. A huge zip was working up and down in the air directly overhead, *Zzrrrp! Zzrrrp!*

I remembered when we'd been watching the earlier Hind attack on the village. One of the Mujahideen turned to me then and said, 'The Hinds churn the world to death.' Now I understood what he meant – the gunships ate the ground, chewing it and spitting it out, shredding humans and weapons alike.

I lay there, frozen. The earthquake moved on. Against all reason, I stuck my head up. It was mayhem. The air was filled with dust and smoke and debris. Through this, I could see the Hinds, spitting orange tracer, the eye-searing flash of yet more exploding rockets. And all the time, that deafening, crushing noise beating down. Unbelievably, one of the Mujahideen was standing out in plain view behind a DshK triple-A gun, pouring his defiance straight down the throat of a Hind. Another ran to his aid. In that moment its quad cannon flicked on to them, almost lazily tearing both men and the gun apart. One moment they were there, the next they had been vaporized.

I recognized one of them – it was Frodo.

Maybe it was that. For a second, the paralysing fear left me. I was still clutching the AK-47. I brought it up, stuck its barrel on the edge of the trench and rammed the butt back hard into my shoulder. There was no need to aim – the closer of the two Hinds filled the sky, big as a truck. I saw no detail, only this huge thundering mass in the air above me. I fired three or four long bursts right into it, until the hammer clicked dry on the breech.

I didn't see the big Gatling move, only the bright flash from under its nose, and a grey blur of shells in the air.

'Oh, fucking hell.'

I rammed my face hard back down into the ground. For some reason, then, I thought about England, and home, and Natalie, the nine-month-old baby girl I'd hardly seen. And now wouldn't see again. I thought about dying where I was, in the middle of nowhere, thousands of miles from home, in an unmarked grave. Would they even bury an infidel? I didn't want to die without anyone to mourn – or even take any notice. I wanted to be buried in the Regiment's cemetery, at St Martin's in Hereford, along with my mates. I was sure I was going to die.

The ground started shaking again. The earthquake was coming back. Cannon shells sliced through the thick shoulder of the run-off channel to my left, blasting the earth and stone of the trench out on to me. I had the *shamag* wrapped tightly across my face, but the dust got in everywhere, in my eyes and nose and lungs. It was hard even to breathe. '*Should I move? Should I move?*' screamed in my head. I had to move. At any moment an armour-piercing round was going to come straight through the dirt and the brittle rock – and straight through me.

I got up and hared for the base of the cliff, racing the gunner. There was another hole, wider than the last, with a big boulder in the middle of it. Curling tight in around the base of the rock, I flattened myself, wedging my body hard up against it, trying to get myself right inside and away from that withering storm of shells.

He'd seen me. Shells crashed and splintered into the great rock, on and on as if it would never end. He was trying to saw through the stone with his cannon. Great lumps of it crashed down into my back and legs – I didn't have to bury myself any more, the gunner was doing it for me. Looking up, I saw long projections of rock sticking out that would crash down on me and finish the job if he put a burst up into the cliff face. This time there really was nowhere to hide, no escape from the creeping death. It was only luck that made the difference between living and dying, the chance flick of a gunner's wrist.

Then, silence.

I lay there for a long while, face in the dirt, not daring to believe they had gone. At last, I stood up. The giddy relief that pumped through me was almost worse than the fear. Then the aftershock hit, a trembling sickness of terror and unused adrenaline. I was covered from head to foot in a thick layer of dirt and dust. It was plugging my nostrils, caked into my mouth. I spat, repeatedly, blowing out my nostrils, shaking myself to get some of the filth off. I couldn't believe I was still alive.

Someone shouted, 'Mig! Mig!'

Oh shit, I thought. That's right. That's what they do – first the Hinds, then the Migs. How could I forget that? When the bombs came, no little hole in the ground was going to save me.

I saw two of the surviving Mujahideen, then, running up around the corner of the cliff to my left. I tried to move, but my legs refused to work. My ears were echoing and ringing as if I'd been shut up inside a giant bell. I felt totally disoriented and I had a strong urge to vomit. Leaning forward, I made myself stumble; the stumble became a trot and then I took off after them at top speed. There might be time. I got down among the boulders at the back of the peak, waiting for the next attack.

PART ONE

The Shooting Gallery

Chapter One

The SAS was my life before I knew I had one. It took my father away from us and made him a total stranger. For Sergeant Kenneth Hunter of the SAS, 12 August 1954 was no different from any other day. His first son was being born, but there was no way he could be there with my mother or celebrate: he was in the jungles of Malaya, helping to counter the six-year-old Communist uprising. And his duty, as always in the SAS, came first, last and always.

Right through the worst years of that campaign, which lasted from 1948 to 1957, Dad was away almost all the time. I was two years old before I remember even meeting him. Then, one day, a dark-faced man turned up on our doorstep, lean and brown and fit-looking. He was hammering at the door and shouting, 'Let me in!' at the top of his voice. My mother was out in the little patch of garden we had at the back, hanging up the washing. My older brother Steven was standing at the top of the stairs; I was a few steps back from him. The roaring giant got in, and came bounding up the steps at us with his arms outstretched. Steven screamed in fear and threw his toy gun. It bounced off the stranger's head, leaving a tiny cut.

'Hands up!' I shouted, pointing my Lone Star Winchester rifle.

'Great!' said my dad, ruefully, rubbing off the blood. 'I survive years of fighting Communists out in the jungle, and get ambushed by my own sons!'

A month later he went back to the Far East – for another two years.

I was used to Dad being away, not knowing what he was doing but being proud of him. I had this picture of him in my mind's eye, a sort of Humphrey Bogart character, hacking through the dense jungle, picking off leeches with a grim smile, harder than steel and ready for anything. You invent a mum or a dad, when they're not there. When he was due home, we'd be screwed up to fever pitch with excitement, and then some new emergency would stop him coming. On the rare occasions we went on holiday, Dad only came with us once. Very few of my schoolfriends ever met him.

In those days the SAS was an unknown army. It fought in unknown wars, with little or no public recognition. There was no Special Forces pay, either, then, the troopers had no spare money to spend on insurance policies, or to put by for a rainy day. So getting killed for your country was a bad idea – not least for the folks back home. Money was always in short supply and Mum would make ends meet as best she could, going without so 'the two boys', as she called us, would have what they wanted.

Our married quarter was on the edge of SAS headquarters, known as Bradbury Lines. The camp lies partially concealed in a long fold of dead ground: it's very hard to see, unless you know it's there. The tiny house we lived in backed on to a field, with a railway line on one side and a stream on the other spanned by a small bridge. It was here that I'd play, most of the time, part of the 'Bridge Gang', camping out in tents on the little spit of flat land by the brook in summer and building snowmen on it in winter. Most of us were children of the SAS: there was Russ, Baz (who was to die of a brain tumour), Duck and Bambi. Also there was 'Pudding Head', who got stung by a wasp on his forehead, which swelled up to a huge size and took days and days to go back down. There was Fisher, one of a pair of brothers, who ran into a sandpit playing in the field at night and broke his leg; so we put him on a bike and pushed him to the hospital in town, a good three miles away. And there was 'Whaffer', who had a beard even at twelve years old, and my own brother, Steven, who was running around the camp playing hide-and-seek one night when an Alsatian guard-dog caught him where he shouldn't be and ripped his side open. He somehow got away from the dog and carried on playing until tea-time, open wound or no. That was Steven, unflappable even at six.

It was a new camp, then, and totally open: there was no terrorist threat to UK bases and we had the run of it. The clock-tower in the middle of the camp fascinated me. Looking like a smaller version of Big Ben, it had the names of all the troopers who'd died fighting for their country engraved on its four sides. They'd fought and fallen in strange, far-away places, like Dofar, that I'd never heard of. I wondered what would happen if one of the Bridge Gang fathers died – would they put his name up, and what if it were my dad?

These were golden days. We'd play on the assault courses, talk to the soldiers, and pretend to be them, fighting our endless battles between the wooden 'spider' huts where the unmarried SAS men lived. One day, when I was seven, the RSM caught me somewhere I shouldn't have been, and placed me under lock and key in the guard-room: 'Not', he barked at me from under a beetling brow, 'for doing wrong, boy, but for getting caught!'

We were always out, in all weathers, Steve and I; my mother had a hard time keeping up with us. We'd 'blaze' the hedgerows and the trees, cutting tiny notches out of the bark with our pocket-knives to mark our trail, roaming the rolling green of the fields and creeping through the coppices, searching for nuts, birds' nests, frogs and toads and mice. One day, I went off with the gang to play by an old well in the woods up on Dindor Hill. For some reason, I left the other boys, and trudged back down to the camp on my own. Sometimes, on cold winter days, I'd go into the Naafi canteen, and try to get the soldiers in there to tell me stories, or maybe even buy me chocolate. Although it was still fairly early in the afternoon, it was already getting dark, with a black sky threatening yet more snow. An hour or so later, my mother looked out of her kitchen window and spotted the gang. Everyone was there except me.

'Where's Gary?' she asked. 'He went off with you boys, didn't he? Where's he gone?'

'He's down the well,' replied one of my six-year-old friends, helpfully.

'Down the well? What well? What do you mean? How long's he been down there?'

'Hours,' replied the boy. 'He was fighting a lion.'

19

My mother pressed the emergency button. Every SAS man who was in camp at the time turned out to rescue me, and half the women on the estate. They all trooped up to Dindor Hill, where they gathered round the lip of this deep well, shining torches down it, shouting my name and wondering how they were going to get me out. Another Bridge Gang kid came up, and stood for a minute, watching all the fuss.

'What's the matter?' he asked, finally.

'It's Gaz,' said another boy. 'He's stuck down the well, fighting lions.'

'No, he's not,' replied the newcomer, scornfully, 'I just seen him. He's in the Naafi with the soldiers, eating a Wagon Wheel.' A crowd of rescuers trooped back to find me there, munching away and wondering innocently where everyone had gone.

I'd have been much better off fighting lions after the roaring my mum gave me. Being a bit of a loner has its pitfalls.

Not long after this, we were all out being Indians, in a war-party hunting for poisons to dip our arrows in, squeezing deadly nightshade berries into a jar and taking care not to lick our fingers afterwards. On the way home, we picked the highest tree we could find to climb for a dare. It was a big old sycamore on the edge of the woods. About half-way up one of the gang, a plumpish, blond-haired boy called Chris, lost his grip. He fell through the tree, bouncing off its branches on the way down. There was a wooden fence on one side of this tree and he landed right on it. He screamed. It was the kind of scream that stops everything dead – the sound I'd heard the pigs make up at Dindor Hill Farm when the farmer stuck his butcher's knife into their neck arteries and yanked it back hard.

Twenty-five years later, I was to hear that sound again, made by a Russian soldier on a mountain thousands of miles away. It's a sound that I don't want to remember; and it's a sound I can never forget.

For a second, we all froze. None of us could see what had happened from the top of the tree. We piled down in a panic. When we got to the ground, we found Chris impaled on the fence. One of the sharp posts had gone right through his thigh, its point sticking out the other side. To take the pressure off his wound Chris was holding himself up by his hands, hanging backwards, crying quietly in agony. The bigger boys got around him and tried to lift him off, but when they saw he was passing out with the pain they lowered him down again and just held him. There wasn't all that much blood, but what there was looked very bright and red against the green grass. Staring at his thigh with this spear-point sticking through it, I was glad when someone said, 'Gaz, you're the fastest, go and get help!' I pelted off across the fields. I was back with a soldier inside ten minutes. To Chris it must have seemed like as many hours. He survived that terrible fall, but he carried the scar for the rest of his life. After that I lost count of the number of times my mother told me not to go wandering away climbing trees.

I suppose our family had always lived with the fear of death – of losing our dad, the real lion-fighter in the family – but I had never believed it could happen to one of us. Chris's accident made me see for the first time that death was even-handed; it could take little boys as easily as it could grown-ups.

A few months later, it came to another little boy in my school.

It was a bright autumn day, with a brisk, fitful wind hurrying the leaves along the gutter, and we were all waiting for the school bus at the bottom of the road. As it came up, we starting running alongside it in our daily frenzy to get on first, pushing and shoving, shouting to our mates at the front to make sure to grab the back seats. The bus came alongside. Suddenly, one of the boys tripped and went down. It was as if the back wheel had grabbed him, pulling him under head first.

I stopped, not quite believing what I'd seen. People started screaming. It was only then that the driver knew something was wrong. He hit the brakes and got off. When he saw what had happened, he went quite still, all the colour draining from his face. By now, some of the mothers, who had heard the screams and shouts, were running down the street in their aprons, desperately calling out the names of their children, praying that it might not be one of their own. I had never seen grown-up people act that way: the fear and the shock they showed made me feel as though the whole world had fallen into little pieces.

No one knew who had been killed. It was almost as if no one wanted to know. Eventually, a soldier came and moved all us kids away. I was glad. I'd seen enough.

When I was eleven, my father was commissioned through the ranks to major. He'd been on countless operations, and earned many decorations. But the MBE was something special. The four of us went up to Buckingham Palace when he received it from the Queen. I can't say if my dad and mum enjoyed the occasion but Steve and I certainly did. As we were waiting for Queen Elizabeth to enter the great hall my brother and I sang very softly, 'Will you come to the palace, will you come? There's a free cup of tea and a bun.' We couldn't know it then, but the two of us would soon have plenty of tea and buns, in the SAS, fighting for that very same Crown.

Chapter Two

When I left school aged fifteen, the last thing on my mind was joining the Army. This might seem strange, given the way I'd grown up with the SAS, but I really didn't know what I wanted to do. The idea of copying my father seemed tame; I wanted to find my own way in life. But getting any sort of job with a future was going to be difficult: I had no qualifications. My mother was always on at me to get an apprenticeship. The only trouble was, I couldn't think of anything I wanted to do for the rest of my days.

To earn some money, I took a job as an errand-boy, delivering groceries for one of the new supermarkets springing up all over the place. They gave me an old-fashioned delivery bike with very bad brakes. I'd time myself over to the car-park where the customers waited. One day, I saw a woman standing by the boot of her car, waving at me furiously to hurry up. I stood up on the pedals, no worries, and went for it. As I raced up I started to lose control. I pulled on the brake levers but nothing happened. A look of horror crossed her face. I wrenched the bike to one side and stuck my feet down, only the woman jumped the same way. I pulled the bike the other way, but she dodged again, too – right back into my path. Still going full tilt, I hit her, knocking her straight back into the boot, followed by myself and half the groceries. That was the end of my first job.

Next, I became a chicken-leg folder at Sun Valley Foods. I lifted the dead chickens off the hooks on a conveyor above my head, shoved their legs up their arses, and placed them on another moving belt. This was definitely the worst job I ever had, but it was also one of the best paid. Only one exciting thing ever happened. One morning, just before break, the lad next to me got his finger caught in one of the hanging M-shaped hooks. The line moved on. He went with it.

'Where the bloody hell do you think you're going?' I yelled, as it dragged him off. 'It's not time for your tea-break yet!' He looked at me, eyes wide with fear. His mouth kept opening and shutting, but nothing came out. I walked slowly along by his side, bantering, 'You can't go for coffee yet, you know, you'll get yourself into serious trouble.'

For some reason, he couldn't see the funny side of it. I couldn't stop laughing. 'Don't worry,' I told him. 'At the end of the line, you'll get a nice new Cellophane bag rammed over your head. Then it's the cold store for you – shrink-wrapped and oven-ready.'

Then I remembered something: a few paces on, at the end of the packing line, the belt swung out over a deep concrete bay. My mate was going to get pulled out into that space, fall, and leave his finger behind on the hook. I turned and yelled to the charge-hand on the other side of the shed, 'Ted! Ted! Stop the line!'

Ted hit the emergency stop button, and we got the lad down.

He came off that hook fighting mad. Ted had to stop him from setting about me with a dead bird.

I stuck the chickens for about three months, until my mum finally persuaded me to take an apprenticeship, as a trainee mechanic, at A. V. Wherley's garage in the centre of Hereford.

If I'd failed to star as an errand-boy, and shown very little talent with chickens, as a trainee mechanic I was a total disaster. Cars and I did not get on. The final wrench came when the man in charge told me to change the oil in his gleaming new Rover. Pulling too hard on the spanner, I broke the engine oil drain bolt. A few hours later when he'd fixed it, having skinned all the knuckles of his right hand in the process, he asked me to park the car for him. He must have been insane. I aimed the big car forwards, revved the engine, and let up the clutch. Only I was in the wrong gear. It went hurtling backwards. There was a horrible rending crunch. I got out to find the boss twitching quietly, staring in shock at his lovely new car, its rear off-side quarter wrapped round the corner of an H-ramp. After that I decided I wasn't cut out to be a mechanic. Funnily enough, the boss felt the same way. Only he put it a little more strongly than I thought was absolutely necessary.

I sat down at home and thought about what to do next. In the two years since leaving school, I hadn't exactly made my mark. For some time, I'd been having a rethink about joining the Army. Almost all the people I'd ever met were soldiers. My dad was a soldier. I'd grown up playing on the Regiment's assault course and begging rides in Army vehicles, and whenever I'd come across an SAS trooper with a weapon, I'd wanted to handle it. The more I thought about it, the rosier life in the Army seemed. Still ringing in my ears were the garage owner's encouraging words as I'd walked away, muttering defiantly about joining up: 'You'll never make it in the Army, boy. I know – I was in it.'

I'd show him.

I walked down to the local Careers Office, which as luck would have it was being run by a mate of my father. 'Hello,' I said. 'I'd like to join the SAS, please.'

My dad's friend smiled. 'Sorry,' he said, 'but you can't. You've got to do three years' service in a line regiment first. You can apply for SAS Selection after that.'

'OK, then, the Paras, please.' My father had also done time with them, which was good enough for me. This time the recruiting sergeant frowned. The look on his face said I was being ambitious. I filled in the forms and did all the tests. A few weeks later, I received a letter accepting me for training in the Royal Green Jacket regiment, with the understanding that I could leave the Army after three years if I hadn't made it into the SAS.

So much for getting straight into the Special Forces – the Army had its own ideas. I went home and told my parents the good news. My mother didn't say anything at all, which meant she didn't want me to join. It was 1972, the conflict in Northern Ireland was at its height, and my father had just left the Army and come home safe. The last thing she wanted was a son joining up in the same year.

'Make sure you look after your kit,' was all my father said. That meant he was pleased.

Maybe.

To celebrate my last days of freedom, my friends Ray, John, Jean and Joan laid on a leaving party for me at the Race Horse, our local pub. The landlady, another Jean, gave us the skittle alley to ourselves. It was great, singing Rod Stewart's 'Maggie May', the girls hanging off my arms like fruit-bats from a tree. Like all my mates, I was completely obsessed with motorbikes at the time – I had a new Yamaha 125. Jean let us park our bikes round the back. But tonight, I thought hazily, she was behaving a bit oddly, catching my eye, and looking at me in a strange way. Towards closing-time, she came up, put her lips to my ear and said, in a hoarse whisper, 'Gaz, I think you should go out the back and make sure the bikes are OK.' Mystified, I went with her. Out in the yard, we turned and looked at one another. I was surprised to see her there, until it finally dawned on me what she'd come for. I made some excuse and walked back inside. The next morning, I went off on the train to become a soldier.

Chapter Three

With my boyhood experience of Regiment life, I thought I knew all about the Army. At 6.30 a.m. on my third day in the Royal Green Jackets, up to my waist in freezing cold water on the assault course, I had this sinking realization: I'd got it all wrong. At Hereford the SAS troopers moved as they pleased. They put their hands in their pockets; they sauntered where they didn't stroll; the parade-ground hardly ever felt the tramp of their boots. This had given me a totally false impression of what Army life was like.

Winchester Depot, the Royal Green Jackets' home base, wasn't like Bradbury Lines. Not one little bit. Royal Green Jackets did everything on the double, which in their case, for historical reasons, meant much faster than anyone else. From dawn until late at night, my feet hardly touched the ground – it felt like there were drills and parades about every fifteen minutes. Keeping yourself and your kit clean and smart seemed to be the entire object of your existence, and getting caught with your hands in your pockets was near enough a court-martial offence.

Our section corporal was a giant, about six foot seven, and a good English cloth yard across at the shoulders. He was a Thing, not really a human being at all. At six foot two I wasn't short, but I had the build of a string bean. When I looked up at the Thing, with these great broad stripes on his meaty arms, I knew the meaning of awe. With a country upbringing and a baby face that stopped me getting into pubs, I was about as street-wise as a Sun Valley chicken.

But, in one way, this innocence worked for me: if somebody told me to jump, I jumped, whereas a lot of the hard boys from the Mersey and the Thames and the Tyne didn't take kindly to all this sudden in-your-face discipline. For myself, though, after that first bucket of cold water in the face, I gradually took to Army life.

Like a lot of people there, I could shoot well, but the difference was I could do it fast. I enjoyed fieldcraft, and was good at it: I'd spent most of my boyhood creeping around in the woods hunting animals, or in the camp hunting other boys. Likewise, the rain and the cold made no difference to me: I'd played out in all weathers. Some of the townie lads in my section couldn't go into a large stand of trees on their own, especially in the dark. When they got out into the countryside at night they were afraid of the noises, and the beasties that might be lurking.

They crammed recruits in like sardines at Winchester barracks, and this had its problems. There was a 'barrack-room lawyer' in our squad called Stuart, a sarcastic bastard who liked everyone to think he knew it all. His favourite trick was to go around smashing bottles with the edge of his hand. He'd boast to anyone who'd listen that he was a karate expert. He was showing off, smashing a beer bottle over a waste-bin one day, when I caught the glint of something metallic falling from his palm. There was a *thunk* as it hit the bottom of the bin. I didn't say anything, but I noticed Stuart moved everyone away from the scene very quickly. I went over and had a look inside. Sure enough, in among the shards of glass there was a large padlock.

A few days later, the Karate Kid was taking the piss out of a recruit called Dave, who happened to be a friend of mine. Dave told our man to bugger off. They squared up to one another. Stuart started chopping the air, threatening Dave with the karate act. Everybody gathered round to see the fight. While he was brave enough, Dave was a quiet man, about to get married. The last thing he wanted was to get into any trouble so he backed down. This annoyed me. I went up to Stuart. 'Want to pick on someone?' I said. 'Then try having a go at me. Because I don't see any padlock in your hand.'

'You what?' he stammered.

'You normally have a padlock in your hand when you're pretending to be a Black Belt. Let's see what you're like without it.'

This time, it was the Karate Kid who backed down. Later on, I heard he was picked up on leave for impersonating a sergeant, and given time in cells. Still in basic training, he'd gone out in full dress uniform, with three stripes pasted up. A junior Walter Mitty, that one.

Ten weeks into our basic training, we had two weeks' leave. I went home to see my parents and friends. It was only when I got home that I noticed how much I'd changed since joining up. Basic training had done its job: I'd filled out physically, and the challenges they set us recruits had done wonders for my self-confidence. The Army had kick-started me into growing up.

But there was one thing I still had to learn about.

I was passing a clothes shop in town on the third day of leave when I saw this girl in the window. She was fiddling with one of the mannequins. She was dark-skinned, with a round, attractive face, glossy black hair and a voluptuous figure. And she was tall, only a bit shorter than me.

I was smitten.

I started going in there regularly, spending hours looking at things I couldn't afford to buy. Quite often, I'd drift off into a trance thinking about her, and come round to find myself sorting through the ladies' dresses. I had a mad passionate crush on this girl and I didn't know how to handle it. What to do?

One morning, Dream-girl caught me going through a row of frocks. She came across and stood right up close to me. It was the first time I'd smelt her scent, and it was wonderful. I could feel my cheeks burning.

'Looking for anything in particular?' she asked.

'Er . . . yes. Something different!'

'Is it for yourself?'

I nodded dumbly.

She picked out the dress I was clutching, looked me up and down with her head on one side and said loudly, 'Well, sir, this one's lovely. And on you it'll *certainly* be different.' From the corner of my eye, I could see some of the other customers watching us. I looked round frantically for the door, which seemed to have vanished while she'd been speaking. 'Shall I wrap it up for you?'

'Er . . . yes,' I mumbled. 'Thanks.' I had no choice but to follow her up to the till.

'Have a lovely time with your new dress,' she said, pushing the bag into my hands.

I stood outside on the pavement for a few minutes, clutching a brand new size twelve dress, and feeling like a complete and utter idiot. What on earth was I going to do with a summer frock? I walked back in. She came up to me at once, an impish grin on her face. 'Something the matter with your new dress, sir?' she asked. 'Doesn't it fit?'

'Er . . . er . . .' At last, from somewhere, I found some nerve. I pushed the bag back into her hands. 'I've bought you a dress to wear. Will you come out to dinner with me?'

'Of course,' she said, taking it gently from me. She smiled the kind of smile that topples empires. 'I thought you'd never ask. And, by the way, my name's Kate.'

How is it that women are always so composed about these things, and always so far ahead of the game? Kate seemed so sophisticated. I was like a big lump of putty in her hands. She convinced me that the next big fashion was a horrible T-shirt she had in the shop, a ridiculous light-blue thing with a stick-on plastic Tom and Jerry motif on the chest. I wore it proudly around the town for a few days. Then I noticed I was getting some funny looks. Why, if they were so fashionable, I wondered, wasn't anyone else wearing one? In the end she took pity, and told me the sad truth. My friends had been in on the joke for some time. I suffered agonies of shame.

We went out to dinner, and met for lunch a few times. Then we arranged to go dancing on the following Saturday night. Kate was going with her girlfriends, and I was going with my mates; but the electrifying thing was, we both knew the time had come to move things on. I sat in the pub where we'd arranged to meet, glancing at the doorway once every fifteen seconds. No Kate. On the Monday, I went round to see her in the shop. Still no Kate. I went up and asked the manageress where she was.

'Who are you?'

'I bought a dress here.'

'Sorry. I can't help you.' And she wouldn't look me in the eye.

That lunchtime, in the Race Horse, I picked up the local paper. There was a banner headline across the top of page one: 'Tragic accident as youths travel to country disco.' The story underneath said, 'A teenage girl was killed and another was seriously injured on Saturday night when their car was involved in an accident on the way to The Park discothèque. Eighteen-year-old Kate X was killed instantly . . .'

I folded up the paper carefully and walked out of the pub.

Just before the end of my leave I had a motorbike accident. While I was in hospital, getting stitched and plastered, I thought, This is it, my leg will never heal in time, and I'll be thrown out of the Army. Even worse, I'll have failed SAS Selection before I even begin. I was determined to carry on and achieve my aim, a bit afraid I would not be able to and be a failure. On my return I asked my platoon sergeant for a week to prove I could catch up on the training with the rest of my intake. He looked at me for a long while, said, 'OK,' then backed me up with the platoon commander, who agreed. Not only did I catch up, but also passed out as 'best recruit' and 'best rifle-shot'.

Chapter Four

We arrived in Belfast soon after Bloody Sunday. From the ferry deck I gazed at Northern Ireland for the first time. I was eighteen years old, and now part of Support Company of the Second Battalion, the Royal Green Jackets. The rain was beating into my face and I was freezing cold. With nothing but the TV news to go on, the Province to me was a place of bombings, shootings and riot, a place of violence. I expected to see burning buildings and rows of tracer arching through the air, but all I saw in the half-dark was Belfast harbour and the city lights glistening in the light rain. It looked just like Liverpool, which we'd left only the night before, and felt like it, raw and hard, with a stark edge to it, brushed out in shades of grey. Dawn was just breaking through the clouds hugging the top of the Black Mountain. As they directed us to our transport, I looked around at all the other soldiers on the quay, dressed in their flak-jackets, loaded weapons at the ready. 'Welcome to hell,' said one of them, encouragingly.

I couldn't see what he was getting so dramatic about.

I looked a bit more closely. All around the docks there were great fortresses of sandbags, massive curtains of steel fencing pierced by high gates. Blazing arc-lights picked out the security checks and road-blocks everywhere in stark detail. We walked outside. Armoured cars – Pigs – roared past, their huge tyres throwing up long mists of spray. There were policemen wearing body armour, carrying rifles, with revolvers in open holsters at their waists: no country bobbies, these, of the kind I knew.

Bomb-damaged, blackened buildings gaped up at the penetrating drizzle. Definitely not Liverpool. Then I started noticing the people: they looked different. There were no smiles; no one was laughing. They looked dull and serious, at war with themselves. This can't be my country, I thought. Look at it! For a long time that's how I thought of Northern Ireland, as a strange foreign land, 'over the water'.

We walked from all that security in the docks straight on to a 'luminous turkey', a big white Army bus. We were in civilian clothes, on our way to Londonderry, where there'd been hundreds of shootings and bombings over the past few months, where the centre of the city had been razed to the ground by the IRA, and our transport to this friendly spot was a big white Army bus with no protection: no flak-jackets, no helmets, no weapons, no armoured escort. Where were our rifles? Maybe the bus was painted white because we'd already surrendered. Or maybe we were in Northern Ireland for the annual IRA turkey shoot. To save us from the combined might of the enemy on the road to Londonderry, through the notorious terrorist enclave of the Glenshane Pass, we had one armed soldier on that gleaming white coach. That was our lot. And he made it plain that he looked down his nose at the 'sprogs'.

Great, I thought. Even our own side despises us. Our escort told us war stories all the way up to our permanent house in Northern Ireland. It turned out later he was a clerk who'd never fired a shot in anger.

We were in rows of long, low Second World War prefabs, shoddily built, but with a great view out across to the mountains on the other side in Eire. As the resident battalion, our job was to cover the county of Londonderry, and to provide support as required to the rest of the North. We were sent to our respective platoons and then issued with our weapons, equipment, and shell dressings for first aid: 'Do *not* use your own shell dressing on anyone else, use the wounded man's first. Someone might need to use yours on *you*.' Next came metal helmets with tilting Perspex visors, cumbersome black rubber gas masks, and thick flak-jackets that might stop a small piece of shrapnel if you were lucky, or a low-velocity round at the squib end of its range. We were also issued with, test fired, and zeroed in our

7.62 mm Self-loading Rifles – SLRs. The weapon sling was fitted to the rifle butt. A while back a young soldier with the sling attached to the barrel end had had the SLR snatched out of his hands during a riot. He'd pulled back on the sling, turning the muzzle of the rifle in towards his own body. The rioter on the other end had pulled the trigger: the soldier was dead.

That was it. Soldiers got killed here.

We'd had hardly any training or briefing on Northern Ireland, least of all on the political situation there. Now, even though we were actually in the Province, the Army still didn't tell us anything about it. We were told only that we'd be policing a 'bad Catholic area'. We knew the IRA were Catholic, so that made all Catholics bad. The best gen we got came from the nineteen-year-old veterans already stationed there, who gave us practical tips on ways of staying alive.

It was at this time that I met the Cat, a big streetwise Cockney lance-corporal who was second-in-command of our platoon. At twenty-three, the Cat was already an old hand, well versed in the ways of the Troubles. He was six foot two and big built, with a broad Cockney accent and loads of credibility from his time served. He had a roundish face and blond hair that made him look younger than his years, and one particular mannerism that was all his own: when he was talking, he brought his thumb and forefinger up in front of his face and stabbed at the listener with them to emphasize his point. The Cat always spoke his mind. He was easy-going, but at the same time he was as sharp as a nut: if he thought someone was a fool, even one of the officers, he'd say as much, straight out, without worrying about the consequences. This didn't always win him friends. But he was a professional soldier and he knew what he was talking about: if the Cat said, 'Do this,' you did it, not because of his size, or his rank, but because you wanted to get home in one piece. His style of positive leadership influenced me a lot in later years: the Cat didn't just bark orders, like most of the junior NCOs, he talked to you, kept you involved in the big picture. This made you much more willing to follow him.

He asked me a few questions about myself, explained my basic duties, and told me to stick close to him on the streets. As the youngest in the platoon, with no experience of urban warfare, I was the most at risk. As the section's guru, he took all the new boys under his wing when they first arrived: 'If I don't get you wised up,' he said, 'they'll only shoot you.'

I was to follow the Cat into the SAS.

There was no mucking about now. We were in Northern Ireland on active service. The next day, I was crammed on to the back of an armoured four-ton truck with the rest of my platoon. We were on our way down to a fort they called the Shooting Gallery in the heart of Londonderry. The Shooting Gallery looked like a little boy's fantasy fort, although it had been converted from a garage by some fevered brain from the Royal Engineers. Every sprawling square inch of the place was covered in sandbags. There were watch-towers, or 'sangars', sticking out of it every twenty-five metres, with narrow sandbag alleys leading into them from the main redoubt. It reminded me strongly of pictures I'd seen of First World War trenches. The whole complex was surrounded by barbed wire and high mesh anti-rocket screens; everything was brown, dismal and dirty-looking. The only light inside its cramped interior was artificial.

On the high ground overlooking the fort were the notorious no-go areas: the Creggan estate on the left, the Bogside on the right. To the rear was open ground backing on to the River Foil. The no-go label wasn't strictly accurate: the Security Forces (SF) ventured into these zones, but they would always come under fire from the people who lived there. The no-go areas were controlled and 'policed' by the IRA, by means of so-called punishment beatings and murders. In 1972, there were still a number of these locations all over Northern Ireland.

The residents around the Shooting Gallery were always spying on the Army's movements, and they gave us new boys a warm welcome. We'd only just arrived when I heard two deafening cracks and thumps: high velocity rifle fire coming in just overhead. It was the first time I'd been on the end of live rounds. A moment later there came more shots, like a giant beating a huge carpet, the bullets thumping into the sandbags in front of us, followed by the sharp cracks of our own sentries' return fire. All the older hands just paused for a second, then carried on with what they were doing. We new boys looked around, waiting for the order to man the walls, pick out the enemy and open fire, but it never came: in the Shooting Gallery incoming fire was an everyday routine.

A lad of about my own age came up. Ginge Meredith had already been in Northern Ireland for a year, which in my eyes made him another oracle. Of average build and on the short side, he had sandy-coloured hair, white, slightly spotty skin that would blister up in any kind of sun, and a strong northern accent. He shook out a cigarette.

'No, thanks. I don't smoke.'

'You will after you've been here for a few days.' We stood chatting for a bit. He had a sharp, terrier face and I noticed his ears stuck out. Apart from that, he was unobtrusive and quiet, in many ways the grey man. He told me he was nineteen, going steady with a girl who was a year older. 'We're getting married,' he said, 'soon as I get back home.' He was due R&R leave in less than two weeks. He stubbed out his cigarette and said, 'Anyway, I've got some more good news. There's a ceasefire starting tonight at 2000 hours. Mind you, before that we've got to go out to the Bogside – show them we're here and we're not going to go away.' Seeing how nervous I looked he grinned reassuringly. 'Don't worry, mate, it's just to put in a presence.'

Sure enough, thirty minutes later we were off to set up a vehicle checkpoint (VCP) at a road junction on the edge of the Bogside housing estate. Ginge was next to me in the Saracen. It was the first time I'd been in one of these armoured cars. I sat there, enjoying the powerful high-pitched whine of the engine as the driver gunned the vehicle through the gears, but still feeling nervous as a cat inside. I had never been tested before. I didn't want to let myself down. Or anyone else, for that matter. My new mate could see how tense I still was, so he kept on talking to take my mind off the coming op.

'Don't worry, Gaz, I'll keep you right.' He explained how the Saracen could be electrified to shake people off it. 'When it was first used on rioters just the noise of it would frighten them all away. Fear of the unknown, eh?' He grinned at me.

They put me on a corner about fifteen metres from the VCP, as part of the protection on it. I got down into a fire position, peered carefully all around the area to work out target indication points, and waited. I felt exposed.

About two hours later, we were all still in the same positions. The lessons I'd learned in training, and the slightly more colourful instructions I'd just received from the Cat, went round in my head. 'Never stay in the same position too long. Change your position frequently. Make it hard for the enemy to set up on you.' Here, in the world's most dangerous urban area, we were making it absurdly easy for them, twelve little army ducks, sitting in a row. The more experienced lads on the patrol started complaining to the platoon sergeant. 'Sarge, we've got to move. Sarge, we're asking for it.'

'Shut up and sit still,' he said. They shut up. We sat still.

Time went by, very slowly: 1800, now, only two hours to go before the ceasefire. Finally, we were all told to move around one position: not to anywhere new – it seemed there was nowhere – just shuffle ourselves one to the right about, like the guests at the Mad Hatter's tea-party. Even I thought it was pointless – and dangerous. Bent low, Ginge ran across to replace me.

He knelt down at my side, took over my position and pointed out where I was supposed to go. As I started to get up, he grabbed my arm. 'Watch it now,' he said. 'Keep low and move fast like I did. We've been here way too long.'

'OK,' I said, and took off at a fair old clip, with my head up, looking all the time in case of snipers. I'd gone about a dozen paces when I heard three very loud thumps right behind me. I dived to the ground, rolled over and turned back to face the way I'd come.

I saw Ginge flying backwards through the air, as if he'd been smashed by a giant fist. He crashed down, his weapon clattering to the ground. For a split second I was confused. I gazed blankly at him: he was just lying there, sprawled, with his arms outstretched, making no sound. One of his hands twitched. Then I understood. He'd been shot.

I ran back to him and took up a firing position by his side, pointing the SLR at where I thought the shots had came from. But I saw nothing. Ginge was half upright now, leaning on his elbows, looking down at his front. Still he made no sound. Then I saw blood welling out of the bottom of his combat jacket.

37

'He's hit,' I yelled. 'Ginge is hit!'

Two other members of the patrol rushed across. Without pausing, they lifted Ginge under the arms as I covered their backs and dragged him across the street into a doorway.

He'd started calling out now.

'I'm hit, I'm hit. I'm dying!' he called softly. 'I want my mum, I want my mum!'

I'll never forget the look of fear and bewilderment in his eyes.

The gunman had hit him with three rounds in the groin and lower gut. The lads had his flak-jacket wide open. They were throwing shell dressings on to the wounds and holding them there to stop the bleeding. It wasn't working. One after another, the thick dressings soaked bright red. 'Give me your dressing,' shouted one of the lads. I ripped the sterile cotton pad from my belt and thrust it at him. I noticed my hand was shaking. In a second, my dressing, too, was soaked and red. We'd used all the dressings we had on us – all four of them were now sodden with his blood. I was very upset by this. I couldn't understand it. The boy was bleeding to death. Why didn't we have enough dressings to stop the bleeding?

Ginge had gone quiet. His eyes were rolling, his face had turned the colour of chalk. With no medical training whatsoever, all I could do was sit there and watch him. I put my hand on his shoulder. 'You'll be all right, mate,' I said. 'The ambulance will be here in a minute.' He groaned softly, then fell quiet.

By now, the rest of the patrol had seen what was going on – but no one had spotted the gunman. Some people came towards us from the nearby houses. I yelled at them, 'Move back or I'll shoot!'

'Don't shoot!' they called. 'We want to help.'

They were people from the surrounding estate, apparently unarmed. I lowered the SLR. One old woman looked at me in tears. 'Son,' she said, 'if those people want to shoot at you boys again they're going to have to shoot us first.' Without flinching, the Bogsiders formed a human barrier between Ginge, the lads trying to save him, and the hidden gunman's line of sight.

We'd radioed out 'contact' and Casevac signals, but nothing was happening. We were no more than five minutes away from the nearest armoured ambulances, which were just over the bridge at the staging-post. But many more than five minutes had gone by already, and there was no ambulance. A man was dying here. Where, I raged inwardly, was the fucking ambulance?

Ginge had stopped looking around now, and his eyes were closed. He seemed to be lying very still. I put my hand on his forehead. 'Hang on, Ginge,' I said. 'You'll be OK. You're not going to die, you'll be OK.' But Ginge didn't hear me. He didn't hear any of us. He was dead.

About fifteen minutes later, one of the ambulances drew up. After Ginge was taken away we waited out on the streets for a few more minutes, until the IRA ceasefire came into effect. They had wanted to prove a point, and we had let them. The shots had come from a Thompson sub-machine-gun. We hadn't heard any cracks, only the thumps of the impact, because the gunman had been close when he fired, and because it was a low-velocity weapon.

An older man among the people standing around us said, 'These bastards are not us, son.'

'Are you a Protestant?' I asked.

'No, we're all of us Catholics, but we don't want this. We don't want you boys here, but we don't want you to have to die for us.'

A woman came up and offered me tea. I refused. I knew troops had been given tea with rat poison or bleach in it before then. Another old lady stepped up, took the tea, drank some, then held out the cup again. 'It's safe to drink, son,' she told me. I smiled, thanked her and drank it. It was hot and sweet, just what I needed, but I was totally confused. What the hell was going on here? Who was friend and who was foe? After that, there were no more Catholics or Protestants for me, no more racism and discrimination: these people here were just like any others, some good, some bad. It wasn't about racism, religion or colour, only about how you behaved. That rule stays with me to this day.

Once the follow-up operation got under way, the Saracens picked us up and took us back to the Shooting Gallery. Everyone gathered around as we walked in. They didn't say anything. They just looked. They had been listening to the contact on the radio net. Word had spread. It hit the Cat as hard as it hit anyone: even though he had been elsewhere when it happened – in fact, because of that – the Cat felt responsible: Ginge had been in his section.

They all knew Ginge better than I did. A tall thin lad with blondish hair called Steve came up to me, patted me on the back and said, in a slightly rasping voice, 'Tough luck, mate, first time out – but it happens. You get used to it.' He paused, as if he were unsure about saying something else, then added, 'You're a lucky bastard. It takes them time to set up on a target. They must have been setting up on *you* for ages. A few seconds earlier and they'd have got the pair of you.' He gave a half-smile. 'I bet they're pissed off about not getting you as well as him. Try not to worry about it. Get something to drink, and eat if you can. You'll be OK.' It was only later I found out that Steve Grange was Ginge Meredith's best friend.

That's just what Ginge said, I thought. You'll be OK. Well, *he* wasn't OK, he was dead – and I definitely wasn't getting used to it. I went off to find somewhere quiet. I leaned my forehead against the cold metal of a locker and told myself not to cry.

Just then, everyone started rushing into the ready room where I was standing, grabbing riot shields and batons. 'Come on, you,' someone shouted. 'There's a riot starting up. Outside – now!' I stood there, staring at the rows of shields and batons lined up on the wall. The shock was going through me in cold waves. I can't go out there again, I thought. I can't do it. I stared at the lockers. The crashing and shouting and banging continued all around me. No one seemed to have noticed I was standing still. Gradually, it fell quiet. Unable to move, I stayed where I was. I knew I had to go outside. I knew that if I didn't get straight back out there I never would. I thought about Ginge, and the confused anger helped. Slowly, I picked up a baton and shield. Kicking open the door, I ran out to join the others.

For a while I didn't really feel anything about Ginge getting shot, I just shut it away. I knew I ought to be feeling something, but I didn't know what that should be. Every time I tried to think about it, everything went blank: I'd been in a contact, and somebody was dead. They'd lined up on me, he'd taken my place and they'd shot him. It

40

was a long time before it sank in that Ginge really was dead and that it could easily have been me. When I did start remembering, I couldn't sleep. My mind kept going over what had happened. I felt guilty that he'd died and not me. But why did any of us have to die? What was it for? I was only eighteen. What had I got myself into? I called my mum and told her a little bit about the shooting, playing it down because I didn't want to worry her. She could tell I was shaken, but not how much. Seeing that kind of death, up close, knocked me sideways. This wasn't a boy under a bus – a terrible accident. These people were out to murder us in cold blood. And they had done just that.

I was just a kid, and not well informed enough to have any reasoned political views but, even so, the shock made me think about the wider situation. OK, the IRA wanted to kill us – but wasn't that because we stood in the way of them killing their real enemy, the Protestants, and so getting the united Ireland they wanted? But there was no way that the Protestants were ever going to give in. The only conclusion I could come to was that we were there to stop the two sides killing one another. The police were good, but they didn't have the manpower to contain the situation. We had to put the brakes on the killing. If we got caught in the crossfire along the way, that was better than all-out civil war.

The next day I was sent back to Ballykelly with Steve Grange. That afternoon Steve had sorted out Ginge's kit so that his effects could be sent home to his family and fiancée. We went into the Naafi and started to drink. The night went on, and we drank more and more. Steve started toasting Ginge, telling me tales of what they used to do together, what things Ginge had planned to do in the future. 'You know,' he said, 'he was going to get married?' I nodded. Suddenly he stopped talking and looked at me: tears welled up in his eyes and he started to cry. All I could do was put my arm around his shoulders. I was too choked myself to say anything.

Chapter Five

Next day they had me out in one of the sangars that protected Sandbag City. What with the ceasefire, and the fact that the location was being abandoned, the defensive wall leading to this sangar had been removed. I had to cross open ground to get to it, and once inside was there on my own. I had been peering through the sangar's observation slits for a while, watching a gang of youths about my own age milling about on the road outside. They were flinging half-bricks at the slits, hoping to land one in on me. The bricks made a dull heavy thud as they whacked into the sandbags. The locals knew there was a ceasefire on, but I was alone in there and they were taking advantage of it.

'Are you in there, Tommy? Are you in there?' they kept yelling.

I didn't answer.

Then one of them came in the back. He was only a few feet away. He had a half-brick in his fist. I stepped round, pointed my rifle at him and said, 'Get back. Fuck off.'

'There's a Tommy bastard in here!' he shouted. The rest rushed forward.

'Get back!' I shouted. 'Or I'll shoot.' They were all around the sangar now, right up close, flinging in rocks through the slits while I was watching my back.

'Get the bastard! He's on his own! Get the bastard's gun!' someone yelled.

I didn't know what to do. I felt fear before my mind went blank. I knew I had to stay in there, make them come at me from the one direction. It was my only chance. If I went outside they'd be on me in a second.

There were two of them at the back entrance trying to get in, no more than a couple of metres away. I started yelling at them, stepping forward and kicking out, but it had no effect. I didn't want to kill anyone, but I couldn't let them take my gun. I reached over with my left hand, caught hold of the SLR's cocking handle, pulled it back and let go. The metallic clash was loud in the enclosed space. They knew what that sound meant: there was a live round in the chamber.

The pair at the door moved back and disappeared. A large piece of wood flew in through one of the slits and hit me on the shoulder. I bent slightly forward to get out of the line of fire. Then two bricks came hurtling in through the back entrance followed by the same two youths.

'He won't fire,' shouted one. 'He won't.'

'Get back, you fuckers! I fucking will.'

They were in a frenzy now, determined to get me and, better still, my weapon. It would make them heroes on the street.

They don't give a shit, I thought. I'm an armed British soldier, the best thing since sliced bread, and they don't give a shit. They're not scared of me, even though I'm armed. *I'm scared of them.*

It was as if I were standing outside myself, watching.

They were still creeping forward, looking to grab the SLR.

I backed into the rear of the cramped sangar and pulled the rifle butt tight into my shoulder. Suddenly I felt a cold, controlling anger – let them feel fear. I took aim just above their heads and fired. The weapon kicked back, the sound was deafening. The muzzle-flash blinded me, the sangar filled with gunsmoke and dust. For a second I couldn't see. I decided if they came again my next two shots would be at body height.

Then I heard people yelling, close to the entrance. The voices were British.

'Security Forces, who's in there? Come out with your hands up!'

I couldn't believe this. 'It's me, Gaz!' I shouted. Steve came in.

43

'What the fuck are you doing in here?' he asked. 'This sangar's been closed down. They shouldn't have sent you out here.'

The reaction hit me then and I sat down with a bump.

Crack! Thump! A few rounds passed overhead. No big deal, I was used to it now, we carried on drinking our brews, squatting on the floor by the Pig.

Whoosh! Something shot into the air leaving a bright trail behind it.

'Incoming mortar!' We shot up, tea going everywhere. Some people tried to cram inside the Pig. The rest of us dived under it, anything to escape the shrapnel rain. 'Move over! Let me in!' We must have broken the world record for getting the most people under an armoured vehicle. There were arms and legs everywhere, stuck into ears and backsides. A second later the sky lit up. I looked out. There was a pair of gaitered shins outside the cover of the Pig. The shins changed to knees and the Cat peered in at the horrible mass of bodies. Half smiling and half sneering, he said, 'You bunch of wankers! Don't you know a fucking Shamulley when you see one?' The rocket flare had been fired to light up the area by a sentry who had seen a suspicious movement.

'Oh.' We crawled out, heads low, feeling stupid. And we'd lost our tea.

A few days later we were called out to assist. There was a riot building up near the entrance to the Bogside. A big crowd was stoning the RUC and the troops. We pitched up in the Pigs and spread out across the road, making sure we stayed well under cover: it was raining stones.

'Fuck off, you Brit bastards!'

A riot was often planned in advance and carefully controlled. It was one of the main ways the IRA set us up as targets: getting the troops deployed and busy, then luring one out into a position where a gunman was waiting. Once they'd shot a soldier, the rioters would close in to hassle the Casevac and cover the killer's withdrawal.

'Get out of our country!'

There must have been hundreds of rioters out on the streets that day, men, women and children of all ages, hardened to this way of life, unafraid of the RUC, the Green Jackets or the Devil himself. This was their ground: they knew every brick of every alley, every stone of every street, they knew the gardens, hedges, walls, gaps and buildings, as well as every trick going in the book.

'The boys killed another one today, Tommy. Was he your friend, Tommy?'

On one side of us was a row of terraced council houses, on the other a scraggle of back gardens. Rubble covered the streets, and two cars were burning out of control; the air was full of black smoke and the stink of burning rubber. There were still traces of the CS gas that had been fired at the rioters before we arrived: it crept into our eyes, making them water, and up our noses, making them run, and burned any exposed skin.

Volleys of bricks and stones kept flying at us, bouncing off the road and the Pigs.

'Stand fast!' shouted the platoon sergeant.

Ozzie, Dave and myself had been detailed off for the snatch squad. The section sergeant identified a ring-leader or someone on the wanted list. Our job was to rush forward, grab him and drag him back. The rest of the platoon would move up in support if necessary. That was the theory. We made ready behind our section, out of sight of the rioters, stripping off our body-armour and belt-kit until we were standing in light order: trainers, no helmets or rifles. Ozzie had an anti-riot gun, a kind of short, single-barrelled shotgun. It fired hard rubber baton rounds about 15 centimetres long by 2 centimetres in diameter, shaped like a long bullet. Dave and I had wooden batons and small round riot shields.

We stood there, getting pelted with rocks and bottles. It was great fun.

A tall skinny bruiser was marshalling events, a few paces back in from the face of the crowd. 'See that shit there, in the blue shirt?' asked the sergeant.

We nodded.

'I want him. Ready? Go!'

Our lines opened up like the Red Sea. We sprinted forward. He was only about fifty metres away. As they saw us charge, a lot of the rioters fell back. But not the shit. By the time he realized we were coming for him it was too late. I got there first and jumped on him, pulling him to the ground. I whipped my baton around his neck and hauled on it. He smelt of old dirt and damp rooms. Dave grabbed his hands and put on a wrist-lock. Ozzie covered. We started to move back, dragging him with us, but the shit was wiry, bucking like a donkey to get away, and he was slippery as a Wye eel: we couldn't get a proper grip. Just holding him took up all my strength.

We weren't covering any ground.

If you're going to snatch someone successfully, it has to be done hard, fast, and furiously. I looked up: a hard core of rioters was edging back towards us, and their blood was up. Dave shouted a warning but they kept coming. I heard a sharp crack as Ozzie fired the anti-riot gun. He hit one. I saw the man go down.

I twisted the prisoner round so I had his windpipe under the baton. He relaxed a little and I had a brief eye-to-eye with him. I'd never felt so much hate. Kicking and struggling, we got him on his feet.

Suddenly another group of rioters appeared out of a side alley between us and the platoon. 'Fuck!' said Dave, as he saw them. They came straight at us from twenty metres, dozens of them, silent except for their pounding feet, charging in a dense mass. I felt everything drain from my body. Maybe, I thought, we could just dust our ring-leader down, hand him back to his mates, and all would be forgiven. Well, then again, maybe not. They came hurtling at us. They looked berserk, like great mad dogs, only well drilled. As they closed in, every one of them was screaming obscenities. At the last second, as if on a command, they let fly with their stones and bottles. Ozzie fired the anti-riot gun into them at point-blank range, but it was no good. They were on us.

We let go of the shit. He turned straight on to Dave and started booting him. There's gratitude for you. My strength came back. I had the adrenaline rush you get when there's nowhere to run and your life's in danger. Things cleared. I may even have smiled, a reaction you sometimes get to intense fear. This time it was different, not like the sangar, I was yelling, 'Come on, then, you bastards!' Blue-shirt was hitting out big time now, flailing at us with his boots and fists. I whacked him one, hard as I could, with the baton, and he staggered back. I adopted the position: legs wide apart and braced, baton resting on my right shoulder for a shorter arc of swing. As the first one came within range, I brought the wood crashing down on his head. It glanced off the side of his skull. *Crack!* He dropped without a sound.

From now on, things came only in fragments. I swung at another head, covered in curly brown hair. I felt it hit, but then I had no more room to swing: they were too close, they were everywhere, hands plucking and punching, swarming all over us. Something hit me hard in the face. My head snapped back, blood bursting out of my nose in a shower. Pain shot through me and I lost my sight, started to fall backwards. Hands were clawing and dragging me down, they wanted me on the floor. I stopped feeling: the pain I already had was too bad. I lost all sensation except for hearing: the thud of the kicks and the punches going in, the rasping noise of my own breath.

Someone was clawing at my hair, trying to pull my face up into the kicks. I could taste the blood in my mouth like a copper penny. I saw a wicked gleam. An open razor swung towards my face. I pulled backwards and it flashed by. The razor slashed again. I felt it slice across my chest and red hot pain shot down my arm. I heard the riot gun fire again and the hand with the razor disappeared.

I couldn't see the rest of the squad, I couldn't see anything – just blackness and boots and fists. I could hardly breathe. I closed my eyes. I was head down, trying to protect my face. My legs were closed and tucked up under me to save my balls. The kicks were still coming into my back and legs, my head snapped back again as someone kicked me right in the face through my arms. My body was too numb to feel much now, my mind too confused to think clearly.

I was being dragged across the gravel on the road. My ears were ringing from where I'd been hit on the side of the head. The kicking stopped. The people who were pulling me let go. I lay back on the road, sucking in breaths. More shots from anti-riot guns, the sound coming from underwater. I opened my eyes and saw a huge pair of black Army DMs boots under my nose. Thank fuck, I thought. Thank fuck for that.

Someone picked me up again and half dragged, half carried me back towards the platoon. As my sight came back, I saw a wall dead ahead of me. Painted across it, in big white letters, I dimly made out the words: WELCOME TO FREE DERRY.

The company took a few days off to train and relax. The Cat came up to me triumphantly one evening, stooping slightly from his great height, pointing eloquently as usual with his finger and thumb. 'Oi! Gaz! 'Ave you 'eard?'

'No? What?'

'Intelligence reckons the bastard that killed Ginge has been shot dead. By his own side, down in the city.'

'Fucking great.'

We had a few drinks to mark that point. The Cat drank beer, and he drank it by the gallon, he could drink me under the table any day. Later that evening, we went on a memorable date with a couple of good-looking sisters. I only remember mine because it didn't last long: about five minutes. We met in the Naafi, and before I'd even opened my mouth this colleen looked me up and down. I was wearing jeans. 'How dare you turn up for a date with me dressed like that?' she screeched, giving me the most almighty roasting, scared me half to death, worse than the company sergeant-major. I decided to give up on Irish girls after that. It was much safer on the streets. The Cat spent slightly longer with his date – she went on to become his wife.

A couple of days later we were sent back to the city. As we were patrolling yet another riot started up a few streets away. We were picked up by a couple of Pigs and rushed to the area, tasked to get in behind the rioters and cut them off. As we closed on the mob we came under a hail of stones, bricks, bottles and paving slabs, which bounced off the Pigs with great crashes and clangs.

Chippy, a rifleman in our half-section, yelled, 'Get the riot guns up on both sides!'

Dave and Russell flung open the side hatches, stuck the guns through and fired. The sound walloped out in the confined space of the Pig. As soon as they'd fired, they pulled in the guns, snapped them open, reloaded, stood straight back up and fired again. They were so skilled it was like watching one continuous movement. Steve and I worked the hatches, slamming them shut between shots to stop people chucking in stones or petrol bombs. Cordite fumes built up inside our little tin shed, along with the empty cartridge cases.

'Give us a go on the gun!' I yelled to Dave.

'Fuck off,' he replied politely.

'Go on, I've never fired one in a riot,' I pleaded. 'What's it worth?'

'Open!' he shouted. I opened the hatch. Boom! He fired again. Boom! That was Russell firing out of the rear hatch. More acrid smoke, the hatches clanging shut. The Pig has great heavy trapdoor hatches and steel doors that can take your fingers clean off if you don't get them out of the way.

'Two pints!' I yelled over the noise.

'Fuck off!' he scoffed. 'Four minimum! Here, it's loaded.'

I took the gun, put the butt to my shoulder and crouched below the hatch. 'Open!' I yelled. I thrust out the barrel, squinting along it for a rioter on the point of throwing something at us. There was one about five metres away. I aimed and fired. The weapon kicked into my shoulder. I peered through the billowing smoke, watching as he went down. When he'd hit the tarmac I pulled back. 'Close!' I shouted, and the hatch banged shut. My eyes and nose were full of cordite fumes, my ears were ringing, I was four pints the poorer – and I was grinning from ear to ear.

With the mob now dispersed, we were ordered to de-bus and make some arrests. The heavy doors thumped open, Russell and I jumped out. There was a high brick wall to our right, and the Pig was under it. Dave and Chippy were just climbing out after us when they stopped. 'Bomb!' they yelled as one.

I looked up. A nail-bomb landed on the road a few metres away and exploded. The shock wave hit my body – it was like having a barn door slammed hard into my face. I was thrown backwards right off my feet. My back hit something solid and all the wind went out of me. Russell landed half on top of me. We lay there for a second in a dazed heap. Then someone lifted him up and over me, the toe-end of his boot kicking me in the head as he went. My helmet had been blown off. Hands grabbed the neck of my flak-jacket as they hauled me up inside after him. My head banged heavily into the door in the rush. Russ and I were thrown to the floor of the Pig as we roared off down the street. Dave bent over to check how badly I'd been hit.

Like Russ, I was peppered all over with nails. But the bomb had caught us at the extreme of its range. Our flak-jackets had taken a lot of the projectiles, and the ones that had hit us had only just penetrated the skin. A few dozen bits of metal were sticking out of my legs and face but I felt no pain, apart from where my head had been knocked by Russ's boots and the steel door. My nose was bleeding and I was groggy. 'Fuck all wrong with you,' said Dave, nonchalantly.

'Nor this wanker,' Chippy said, poking at Russell with his finger.

I looked across at Russ: his glasses were smashed and hanging off one ear, his hair was standing straight up on end, and his eyes were like dinner plates. I knew I must look the same. I started laughing. He stared at me as if I were mad, then burst out laughing too. The others looked at us and then at each other.

'Nuts!' said Dave. 'They're both fucking nuts!'

As dawn broke Operation Motorman began. I was point-man in a 'brick' – four-man patrol – sweeping through the city, part of a huge deployment to reclaim the no-go areas once and for all. Approaching the junction of a main road I crouched, stuck my head round the corner, and had a quick squint. I pulled my neck back in again sharpish. There was a gunman standing just outside a doorway up the street, holding an Armalite at the high port. No, I thought, surely not. I must be seeing things. In broad daylight?

I peered round again. There he was, posing for a small crowd of admiring locals. At that time, there was a lot of IRA-friendly coverage in the Catholic press of the our-men-are-still-dominating-the-area type. We had stumbled across a propaganda exercise. I brought up the SLR and released the safety-catch. Then I made the mistake of looking over my shoulder, to see where everyone else was.

This kind of contact happens in fractions of a second. By looking back I had taken just a fraction too long. The gunman saw the movement, turned and ran.

As he ducked back through the doorway, the quicker-witted – and braver – members of the crowd started coming towards me, yelling and waving to put off my aim. I stood up, had a clear shot and fired. The bullet just missed the gunman's head. It thwacked into the doorpost, leaving a long yellow-white gash in the wood. Everyone in the street hit the tarmac. At my back, a voice yelled, 'Contact!'

The man right behind me raced over to the other side of the street. 'Come on!' he cried. We steamed through the house and out the back, smashing past a woman who tried to block the way. Action Man had gone. We came out again to find rent-a-crowd covering the escape.

Normally, for such a calculated exercise in public relations, the IRA would have cleared the area first. Catching one of them cold and unprotected like that was a chance in ten thousand. I was eternally pissed off about missing him.

We secured the Creggan with no major problems, the engineers moving in behind us and building temporary defensive positions in schools and other such locations to consolidate.

Tucked away in the bottom corner of the base there was a building we called the Funny Farm. This was where the Military Reaction Force (MRF), was based. It was made up of people seconded from various units, not just the Green Jackets. They spooled around the Province in civilian vehicles, operating undercover in nondescript plain clothes, usually unshaven and with long hair, mostly in support of the SAS.

They also collected intelligence, and they had a pretty good success rate. One time they'd had word about an IRA meet in a farmhouse on the moors south of Londonderry, up on the road towards Glenshane. We arrested eight or nine of these guys, handcuffed them, and drove them back down for questioning, one to each of the Kevlar-reinforced LWB Land Rovers. I'll always remember the look on this prisoner's face as we walked him up to the door of the Funny Farm. None of us knew what went on in there but, as far as he

51

was concerned, he was about to get the beating of his life. He was babbling like a brook by the time the MRF reception committee met us at the door – and they hadn't even asked him a question.

I liked their style. I thought it might be interesting to be a part of that while I was serving out my time before I could apply to join the SAS.

Chapter Six

The battalion's two-year tour of Northern Ireland finished a short while later. The Regiment had done well and was leaving with a sound record. I'd arrived as a young, immature, inexperienced soldier. In six months even I could see I'd changed beyond measure.

The battalion moved to Catterick, where I was posted from Support Company to the Reconnaissance Platoon, and promoted to lance-corporal. No sooner had I got used to having a stripe on my arm than we were sent to Belize for seven months' jungle training. I was interested in doing this because my father had spent years in the same environment. He'd never spoken about it but now I could find out for myself what it was like. What we actually got, though, was seven months' chasing the Army nurses out there, seven months' drinking, and the best part of a year learning how *not* to operate in the jungle. I'd find out how that was done later, in the SAS.

We returned from Belize in 1974, when the battalion went up to Catterick for more infantry training, which in my case included a corporal's course. It was at this time that I met Margaret, my future wife. I was standing in a pub with a few mates, chatting, drinking and looking around for the ladies. I noticed two girls at a table, one with a very pretty face and long brown hair. I grabbed Stan and nodded towards them. 'Forget it,' he told me. 'You've got no hope. Those two won't even look at a soldier.'

I carried on drinking. A few pints later, and feeling much braver, I thought, Who dares wins, an expression I'd got from my father. At the same time, a very original chat-up line came to me. I went over and asked the pretty woman if she'd like to have a drink. She told me her name was Margaret, and that she was a civil servant working for the military. I asked her for a date. She said her father was a soldier who would not, under any circumstances, allow her to date a serviceman. Four months later we were engaged. In the meantime, the battalion had started build-up training for a four-month emergency tour over the water.

By now, the Army had a much more professional Northern Ireland training act. The Northern Ireland Training Advisory Team (NITAT) was based at a secret location in the south of England. It was staffed with experienced veterans of the Troubles dedicated to passing on best practice over the water to troops about to go there. This specialist training lasted for a little over two weeks, and at the end of it I'd learned a lot more about how to command a section on the streets of Belfast or Derry than I had at Catterick. A lance-jack on my second tour in the Province, at the ripe old age of twenty, I'd be leading my own brick. I was becoming a professional NCO in an increasingly professional Army. I felt confident. In fact, by the end of the NITAT training I was raring to get back out there. There'd be no more deaths like Ginge's, if I could help it, with the boys playing sitting duck for the IRA.

There had been no let-up in the level of violence in the Province while we'd been in Belize, but the Security Forces in general were by now much better organized, much more businesslike in the way they conducted operations. I noticed at once that everything was much more controlled, the Wild West atmosphere had gone. Having said which, we had no sooner arrived at the Moyard Park RUC station than three shots thumped into the sandbags out front. Just like old times, I thought. The IRA making us feel at home.

We were based in another hot area, with the Ballymurphy estate to our front, and the Springfield Road outside the main gate. The Army was still in the Province in huge numbers, acting as a police force as well as a security force, but there was a feeling that the police should begin taking back some of their proper law-enforcement functions, as the situation settled. Four years later, in 1978, this feeling resulted in the policy of Police Primacy.

By this time I was a bit more realistic about what the Army was doing in Northern Ireland: I knew that we were never going to change anything fundamental. Who could, apart from the Irish themselves? But, for my own part, I was happy. Gradually our section corporal, Chris, was being used more and more in planning ops, in itself a good sign of the newly de-layered management. It also meant that I was getting more responsibility out on the streets, regularly leading bricks, which was great.

After a couple of months in Belfast, they sent us down to Crossmaglen. The Ballymurphy was hostile ground, no question, but 'XMG' was something else. Everybody there, without exception, hated us and the IRA had massive community support. Just by being there, we were providing the 'players' – the IRA – with a target-rich environment. And they kept scoring.

The police, who couldn't go anywhere unsupported, operated from inside our barracks. We all moved in armoured vehicles or by helicopter. It was ironic, after all the confidence I'd felt before coming back. We were playing cat and mouse down here, and it felt like we were the mice.

Not that we didn't sometimes come to grips with the enemy. Half the section was on stag in an OP sangar overlooking the border from high ground. The weather was overcast, with the rain only just holding off. The day dragged by. It was very quiet and nearly last light. One of the lads was pouring hot tea from a flask into two mugs for the five of us to share.

The silence was shattered by cracks and thumps. Someone shouted, 'Contact front!' The tea hit the floor along with the rest of us. A sharp burst of automatic fire blasted overhead. Watching their tracer and spotting their ground strike, the IRA gunmen corrected their aim. The next burst ripped into the sandbags in front of us.

Then we were up on our firing parapet. Dave had the GPMG locked into his shoulder. We were watching for muzzle-flashes, smoke and dust to locate the IRA's fire position. Stu saw it first. 'Four hundred, barn, right twenty-five! Hedgerow near track! Smoke and flash!' he yelled. We took aim, adjusting our weapon sights to four hundred metres. Chris, the corporal, shouted, 'Fire!'

He didn't need to tell us twice. The noise from the GPMG went right into me, making my bones vibrate. My mouth dropped open in surprise. I shut it with a snap. Shock waves of hot air from the roaring machine-gun smacked me in the face. Our whole position was shaking, filling up with dust and cordite smoke. I was half blinded by the lightning-white muzzle-flashes all around me. Hot empty cartridge cases were spinning and flying everywhere, bouncing off my head and stinging my nose and cheeks. I heard someone yell out, 'YAH-HOO!' at the top of his voice. Yes! I thought, aiming at a distant flash and squeezing off a round. Yes!

My ears were ringing. I was deafened, my nostrils full of the clinging stink of gunsmoke. I leaned across and bellowed in Dave's ear, 'Give us a go on the Gimpy!'

'Fuck off,' he shouted back. 'I carry it, I'm using it!'

Every few seconds, someone shouted, 'Changing mag!' With the noise and dust and confusion, it was impossible to know if the players were still firing at us. All I could see, through the smoke and dust, was our own tracer, flashing across the sky in brilliant slow-motion beads, hitting the target and whanging off high up into the dusky air. We'd been firing continually for more than a minute, a very long time. Chris shouted, 'Cease firing! Cease fire!' Nobody heard him. He tried again. 'Cease fucking fire!'

We stopped. Fumes and disturbed muck hung in the air about us. Our ears were ringing and our eyes were red. I looked around. Every single one of us was laughing, elated, eyes wide open and shining with excitement.

My brother Steve joined the Royal Marines that same year, 1974, arriving in Northern Ireland on his first tour in January 1975. He was stationed in the Turf Lodge right next to our area. I managed to cadge a lift in a Saracen to visit him. Last time we had seen each other we had been out on the town in Hereford. Now we were in a war zone. What our mum thought about us both being there, I can only imagine. Two sons to worry about patrolling the terrorist turf instead of one. Dad was always telling us to make sure and ring up as often as possible or Mum worried herself sick – she dreaded the sound of the mail arriving or a stranger knocking at the door. She never let us see it, though.

Having predicted the likely loss of six men, the battalion finished that second tour of Northern Ireland without the loss of one. I hoped Steve's unit would have the same luck. We returned to Catterick by train, and when we arrived at the station the regimental band was thundering away on the platform to greet us. And so was Margaret.

There was little time to exchange sweet nothings. As soon as we got back into camp, I was told I was on CO's orders. I couldn't think what I'd done wrong. They marched me in. A few moments later I marched back out under my own steam, a full corporal. I went out at lunch time for a quick drink to celebrate. I arrived back in camp three hours later, having missed the CO's briefing and drunk as a skunk. The platoon sergeant found me rolling around on the grass, filled to the gills with Pernod, gurgling happily. He put me to bed and said he'd see me later.

Great, I thought, when I woke up holding my head the next day. A corporal for less than twenty-four hours, and busted. But Bill, who'd been the platoon sergeant on the last tour, never mentioned it again. I've avoided Pernod ever since.

A few weeks later, in March 1975, Margaret and I were married in Catterick. The ceremony took place in a military church, but we all wore civilian clothes. Paper Lace was top of the charts with 'Billy Don't Be A Hero'. I had a shirt with a huge collar, a kipper tie, billowing great flares and bulbous two-tone platform shoes. It snowed. My brother came over on leave, my mates came up from Hereford, Margaret's mother cried and we all had a right old time of it in the sergeants' mess afterwards. A friend of mine, Taff, threw a snowball at the windscreen of the car when we left. The only trouble was, it had a stone in it, which crazed the glass.

My next posting, my first as 'married accompanied', was to Gibraltar. Margaret and I had a room in the Hotel Mediterranean on the seafront. Encouraged by my tales of derring-do, Ray, one of my mates from Hereford, had joined up in his turn, and he was here with his wife Jean in the same hotel. We spent a lot of our spare time together, swimming and sunbathing, or sitting drinking the duty-free and shooting the breeze. Things most definitely could have been worse.

The odd bit of work got in the way. One of the battalion's duties in Gibraltar was to provide the ceremonial guard for the Governor's residence, which in practice meant three soldiers all dressed up in their best green uniforms standing for long stretches outside the main man's house. The residence was at the back of a little square fronting the main road through the centre of the town, with the guardroom on the far side. Tourists and local children would line the sides of the square and the street, waiting to see the changing of the guard, which as a corporal was one of my duties. I had to march behind the relief sentries, changing them one at a time with the men who were already on duty.

Because of a historical quirk, the Royal Green Jackets march at a hundred and eighty paces to the minute, or about twice as fast as normal. On this particular occasion one of the Governor's adjutants, a young captain from a different regiment, decided he was going to follow me around. His presence was surplus to military requirements but his girlfriend was there that day and he wanted to impress her.

I set off at the usual very smart Green Jacket clip. At once it became clear that the captain, who was short, couldn't keep up. His hat kept falling off and he was continually getting his sword tangled between his legs. 'Slow down, Corporal,' he hissed, in a stage whisper, as we were making the first change. I carried on as if I hadn't heard. We were Green Jackets. We marched at that pace, and that was the pace we marched at. If he couldn't keep up, tough.

'Corporal!' he spluttered, at the second changeover. 'I said slow down!'

'Sorry, sir,' I replied. 'Can't slow down. Green Jackets march at a hundred and eighty paces per minute.' Under my breath, I murmured, 'Speed up, lads!'

The lads were only too happy to obey. Around the front of the residence we raced, like so many overwound clockwork soldiers. Scuttling and scurrying along in our wake, the captain wasn't quite cutting the dashing figure he'd hoped. It was a very hot morning, with a full sun striking a brilliant white light off the pale-coloured flagstones. He was getting cross and bothered – and very red in the face. His neck was sticking out with the effort to keep his cap on, control his sword and keep up; he looked more and more like an enraged turkey-cock. With every changeover he'd come puffing up behind us and give me a bollocking. Every time, we rocketed away as if nothing had happened. As I marched the lads coming off-duty back into the guardroom, the captain came rushing in behind me. 'Carry on marching, Corporal!' he shouted. 'March into jail!'

'What?'

'What, sir!' he snapped.

'What what?'

'What, *sir*, what, *sir*!'

'What, sir?' I gazed over the top of his head.

'You heard me, Corporal! Get into jail.' By now, he was quite purple in the face.

'Jail? Why?'

'Why, sir!' Silence. We exchanged looks.

'Why *what*, Corporal?'

'Why what?' I asked, as if mystified.

'Why what, *sir*! CALL ME SIR!' he bellowed.

'Why what, what, sir?'

'Shut up, C-Corporal!' he screamed, 'You marched too fast!'

I looked injured. 'No, I didn't.'

'No, you didn't, *sir*,' he yelled.

'No, I didn't what?'

'No, you didn't march too fast, sir!'

'Yes, sir, that's right, sir, no, I didn't march too fast, sir. That's just the pace we march at in the Green Jackets.' He had cracked, now: his fists were clenching and unclenching, and his arms were flapping up and down. 'Shut up and tell me your name!'

I looked at him in mock-puzzlement. 'What? Shut up *and* tell you my name? How can I do that?'

'Sir, *sir*! I'm an officer! Address me as sir!'

'Sir?'

'You're for it, Corporal. Your arm was bending in the middle when you marched.' He was so upset that I thought he was going to throw his teddy bear into the corner.

'What?'

'What, *sir*! What, *sir*!' I smiled at him. He was either going to burst into tears or explode. 'Get – into – jail!' he screeched. I went. The door clanged shut behind me. I must have been the first Corporal of the Guard in Royal Green Jacket regimental history to be marched straight off the parade-ground and into the guardroom. There I sat, in full ceremonial rig, kicking my perfectly polished heels. It was dark in there, and beautifully cool. Maybe now I'd get a bit of peace and quiet. But no. The captain was still jumping up and down outside. He hadn't finished with me. His voice cracking with rage, he stuck his face right up to the viewing grille and yodelled, 'I'll make sure you never do this duty again!'

'Oh, no,' I protested. 'You wouldn't do that, would you?'

'Would you, *sir*!' he squawked.

'Sir?' I replied.

'Yes, I bloody will.'

'OK, sir, if you must.'

'I bloody well will, too. You see if I don't, Corporal!'

I'm happy to say he was as good as his word: for the remainder of my time in Gibraltar I never did guard duty at the Residence again.

What a bummer.

Chapter Seven

It was in Gibraltar that I applied to join the Special Air Service. Once you've applied for Selection, only the Regiment itself can stop you doing it, unless you've just been advised of a new operational posting. The battalion CO agreed to let me go, but asked me if I'd do a short stint training recruits at the Green Jackets' Winchester depot first. I could have refused, but the Green Jackets had been good to me: I felt I owed them something back. While I was at the depot, my third stripe came through. I was now a sergeant.

Margaret was against my trying for the SAS: she knew that if the Regiment accepted me, I'd be away a lot. And if she were in any doubt about this, my mother quickly set her right. 'He won't be away a lot,' she told Margaret. 'He'll be away all the time.' Which turned out to be perfectly true.

To train for the SAS I went out on the hills with weight on my back, alone. I walked and ran for miles in the sun, rain, wind and fog, navigating up, over and down the high, steep, uneven and boggy ground of the Welsh hills: ground where so many leave their hope behind.

I never ever trained without navigating. I came to see that a two-minute map study could be worth an hour on the ground. I had to improve my stamina and determination, learn to read the land – and I had to do it on my own. A lot of soldiers who can run for miles and lift heavy weights fail Selection. It's as much about the inner game as it is about stamina and strength.

In August 1977, two years past the deadline I'd originally set myself, I set out for Hereford on one of life's hardest tests. I was twenty-two years old. As I was leaving, the OC of the Green Jackets said, 'Good luck, Hunter. I'm sorry to see you go but I hope I don't see you back!'

'Thanks, sir,' I said. 'I hope I don't come back.'

I didn't know it then but the regimental clock that records and keeps watch over all the SAS dead in their Hereford graves was ticking for me. I'd already used up at least two of my nine lives over the water with the Green Jackets. During the next eighteen years with the SAS, I'd use up all of the remaining seven – and then some.

SAS Selection was becoming a family tradition. My brother, Steve, had done Selection a few months ahead of me, but he had had to pull out with knee problems. He was devastated. I felt for him, but it wasn't over yet. He would still get another chance – and take it. As for my father, the one thing he wasn't going to do was help us out. But when I got to the camp, all the Directing Staff (DS) knew exactly who I was.

'Hoping to follow in your father's footsteps?' asked the OC.

'That's why I'm here, sir,' I replied.

'Good luck, then,' he said. 'We're always short of numbers.'

Looking round then at the enormous group of other hopefuls on Selection, hard-looking guys to a man, I found that difficult to believe. A few days later I understood what he meant.

I went and had a look around. The camp hadn't changed much from when I'd run around in it as a boy; the only noticeable difference was the perimeter security fencing, which was some of the most fearsome I'd ever seen. The place still had that strange, slightly empty feel to it, as if nothing much ever happened there – and for the exact same reason: the Regiment spent most of its time overseas.

The first person I met in camp was the Cat, who'd passed winter Selection about six months previously. The weather had been so severe that out of one hundred and seventy-five men, only seven passed. They became known as the Magnificent Seven – and the Cat was one of them. There he was, smiling and pointing as usual. 'This time, Gaz, you're on your own,' he said. He'd changed. He looked much more confident even than he had before, stronger than ever and super-fit. His shoulders no longer drooped, and he was much less casual. His uniform still looked as if he'd slept in it, though. He showed me the sand-coloured beret with its winged-dagger cap badge. I turned it over in my hand. I wanted that badge – more than I'd wanted anything in my life.

'Listen,' said the Cat, watching, 'never mind that Magnificent Seven shit, if I can fackin' do it, you can.' And, deep down, I thought he was right: I was as fit as he was, and I had the confidence now.

That evening, we went out for a quiet drink, me wanting to stay fresh for the off in the morning. We were in a pub I'd known since I was a teenager – only this time when we walked in you could tell straight away it had become an SAS drinking den. Lots of fit-looking men were standing about in desert-boots, jeans and crew-neck jumpers, drinking half-pints. I noticed one guy keeping a close watch on the door. The Cat told me the SAS always maintained security, wherever they were, no matter how few in number; every man looked out for the rest.

The more horror stories he told me about how hard Selection had been for him, the more we drank. I was very aware of all these guys looking at me, sure I was already undergoing some kind of test, right there in the pub. 'Say the wrong thing in town, and they'll fail you before you even start,' I'd been told. Well, it wasn't true that the Staff would be out watching us, but Hereford is a small town: most people know someone who is 'in' or 'badged'. If you had too much to say about it, the Regiment would certainly find out.

The next morning I sat in the lecture hall, holding my head in my hands, and praying they wouldn't ask us to do any running around until my hangover cleared. The OC of the training wing, a major, came in and introduced the training officer. I did a double-take: he was a great friend of my father's – from my earliest years I'd known him as Uncle Bill. It occurred to me that Selection was a bit of a family affair – I'd never looked at it before in that light.

I thought, That won't help me – the complete opposite, in fact.

Uncle Bill said he wanted all one hundred and seventy-five of us there to pass, but that nineteen in every twenty of us would fail, for one simple reason: ourselves. One by one, we would quit, under the

63

physical and mental stress. 'There's also dying on the hills,' he said. 'That's nature's way of telling you you've failed Selection. Of course, we'll do our best to prevent that.' But he didn't look concerned.

The first four weeks of Selection were split up, the first big test being the Fan Dance, to sort out the people who wanted to carry on and meant it. We were up at 5 a.m., and it was cold and dark. We climbed on to the canvas-covered trucks and set off. Every morning there was one truck less, reducing the odds and getting me closer to being badged. The Cat went out with one hundred and seventy-five and came back one of seven; I meant to do the same – be in that last 5 per cent. An hour and a half later, stiff and cold, we arrived at Pen-y-Fan, a mountain I knew well. I had first walked it years before with my father, mother and brother.

Uncle Bill was right: I could do it, but I had to fight the voice inside me all the way that was telling me I couldn't. Once the Fan was cracked, though, I felt better: I had the feeling I was going to get through.

We had two more weeks of mountain navigation, over longer and longer distances with ever-increasing weight on our backs, alone. The final week was called test week: this was the worst week of all, the marches were all long and with a set weight of 30 kilograms plus all the belt-kit and weapon. Every day that passed was one less to do, that's how I looked at it, every day I was getting nearer to being part of that successful 5 per cent. We were allowed a part day off before Endurance, the final test of the first phase of Selection, 64 kilometres in eighteen hours with 30 kilograms of weight over the worst country they could find for us. When we got back from Endurance, the Cat met us with the words, 'The Regiment is short of men – that's the only reason you wankers are still here.' Then he winked.

I rang home. 'Well done,' was all my father said.

During the week's leave the SAS gave me before Christmas, Margaret and I moved into a married quarter in Hereford. We spent a happy, frantic week doing it up. But for Christmas itself I was being posted to Belize again, on my first operational tour with the SAS: new-comers have to go straight out and relieve the people who have

Over the water. A Company

The Shooting Gallery, Londonderry 1972

Above My only photograph of Ginge Meredith

Below Jungle training, still Green

Opposite above The final hurdle: Combat Survival

Opposite below Freefall training, Air Troop

Back across the water. Blending in with the scenery . . .

. . . and (some years later) in command

Left Jungle training. Lunch

Above Motorized transport. Note the speed goggles

Below On the Guatemalan border. The Cat is far right

Above Unscheduled stop: CRW training

Below CRW ticket holders only!

Convoy attack, Afghanistan

been stuck in the jungle for three months.

When Margaret heard the news she looked at me sadly. 'This is what it's going to be like, from now on, isn't it?' she said. There was nothing I could say. I didn't even know when I'd be back. We had started years of more or less constant separation.

The first person I saw at Airport Camp when we got off the plane was the Cat, always that little bit ahead of me wherever I went. Having already been to Belize with the Royal Green Jackets, I knew the type of terrain we would be working in. I liked Belize. To the north of the country the land was like the Welsh hills, and just as wet: a spectacular folding green landscape cut by rushing streams. It was about ten times hotter than Wales, though. Further south, in the interior, the country grew more mountainous still, covered in thick jungle sprawling out to the east, then breaking down gradually into low hills and flatlands. The coast was a mass of dense, knotted, mosquito-infested mangrove swamps.

A muddy main river fed by the hills ran through the middle of Belize City and out into the sea. We were there because, in theory, the former British colony was under a low-grade security threat from Guatemala. The city centre was full of old stone colonial-type buildings, most of them in a pretty bad state: rusting ironwork, broken pipes, sieve-like roofs, peeling stucco. But these archaic piles looked handsome compared to the shacks that meandered out from the city's core. These hovels were thrown together out of anything and everything that came to hand, mostly bits of wood and wriggly tin, all falling down, a shanty-suburb that stank of human sewage and the fish market. The people ranged from African and European in the towns to Mayan Indian in the jungle villages.

There were dozens of bars in Belize town, from the semi-decent hotels to the outright whore-houses. This time round, with the SAS, I wasn't going to get much time for recreation: we were detailed off at once for a nine-day border patrol. It was to be my first task with the Regiment. And it was almost my last.

In joining the SAS I'd lost my stripes; like everyone else I'd have to start from scratch. Besides the Cat and myself, our patrol consisted

65

of another new lad, John, a warrant officer, second class, I'd done Selection with, also ex-Green Jackets, and a staff-sergeant called Brown, who was supposed to be in charge. Slim-built and with dark hair, Brown was in his late thirties, standing about five foot nine. What he lacked in height he made up for in sheer bloody-mindedness.

We jumped off the Puma down in the south near the Guatemalan border, and tabbed off into the jungle. Brown hadn't bothered fully briefing us, which I thought was not only unprofessional but strange. After a couple of kilometres, it got stranger. He stopped in the middle of the track – which we weren't supposed to be on anyway as the SAS doesn't use trails.

'You do realize', he said, looking us up and down with open contempt, 'that for your first three years in the Regiment you're just going to be a bloody nuisance to the troop?'

John and I looked at each other. 'What the fuck's he mean by that?' I muttered.

Those were the first, and virtually the last, words our staff-sergeant said to us for the entire trip. From that moment on it was the Cat who had to relay any information to us, while Brown held himself in splendid isolation. Although he thought himself a brilliant soldier, our leader was one of the worst I'd ever met.

Off he strode, straight down the middle of the track, in breach of all standard operating procedures (SOPs). In a real war, against any kind of clued-up opposition, we'd have walked straight into a booby-trap. We would walk for a bit and then, without a word or a sign of warning, Brown would shoot off at top speed into the jungle. We would follow, wondering what was happening. There would be no message back. This went in the face of everything we had been taught: in any kind of infantry, communication is key. We were supposed to be an élite force.

We arrived outside a village. Expecting to set up an OP, I stopped – but our intrepid leader strolled straight on in. Luckily the people were friendly, squat and broad-faced, proud, polite and smiling. They looked like a forgotten tribe, their faces like the ones carved on the ancient Mayan ruins in the jungle.

The villagers offered us the guest hut. Brown hadn't told us to go non-tactical, so John and I stood to, with our packs on, waiting for orders. None came. After about an hour, we smelt tea brewing. The Cat peered out of the hut and shrugged his shoulders, as if to say, 'Don't ask me.'

We waited another hour. Eventually, we were both called inside and told to put up our hammocks. The Cat came out, thumbs a-flying. He didn't have to say anything – John and I could both tell he was as pissed off as we were. This wasn't just unprofessional: it was ludicrous.

'We'll cook in twos,' he said, 'and do our weapons in twos as normal.'

Our leader sat at the end of the hut, with his back to us, in magnificent silence. The next day we got more of the same treatment: Brown strode off into the undergrowth without so much as a glance in our direction. We had advanced a couple of kilometres when, quite suddenly, he stopped dead in the middle of the track.

Then he did something I'll never forget. He put the side of his clenched fist up against his nose, and twisted it backwards and forwards. The rest of us stood and stared. If this was some kind of tactical signal it was a new one on me. Still twisting madly, Brown glared at us.

Tentatively, the Cat raised his fist to his nose and gave it a bit of a tweak. John and I looked at one another. Here we were, a tactical SAS patrol, in the middle of the jungle on the border with a potential enemy, and we were all standing around making secret signs like something out of Enid Blyton's *The Secret Seven*. Oh, well, I thought, if you can't beat them . . . Nose twisting had to mean something deep and profound, something that only a veteran SAS man, steeped in the mystic lore of the Regiment, would understand. Either that, or it was complete bollocks. In a while, Brown dropped his hand, plunged back into the jungle and we carried on patrolling.

The next morning, unable to contain his curiosity any longer, the Cat went over to Brown and made the secret sign. 'Sarge,' he asked, 'what does this mean?' Brown looked at him as if he were a complete fool. Turning to us, he stuck his fist up to his conk and did the mystery twiddle.

'Any of you cunts know what this means?'

'No.' We shook our heads.

'Pig!' he barked. 'It means wild pig!'

Oh, we thought, that'll come in useful when the Guats steam across the border.

John and I were totally disillusioned. We were in our first operational Sabre squadron, on our first operational mission, and we were having to put up with this unadulterated bullshit from an all-round fool and incompetent. We had been on far better-led patrols in our Green Jackets days.

From this point, things got even worse. Before setting out, Brown had told the Cat we were not to carry more than two days' rations as we'd be able to buy food in the villages. This turned out to be completely untrue. It was sometimes possible to buy pig off the villagers (make the secret sign) but we didn't want to risk it – the meat is almost always full of worm. What we needed was a large village with a rudimentary shop in it, a branch of Tesco's, say, or a nice big Sainsbury's. Unfortunately, these were few and far between so, on the third day of the patrol, we ran out of food. Against SOPs, we broke into our emergency rations. Brown, meanwhile, had Pandora's Bergen: every time he put his hand inside, another fistful of food came out. In the villages, he would reach into his pack and fling biscuits at the kids who came up begging. John and I ran after them and grabbed them back.

At the end of the nine days, the three of us were starving. The pick-up time came and went. The RAF radioed there would be a twenty-four-hour delay. We sat there with our bellies rumbling, waiting for the sound of the rotors, imagining huge feasts: bully beef, biscuits, baked beans – anything would have done. Brown decided the delay was all our fault, so he said, 'Right, hard routine.'

I said, 'We've been on hard routine for five days already. We've had no food.'

'Right. Well, now it's no fucking brews either,' said the Jungle Master.

'Haven't got any stuff to brew with, anyway,' drawled John. 'I ate the fucking tea.'

★

I've dwelt on this story because for me it was a formative experience. Brown was an example of a tiny minority in the SAS, the dinosaurs, who couldn't change to suit the new demands of the job. He had been promoted under the system of dead men's shoes, as a function of time served, instead of on merit. But in the 1970s, like the rest of the British Army, the SAS had to change. We were up against the IRA. There was no choice. We had to become quick-thinking, fast to act and react, responsive to change in procedure and new technology, highly professional, efficient and extremely well disciplined. The Army had been changing gradually, in the decades after the Second World War but the Troubles put that process of change on fast forward.

It took me a while to see this. After that Wild Pig patrol, when the SAS parked me and some of the other new lads in the jungle for another three months with no operational tasking, I got so fed up I wrote asking Margaret to find out for me about joining the police or the fire service.

But once we got back to the UK, and I met more of the Regiment's NCOs, I realized that Staff Sergeant Brown was the exception, not the rule, and the experience had been useful: it made me determined that if I ever rose up through the Regiment's ranks, I was going to blow away the old system of 'Buggins' turn' and make sure that only the best got to the top. I'd learned at the bottom how critical that was.

Chapter Eight

After Belize I was sent back to Northern Ireland, but this time as a fully trained member of the SAS. If I'd thought the Green Jackets tested my skills and initiative, this was something else. It was like joining a completely different Army.

We were in the middle of one of the most vicious phases of the Troubles. Two years before the new British ambassador, Christopher Ewart-Biggs, and his secretary had been killed by a land-mine. It was not long before the Second World War hero Earl Mountbatten, the last Viceroy of India, and cousin of the Queen to whom we'd sworn allegiance, was assassinated in a bomb attack in a fishing-boat off the coast.

But no longer would I be one of the Green targets, walking around waiting to get shot at. I was with the best in the business – and I meant to live up to that. We were trained in covert warfare by our own Counter-revolutionary Warfare (CRW) instructors, as well as by members of '14 Int & SY' – 14 Intelligence and Security, otherwise known as the Det. 14 Int & SY is the principal long-term clandestine surveillance unit in the Province.

In comparison with my Green Jacket days, the quality of the intelligence we received now was superb. We were briefed directly by a whole new set of people, the key specialists within the RUC Special Branch, Army Intelligence and MI5. We came under the direct command of the Commander Land Forces (CLF) and the RUC's Tasking and Co-ordination Group (TCG), which oversees and controls all anti-terrorist operations in Northern Ireland.

Right from the off, I liked the atmosphere. It felt like we were winning the argument.

For obvious reasons, we dressed pretty scruffily over the water: most of us let our hair grow long, sprouted great bushy sideburns and droopy moustaches. The less neat and military we looked, the better. This was 1978, the time of Cash 'n' Carry, *Charlie's Angels*, the string bikini – and, I still cringe to think of it, mega-flared loon pants. We kept the local Oxfam shops in business for miles around. Which brings me to the one area in which our mighty intelligence sources failed us miserably. Fashion.

One night we were out for a quiet drink in a 'safe' club. There was nothing much to do except watch the colour TV, which was still a bit of a novelty. What did it for me was the sight of some punk rockers on *News at Ten*. These people had gel-spiked hair dyed purple, they spat rather than talked, they wore bondage gear, and the boys led the girls around in handcuffs and chains. Sometimes they even reversed roles. The world had moved on!

I started looking around. Everyone in that room looked like a stunt man for Engelbert Humperdinck in a bad action movie. 'Bloody hell,' I said to myself. 'The only people left in the world with big hair, bandido moustaches and hedgerow sideburns are Regiment!' It made your flesh creep. The whole idea was to blend in, be the 'grey man'. We might as well have been wearing neon signs on our heads saying, 'SAS . . . SAS . . . Trying to look ordinary.'

When we were safely back at base, I pointed out that fluffy hair, Zapata moustaches, sideburns and all the other horrors of Seventies Man were out. We had just been rendered visually obsolete. We had to get with the new look: the age of the skateboard was upon us. The guys looked at me. Someone said, 'Bollocks!' Then they looked shiftily at one another. Nobody said anything. But gradually, one by one, they all sneaked off to the washrooms to shave, trim and snip.

When you're undercover, it pays to be a dedicated follower of fashion.

Even in the SAS, a lot of soldiering is routine. But working with the SAS troop and the Det is anything but. What was striking was the freedom we had as small teams or individually. To start with this was a bit scary: there was no one else to blame if you fouled up. But it had its uses.

Shortly after arriving back in the Province I happened to be in Gough barracks one evening. Special Branch was charging an IRA member for possession of firearms. He was talking a lot, hoping to get a reduced sentence by giving the police useful information. He was a wiry, skinny character, in his mid-twenties, with lank dark hair and a face fit for the hangman. I don't think any of us trusted him for a second. It could just have been a set-up. He said he knew of an IRA weapons cache, up in the mountains west of Armagh town. The RUC decided to check out his story. I went along as protection and to see if we could elaborate on the find.

We drove for about an hour and a half out of Armagh, stopping high up in an area of thick pine forest when he gave us the nod. Our informant didn't seem all that sure of his directions. I was getting a bad feeling from him. He kept asking the driver to go on a bit then stop, casting nervous looks all around but never appearing to recognize anything. At our fourth or fifth stop he made another show of looking around. 'No, it isn't here,' he said slowly. 'We need to make a right and then go on up that track.' We bumped up the forestry road until he made another sign and we stopped yet again. This, he thought, might be the place. We all got out. Our passenger walked about, grubbing at tree roots with his foot.

'No, I thought this was it,' he told Ian Phoenix, the RUC sergeant in charge, 'but I've gone wrong again.' He smiled, ruefully, as though we were all great pals out for a picnic in the woods.

This same stop-start malarkey went on for another twenty minutes. It was late at night and dark. I turned to him, said, 'You know what I think? I think you're messing us about.'

'Oh, no,' he said. 'I know where it is. Just carry on as you are.' We drove on in the direction he gave us. Eventually he told us to pull up. We put out all-round protection and I followed our informant into the forest with two of the RUC officers. He led us down a steep bank to a partially filled hole at the base of a tree. To me it looked like a half-collapsed badger's set, long since abandoned. A lot like. The last

72

thing it looked like was a recently excavated weapons cache. Even so, we had to take him seriously. The RUC men got busy with their shovels.

After about fifteen minutes' hard sweat, they stopped digging. There was nothing in their hole except earth.

We had wasted a whole night. The only remaining question was, did the suspect actually know anything worth finding out? I went over to the RUC officer. 'Ian,' I said quietly, 'could you give me a minute alone with him?'

Ian didn't say anything. He just ground out his cigarette and moved his men away out of earshot – and sight.

The IRA man was lounging in front of a tree. When I was sure they had gone, I turned on him. With one hand I grabbed him by the throat, lifted him right off his feet and slammed him back up against the trunk of the tree. His teeth clicked together with the force of the impact. 'Now then,' I said quietly, 'you're going to tell us what the fuck's going on. Is there a cache? If so, where is it?' He hung there, feet dangling in mid-air, unable to believe what was happening. His eyes bulged out of his head. He made a strangled, bleating noise.

I stared into his eyes. 'You know who I am, don't you? What I am?' He made a slight nod above my bunched fist. 'Good. So, tell me.'

I waited for a few seconds, relaxing my grip on his throat very slightly so that he could speak. He was looking from side to side – he actually wanted the RUC now to come and save him. He was scared – but not scared enough. He still wasn't talking. I reached round, took my pistol out of its belt holster, and shoved the muzzle hard up under his chin. His head went back but he tried to keep his eyes on me. There was a sharp smell as he pissed himself.

Now he was scared.

'Last chance, sunshine,' I said. 'We're fed up buggering about. I'm not the police, and I don't have to worry about the law.' I did. 'Now, do you know anything worth the shout? Yes or no?'

'No,' he said. 'There's no cache. I don't know anything. I swear I don't.'

I dragged him back up the slope and slung him into the car. In

73

silence, we drove back to Gough barracks. The player never took his eyes off me once during the entire journey.

Ian Phoenix gave me a knowing look and his wry smile. This was my first contact with him, a man I came to know and admire over the next decade.

Only once did I really overstep the mark.

For some time the RUC had been watching two groups of IRA men, letting them run on for as long as possible in the hope that they might lead to a weapons cache or a new cell. But the players had gone to earth in some isolated farm buildings in the remote countryside of South Armagh. There were at least six of them, in a pair of adjoining two-storey cottages built out of old dark brick, the gardens over-grown with weeds and soft green carpet-moss all over their patched and staggered slate roofs. The IRA men were armed, and we were expecting resistance.

They had been in there for two days, and they showed no signs of moving.

It was time to go in and take them.

We split into two assault teams of four men, one team to each house. I went to the rear of the northernmost house along with Frank White, to cut off any runners. The other two in our team were at the front. On the word, we were going to hit them from both sides. As always, we had the QRF at hand, positioned so they could get to us within five minutes. This time, as soon as we started moving in, the QRF was going to move with us. There was no point in taking any chances.

'Go!' I slipped the armband (to sort out the good guys from the bad guys) on over my civilian clothes. It was just dark.

I ghosted up to the back door. Strangely, it was slightly ajar. I eased it wide open and stepped inside. Frank was at my shoulder. The house smelt of decay and cigarette smoke. We were in a broken-down kitchen. All the lights were on. Half-finished drinks lay on a Formica table in the middle of the room, and a dog-end was still burning in an ashtray. We stood for a few seconds, listening hard. We knew they were in there. But what did they know?

Soundlessly, we moved into the living room. I was aware they could fire straight through the ceilings and walls at us. We cleared through. There was no one on the ground floor.

Jimmy and Chris had gone in the front door. They were upstairs ahead of us. I heard Jimmy roar, 'Up against the wall!'

We raced up to the first floor, the shout still ringing round the walls. I could see Jimmy's back in the doorway of the end bedroom. That left two bedrooms to clear. I signalled to Frank that I'd take the one on the right. He nodded and was gone.

The door to the bedroom was in front of me. I kicked it open, whipped round into the room and dropped on to one knee, Armalite up. There was a man half in and half out of the window, with his back to me, trying to make a run for it.

I put my sights square on his head, and took up the first pressure on the trigger. 'Security Forces!' I shouted. 'Halt!' He climbed back into the room, put his hands up slowly and turned to face me. Next door, I could hear thumping, banging and loud yells, the wall shaking with the sounds of a full-scale scrap: that was Frank taking care of business.

'Don't move unless I tell you,' I said. 'Put your hands on the top of your head and keep them there. Move away from the window.' Slowly, watching me intently all the time, he moved.

Keeping the Armalite on him, I backed up to the doorway. Glancing along the corridor, I could see the rest of our team showing themselves in the doorways. We had cleared the house, we were in control.

Just then a single shot rang out from the next-door house. At the sound of it, my prisoner got scared.

'We're all soldiers together, boy,' he babbled. 'Aren't we the same? If you let me just slip out of the window? Give me a chance? What d'you say?'

'We're not the same, sunshine,' I told him. 'Shut the fuck up.'

'Come on now,' he wheedled. 'Give a man a break.'

I took him in. He was a skinny-looking bastard of about twenty-five, with scruffy jeans, a dirty-looking light-blue polo-neck jumper, scuffed trainers and a newish, military-style, thigh-length cotton-canvas jacket, straight out of the Che Guevara book of revolutionary in-wear. He had light brown curly hair and a clear complexion. Suddenly I recognized him from one of the 'brief' books: he was on the 'Most Wanted' list. He was a suspect in numerous shootings and bombings, all against civilians. He had a lot of deaths to answer for.

And now he would.

As I watched him, his eyes flicked to the floor. Something was wrong. I'd missed a trick. I looked down, and saw the butt of an AK-47 assault-rifle sticking out from under the bed. Great, I thought. A weapon. Got you fair and square, you bastard. Seeing I'd spotted the long, he piped up again, 'Come on now, boy, fair's fair. Would you give me a chance?'

When he said this I started losing my sense of humour. That AK-47 was at the end of a killing chain stretching all the way back to the Russians. There was strong intelligence suggesting the IRA came by much of its weaponry and explosives from the Soviet Union, via (then) terrorist front countries like the Lebanon and Syria. For the old men in the Kremlin, it was another way of fighting the Cold War.

I wondered what had happened to the QRF. I'd had about enough of this player. He was getting to me, which was bad. 'OK,' I said. 'I'll give you a chance. Go for your weapon.'

It was against every rule in the book.

'What?' he stammered.

'You heard me. Go for your weapon.'

He stared down the barrel of my Armalite. 'No,' he said. 'No, I can't.'

'Tell you what, I'll put my gun down. Then you go for it.'

He looked at me.

'Do it,' I said. 'You talk about being a soldier but you're afraid to take me on man to man.' I brought the Armalite down, rested its barrel against the end of the bed, and stepped away from it.

'Look,' I said, pointing at the AK-47 on the floor in front of him, 'equal distances. Now, *go for it!*' Slowly, staring at me all the time, he lowered his arms to his sides.

I gestured at his weapon with my left hand. He didn't move. 'So much for you then, *soldier.*' With my eyes still on him, I reached round and drew the Browning from my belt-holster. 'Just as well you're a fucking coward, eh? Now turn round and put your hands on the back of your head.'

Outside, in the fresh night air, I took a deep breath and thought about what I'd done. It had been against all the SOPs, against everything I'd been taught. But I was still glad I'd done it.

The other team had made three arrests in the next-door house. On their way in, a large German shepherd had come hurtling down the stairs at them. One of our guys, Pete, had shot it, and called in a contact report. That was the shot we'd heard.

'Pete the Dog-Shooter' never lived that particular 'contact' down.

Six in one hit, which is about as good as it gets – but we don't walk on water. Word came through that the IRA was planning a hit on a UDR man in his home. We decided to put in a reactive OP, hoping to lift the players as they moved in. The UDR officer lived on a well-lit estate, making his house difficult to reach undetected, but we dropped off in the small hours and started in along a planned route.

I was number two in a patrol of four. We were advancing along the side of a high stone wall, which, in the light of the full moon beaming down from a clear sky, was very bright, almost white.

'Contact!' hissed Morris, who was leading.

We froze.

'What?' I breathed. 'Where?'

'Armed men, there, on our left.' We dropped flat, and put out a 'possible contact' report over the radio. We lay tensed and ready, peering across our sights. The seconds ticked by.

There was no sign of them. 'I definitely saw longs,' said Morris. 'They were moving that way.' He pointed in the direction we'd been travelling. 'OK,' I breathed. 'Let's take a look. We'll move in twos.' As we got to our feet, I saw two armed men rise up out of the ditch across the road. 'Get down!' I hissed. I trained my long on them. Then it hit me.

'No, wait,' I said. 'Everybody stand up.' I got to my feet. They looked at me as if I'd gone mad. You don't stand up in these situations. Cautiously they followed me. Four men with rifles were standing directly opposite. 'Christ,' said Jimmy at the rear, bringing his Armalite to bear.

'No,' I told him. 'Wait! Watch.' It was an effort not to laugh. I squatted. One of the men across from us squatted. I stood up. The fellow by the wall stood up. Finally, somebody laughed.

We bobbed up and down for a while in front of this white wall. We'd called in a contact report on our own shadows.

Chapter Nine

———————————

We were going to call the baby Andrew. Somehow we both knew it was going to be a boy. More than anything I wanted a child. I knew Margaret felt the same way. I had been with the Regiment for five years, I'd been promoted to lance-corporal, I was well settled in, and while our Labrador, Lady, had been a pretty good child substitute, the time had come for the real thing: we were ready.

For a year, we had been preparing, working out our finances and finding a suitable home. We had moved into a new house in Hereford, done out one of the bedrooms as a nursery, Margaret had been through a perfect pregnancy. Everything was looking good. We went down to the hospital, and the labour was mercifully short.

It was a boy. As soon as he was born, they placed Andrew on Margaret's chest. She'd had gas and air, and she was still a little bit out of it, but she held him in her arms for a while and hugged him. It was an amazing moment. I bent over them, trying to see his face but he was covered in the usual goo. The sister came up and took him away. I gazed at her while the other nurses attended to Margaret. There was something wrong with the way she was staring at the child. I didn't like the way she was holding him, either.

'What is it?' I asked, stepping closer. She made some evasive reply, trying to turn away. I stepped up, looked down into the face of my newborn son and saw what the sister's strange expression meant.

All the joy went out of me. 'He's got Down's syndrome,' I said quietly. 'Hasn't he?'

'We don't know that,' she said briskly. 'Not for certain.' I searched her face. She was trying to save my feelings. 'We'll need to get someone in to have a look at him. An expert.'

'Then please get him,' I said.

'Today's Sunday,' she replied. 'He won't be in until Monday.'

'I want to know now. Please get the specialist in.' She looked at me, and moved quickly away. I followed her out into the corridor. 'Get him in now,' I insisted. 'Listen, you think there's something wrong, I think there's something wrong. My wife's in there, she hasn't got a clue what's happening. She deserves to know, she's the mother. Why should we have to wait?'

But, whatever I said, they wouldn't call in the consultant on his day off. I went back to Margaret. Despite her exhaustion, she was sitting up. 'Where's the baby?' she asked anxiously. 'Why can't I hold him?' I called to one of the nurses, who brought our newborn baby back.

'Margaret,' I started, 'Margaret . . .' There was a note in my voice that I didn't recognize. I took her hand. 'They're going to get a specialist in to look at him.'

'Why? What is it? What's wrong with him?'

I met her eyes. 'I think it's Down's syndrome.'

I can still see the look on her face now.

I went back home. There was a list of names by the phone, people I was supposed to ring with the happy news. I told Lady to sit and put my hand on her head. It was a very long list. Unable to focus on it, I sat holding the receiver for the best part of an hour. In a little while, Lady laid her head in my lap.

At last, I started calling – but only our immediate families. When they picked up the phone, I said, 'The baby's been born,' and rang off.

When I'd finished, I grabbed Lady, crawled into bed with her, and lay there sleepless all night, thinking about Andrew, our newborn child. Every so often, Lady would nuzzle me or lick my hand, as if she understood the pain I was feeling and was trying to make up for it.

Early the next morning I went back into the hospital. The specialist took us into a private room, where he quietly confirmed our worst fears. Andrew was a very severe case. Margaret and I discussed what to do between ourselves and came to a decision.

A little while later, our respective parents came to see us. I met them at the door. 'Look,' I said, 'we've talked to the professionals about this, we've had counselling, and this is what we've decided to do. Andrew's going to have full-time professional care. Please don't put any pressure on us to change our minds.' To our relief, they never did.

I went back into the room we had decorated for Andrew, looking at the toys and all the normal things you get for a child. He'd never use them now. I stood in the room and tears filled my eyes. Slowly, I packed everything away into black bags, and put them up into the loft. Our dreams went into the bags with them.

As for the people who looked after Andrew, I can feel only admiration: I thought I could face any enemy, confront any fear or situation thrown at me – but I couldn't face what they took on, on our behalf, for years on end, and not for the few days or weeks the situations I'm in normally demand.

Some people look at the Regiment and wish they could do it: I believe a lot of people could but never try. I know there are many jobs that I couldn't do, like that one, taking care of a mentally disabled child. That takes a different kind of courage.

Chapter Ten

It was night and the weather was bad for parachuting. I was in a four-man stick (all members of 2 Troop, of which I was then a member) in a big Nato exercise, codenamed Flintlock, testing the ability of regular forces to withstand covert Special Forces attack.

We got to the tail ramp, not bothering with our last-minute safety-checks. There was no time. They just wanted us out now so that the exercise could go ahead as scheduled. We had been flying since mid-night, on and off oxygen, up and down to the tailgate, ready to go each time and then being cancelled, bent double under an all-up weight of about 50 kilograms, made up of the Bergen, weapons, belt-kit and an extra pack, all strapped on around the legs, the pack and parachute straps ferociously tight for free fall. The aircraft dropped lower at every attempt so that from our original jump height of 6,000 metres we were down to 2,000. At four in the morning, physically and mentally drained, we jumped.

As I came out, all I could see was light. There were lights everywhere I looked – the whole German countryside was ablaze. I shook my head, closed my eyes, then opened them again. This wasn't sup-posed to be happening. No, this wasn't a horrible dream: forgetting how much lower we were than the originally planned jump height, the navigator had failed to adjust the exit-point. He should have recalculated the drop, allowing for a much shorter distance of forward travel in the air. Instead, he had put us out right over the middle of a small German town at very low altitude.

Still, I had a stable position in the free fall, my legs were tucked up, my straps were secure, everything was OK. All I needed now was the canopy, and I could scan for a clear space. I watched the altimeters unwind. A thousand metres. I waited for the height-finder (HF) to auto-release the parachute. It failed. No dramas, this had happened to me before. But I wasn't going to wait.

I hit the parachute with my elbows, trying to smash it free, knowing this would set me spiralling. I was head down, hoping the faster airspeed might drag the chute out. I reached across to dump off the main rig manually. No handle, it had moved. In the dark, with all the clutter of the oxygen mask I was blind, but my hands were searching frantically, my life depended on it.

I found the handle, ripped it out, down and away, and waited. No canopy. Furiously, I rolled in the air and pulled at it again and again. I was through 700 metres, falling at terminal velocity. I twisted frantically, smashing and elbowing the lump on my back. I went head down again, this time against my will. Looking out, I saw ground-rush. I was below the horizon-line. Unless I cleared in the next few seconds, I was going in.

I felt a flash of panic.

I went for my front reserve handle, and as I pulled, the weight left my back and the canopy rushed away into the night sky with a great swirl. It snapped me vertical with an almighty, back-breaking jolt, but that was the least of my worries. Glancing at the altimeter, I saw I was at about 300 metres. I had seconds to pick a safe-looking spot. For me, the training exercise was over. The essential and only thing now was to avoid hitting anything on the ground that would kill me.

All around me were lights from the houses, I could see the roof tiles gleaming, I was about to get castrated by a television aerial. I scanned frantically: there had to be a patch of open ground somewhere. To my right I saw a dark space. My steering-toggles were still locked up. Snatching them down and steering towards that one solitary black patch in the sea of light, I swung round into the wind ready for landing.

All the extra kit and my Bergen were still bundled up on the back of my legs. This had to hit the ground before I did, or the huge weight would snap my ankles on landing. I let go of the steering-toggles and pulled up on the pack-release hooks. The Bergen and the rest of the kit dropped a fraction. I wriggled it down my legs, manoeuvring it out on to my feet. The kit was still attached to my body by a line, which had to be released so the packs would fall away under me. I could still see the clear black space below. At 20 metres I tipped the Bergen off my boots. There was a massive downward tug as the line caught the weight and held.

At that moment there was a huge flash in the sky. A brilliant arc of white-blue light shot out into the darkness, followed by fountains of yellow sparks. There was a weird fizzling sound. The air all around me crackled and hissed, I smelt burning. Then something hit me hard on the back of the legs. I flipped over backwards into the void, and caught fast. For a second or two, I lost consciousness. When I came round, I found myself hanging upside down in the pitch dark, snagged on something. I reached forward, trying to feel what had happened. A cable. Steel wire. My right leg was twisted around some sort of steel cable. Another thick wire was digging into the small of my back. The parachute was draped all around me. I had no idea where I was or what was happening.

Pushing away the folds, I could just make out the Bergen. It seemed to be hanging in front of my eyes, like an apparition, on the same level as I was but a good two metres away. How could that be? I dangled there, like a bat, trying to work it out. Tracing the pack attachment line back up above my head I saw another thick wire cable.

Screwing my head round, I saw the town behind me, a vague black mass. Wait a minute, I thought. It's dark. Where have all the lights gone? Close by, I could just make out a tall metal pole of some sort. I thought about cutting the line. But I couldn't see the ground, I had no idea how high up I was. I could fall and break a bone, or worse. But, on the other hand, I couldn't just hang where I was all night. Should I cut the line?

I reached down and took out the knife.

As I reached forward a torch came on right below me. Someone shouted: it was Morris, part of our four-man stick.

'Morris,' I shouted, 'look out! I'm just going to cut.'

84

'No, you're not!' he yelled back. 'Don't cut! You're way up in the air! Over ten metres! You're across some power lines! Don't move! Stay exactly where you are and don't move a muscle. I'll go and get help.'

Power lines, I thought. High-voltage electricity. I'll stay exactly where I am, then.

I managed to make out the time on my watch. It was nearly five. Already I'd been upside down for the best part of an hour. More than anything, I wanted to go to sleep. Now I knew why bats went to sleep upside down – it's the perfect position. Half an hour later I was still there. From time to time, Morris called up encouraging comments, like, 'You look like a bauble on a Christmas tree!'

'Cheers, mate,' I shouted back. 'Thanks a lot for your help.'

In dribs and drabs, a small knot of German farmers, the rest of my stick and the odd stray dog gathered underneath Gaz the Giant Bat Impersonator. The red tips of cigarettes glowed in the darkness. Why weren't they doing something to help? Then it dawned: they were waiting until the engineers arrived to switch off the power.

A US Army ambulance rolled up. A sergeant got out. Upside down, I watched him, warily. He clambered up on top of his ambulance and started jumping for the folds of my parachute. No one else seemed to have noticed what was happening. 'Help!' I squawked, 'Someone stop him!'

Suddenly Morris looked up. At once, he saw the danger. He raced forward, grabbed the sergeant's ankles, and jerked them hard back. The sergeant came off the top of his ambulance as though he'd been shot. 'What the fuck?' he spluttered. Morris had seen what I'd seen: the instant the American touched me, he would complete the circuit to earth, and we would both get sixty-four thousand volts through us. I'd stick with impersonating a bat every time. Someone else could try being a potato crisp.

Next on the scene was the local fire brigade – part-timers, I later found out. As the fire truck rolled up, the power company finally gave the all clear: the current was off, this time officially. One of the German firemen got up on the fire-tender's hydraulic platform. Slowly, he began rising up through the air towards me. As he came nearer, I noticed that he had a large serrated knife in his hand. I could see him eyeing up my Bergen. Oh, no, I thought. He's going to cut the line!

'No, no, no!' I shouted, at the top of my voice. '*Nein*! It's holding me up! It's holding me up! Don't cut it!'

The fireman had no English, and I had no German. '*Ja, ja, ja,*' he replied soothingly. 'Cut it, *ja*!' He reached forward with his knife.

'No!' I yelled desperately. '*Nein*, don't cut!'

He cut the rope.

I sat bolt upright for a moment on the power line, then dropped like a stone into space. Something stopped me in mid-fall. I swung wildly for a moment, then steadied. I heard the packs thud into the earth below. I was dangling upside down from the rescue platform. The fireman had caught my feet, trapping them against the rails. Slowly, the fire-crew lowered us both to safety on the boom.

Next day, the whole episode was the front-page headline in the local newspaper: 'British soldier blacks out town.'

As an exercise in covert infiltration, you had to say this one hadn't gone particularly well.

Back in Hereford, a few days later, the colonel of the Regiment introduced me to the Prime Minister, who happened to be visiting. 'Ah, yes,' said Margaret Thatcher thoughtfully, as we shook hands, 'so you're the man who blacked out half of Germany. For a while there we were worried about you.'

My next parachuting disaster came in Oman.

The SAS spent years during the sixties and seventies helping the Sultan's forces overcome a long-running Marxist rebellion. My father was very much a part of this: in one of the critical engagements of that war, the SAS had proved decisive, scaling the Radfan Ridge, a rebel stronghold, from its so-called 'impossible' side, and winning the battle through a combination of ferocity and surprise. Dad had been well to the fore.

My brother, Steven, who'd passed Selection at the second attempt, was now in A squadron's Mountain Troop. During his troop training, he climbed the Radfan Ridge, following literally in Dad's footsteps. I had no time off to follow suit, but being there meant a lot to me all the same.

By now, we were jumping with high-performance rigs. Instead of pulling out a pin, there was a tiny parachute, called a throw-away drogue, attached by a line to the main canopy's extractor pin. Having jumped, you pulled on a small toggle, which released the drogue chute into the airflow. This, in turn, pulled a pin releasing the main canopy. There was no need to rely on the automatic height-finder, which, as I knew only too well, was prone to failure.

You might think the desert is easy to jump on, but in fact the opposite is true: the flatness gives a false sense of height, particularly in comparison to Europe, where there's always a tree around to help. In the Oman, the desert is littered with stunted bushes, which from the air look confusingly like trees. You can think you're at 200 metres when in reality you're at less than half that height.

We made the first jump from the Skyvan without any problems. There were six of us in the next stick – myself, Geordie Barker, Morris, Gill, Dave, 'Tug' Wilson, who was one of B squadron's sergeants, and an RAF man, Don.

Geordie was a sergeant who had come from G squadron. I'd first got to know him on a demolitions course, in 1980, when he had instructed me. He knew a lot about demolitions, and he had helped me get up to scratch. Any time after that, when I was going out on a team job and needed to teach demolitions, I would go back and see Geordie to make sure I knew what I was talking about.

Geordie had been posted across from G squadron because he was a first-class sergeant, whereas the two we already had weren't quite up to the job. He was one of the first examples of the cross-fertilization that started taking place in the squadrons around this time. He was just what we needed in the troop, a breath of fresh air, an excellent leader who listened then delegated, and he kept Tug Wilson firmly in check.

Geordie was about five foot eight, stockily built, with light-coloured hair. Although he came across as a quiet northerner, he was a great story-teller. Once he got going, he could sit and keep you in stitches for hours on end. One story he told about himself was typical: he'd been out drinking heavily one night, before a HALO jump scheduled for the next morning. He got up in the back of the aircraft, and his stomach started playing up. He had the spew-bags out, filled a couple, and then he developed the shits. Just before the stick was due out, there was a horrible stench. Everyone moved away.

'Fucking hell, Geordie,' someone said. 'A rat's crawled up your arse and died.'

'Bollocks,' said Geordie, 'I've shit myself.'

In free fall, Geordie went head down, reached terminal velocity and did a few spins. When he got to the ground, the others stood and looked at him. The air pressure had forced the shit up around his neck and on to his face, it had squirted out of his cuffs and over the tops of his boots – anywhere it could come out, it had.

That was Geordie.

On the way down, Geordie and Gill practised doing a free-fall link-up. I was just above them and off to one side, observing. Geordie took out his drogue and held it in his right hand. (Holding the drogue parachute bunched up in your fist and throwing it away into the air-stream when you wanted the main canopy to come out was common practice.)

The drogue had a bridle-strap attaching it to the main parachute's pin. Made of closely woven nylon, this bridle-strap was a couple of centimetres wide. There was a problem with this, as we were about to discover.

At around 600 metres the two men separated, ready for the pull. Suddenly, Geordie went head down. There was something wrong. I could see that his main rig had come partially out but, instead of streaming clear, the canopy was somehow caught up around his back and legs. He'd thrown the drogue OK, I could see that wobbling about in the air, but the main rig was seriously out of order. I put my head down and dived hard towards him. As I came up close, I flared slightly to keep station with him. His main rig was plastered over his back-mounted reserve chute and all around his legs.

That was a disaster. He was in mortal danger.

We were below 300 metres now, still in free fall. Glancing at my altimeter, I tracked a little closer as Geordie struggled and kicked. I didn't want to watch this man die. I had to get hold of him, grab his rig and pull it clear myself or, if that didn't work, hold on to him and let him share my chute. I sensed the others around me in the air trying to do the same. I got ground-rush, then, and knew it was too late. We'd run out of ceiling: it was time to dump or die. With everyone else, I dumped. For a second, I was disoriented by the massive upward jerk. I looked around frantically, counting chutes. Including my own, there were five: five orange-white canopies against the blue sky.

Six of us had jumped in the stick.

As we came in to land, I saw Des McAlpine, the RAF jumpmaster, driving like a madman across the desert in the Land Rover. Then I saw what I'd been dreading, a long swathe of tangled nylon, strung out across the hard-packed sand, at the end of which was Geordie. I landed nearby. Des was walking around in small circles, repeating the phrase, 'He's gone in. He's gone in. He's gone in,' over and over.

I said, 'Shut the fuck up, Des.' Dave and I ran across. Geordie was lying face down in the desert. His twisted reserve parachute was laid straight out, like a pointer, from his head. He had his right hand tucked in underneath his body; his left hand was slightly forward and out, with the palm turned up, as if in supplication. His legs were bunched up, hidden under the nylon folds. His helmet had come off and rolled away.

I looked across at Dave. 'We don't need a doctor, do we?' He shook his head slowly, and sadly. Another friend who had run out of lives. Another name on the Hereford clock-tower.

Together we gently turned Geordie over. His features had been squashed flat into his face: it was as if the nose, eyes and mouth had been drawn on his skin, making him look two-dimensional, not like a real person any more. Every bone in his body was shattered, only his jump suit was holding him together.

For three hours, we sat there at the dead man's side, keeping him company until a doctor came out to certify him dead. Then we gathered him up and took him over to the Skyvan on a stretcher.

Examining Geordie's gear later on, we discovered that the airflow tugging on the drogue's bridle-strap had pulled the pin out of his main parachute *before* he had chucked the drogue. The main canopy had come half out, caught the slipstream vortex behind his back, and promptly tangled. Geordie must have been horribly aware of all this. But he had been unable to free the mess that had eventually killed him.

The next day we burned his parachutes.

Shortly after this accident, drogue bridles throughout the armed forces were replaced by thin, round paracord, which induces negligible drag. But for one good man, it was a change that came too late.

I've always had a love-hate relationship with free fall. Not long after joining the SAS, I had very nearly been killed training in Canada: the old TAP parachute failed to come out, I couldn't pull the reserve because I was head down and in a spin, and when I did finally succeed in getting the main rig out it jerked me upright with such force it put my heels on to the back of my head, cracked my vertebrae and ripped three panels out of the chute. Result: several days flat on my back in hospital, and lucky not to be paralysed or dead.

And yet, when you're jumping in the beautiful mountain country around Pau, in the Pyrenees, where the French forces have their main training ground, falling free as an eagle between those spectacular peaks, there's no other feeling in the world like it. You land and think, I want to do that again – straight away. It's worth the risk!

While we were out in the Omani desert losing valued friends, we had a visit from a two-star general. It was a fairly standard staff-officer visit: the great man arrived, pretended he'd met us all before, and asked a series of more or less fatuous questions, what rank we were, what we were doing, and so on. We waffled back at him, and he toddled off happily with a nod and a vague smile. At the last second, he stopped and came back. Morris was trying to talk to a local in broken Arabic. The general thought this was interesting. 'Can you interpret for me?' he asked.

'If you like, sir,' Morris said.

This should be good, I thought. Morris is a chronic linguist.

'Good, good. Splendid. It just occurred to me . . . I wonder if you could ask that Omani fellow you're talking to how the rebel attacks by the Adu have affected the Omani economy and how, in particular, they have impacted on him personally?' Morris was a baby-faced northerner, with very wide eyes who had been, in his own words, 'a

90

tubby little radio repairman in the RAF' when he had suddenly decided to get up and join the SAS. We had been on Selection together, and it was out in Belize on continuation training that I'd got to know him. His hair was always standing on end, and he was one of life's born anarchists: he always wanted to know *why* we had to do anything. Even in civilian life he ignored the rules – he was always getting nicked for not having his car taxed and things like that.

Morris looked intently at the general, to see if he were taking the piss but he was serious.

'OK, sir, I'll try.' Morris turned back to the Omani, and held out a cigarette. I could just follow the conversation. 'All right, mate? How's your camels?'

'I have no camels,' said the Omani gravely.

'Really? Spot of bad luck.' They both lit up. 'The, er, the weather's very warm for the time of year, isn't it?' Morris continued.

'Yes, the weather is indeed very warm for this season.'

'Your family is well?'

'Yes, my family is very well, thank you. How is your own?'

'Oh, not so bad, you know, mostly dead.'

'Oh dear,' said the Omani, who like nearly all Omanis was extremely polite. 'That is not so good.'

Morris nodded, and turned back to the general. 'Well, sir, what he tells me is quite complicated, but I'll do my best. When the enemy first attacked, many people, including this man, fled their homes. Clearly this had a catastrophic effect on the economy as a whole, and he was no exception. Having been a settled and prosperous farmer, he was forced by these tragic circumstances to lead a semi-nomadic existence with his family, essentially reverting to the traditional way of life carried on by his ancestors since time immemorial. However, as time went on, and the situation stabilized, he was able to settle back down, and . . .' Morris went on like this for about five minutes, giving the general a complete breakdown of the Omani economy, which he had just made up on the spot.

At the end of this briefing, the general, clearly impressed, shook Morris warmly by the hand. 'Well,' he said, 'jolly good. Really that was jolly good. Very, very interesting. Splendid stuff. Thank you very much.' And he went away a happy general.

Morris, unfortunately, wasn't quite so happy. He had come from sitting on a chair mending radios in the RAF, and what he wanted was to be on operations, full time. But the SAS isn't like that: sometimes – in fact, quite a lot of the time – you have to do little things like training. Also, much like the Cat, Morris wasn't one to suffer fools. Although things had changed a lot since I joined, the Regiment still promoted a few people on the basis of dead men's shoes, regardless of their ability and experience. Consequently, and often through no fault of their own, a few of the NCOs were incapable of planning exercises, let alone leading live operations. There were no internal command courses, and attendance at external Army courses was rare. Sometimes there were operational fuck-ups. Most of these were avoided because the junior members of the troop would use their initiative and save the day. But, to a very bright guy like Morris, this situation was unacceptable.

I understood how he felt. I was still dissatisfied with the less-than-competent minority, and with the question marks hanging over the Regiment's future.

Added to the internal problems faced by the SAS, there was the question of its wider operational role. In the late seventies and early eighties it was only the counter-terrorist operational role that had saved it from being disbanded. It took the Falklands War to ram home the need for Special Forces. And, in a way, it was the Falklands War that gave rise to a major new SAS role.

The Falklands conflict sent shock waves through the British political and military establishment because we had been caught napping. This applied in particular to the Secret Intelligence Service (SIS) and to its masters in the Foreign and Commonwealth Office (FCO). The foreign secretary, Lord Carrington, had felt obliged to resign over the intelligence failures prior to the invasion. The SAS felt it should have been in there much earlier, destroying Argentine aircraft on the ground before they could get anywhere near the British fleet. What if there had been a sudden pre-emptive strike by the Warsaw Pact countries? It was clear that something needed to be done to ensure we stayed much more alert to potential threats.

Chapter Eleven

In the early 1980s, right after the Falklands conflict, the Cold War plunged into a deep frost. The old guard in the Kremlin, headed by Andropov and then Chernenko, decided to play hardball with the West. The Soviet economy wasn't in good enough shape to keep up in the arms race, and the Russians were way behind the weapons technology curve. They had no answer to the Star Wars initiative. But they could deploy the resources they already had, both as a warning and as a threat. And in the new SS-20 intermediate-range ballistic nuclear missile, they had the perfect weapon.

The point about these missiles was that they were medium and not long range. Their only possible targets could be Western European capital cities – London, Paris, Brussels, Copenhagen, Rome and the rest. With hindsight, we can see that perhaps the Kremlin's deployment of the SS-20 was one last, desperate fling of the dice by a leadership that sensed its days were numbered. But to Western eyes at the time, this action was seen as an aggressive policy, which needed a firm response: if the Russians wanted to play hardball, then the SAS had to get out on court. Just as they'd done in the nineteenth century, the big powers were using Third World countries such as Afghanistan as proxy battlegrounds in their struggle for power and influence. The place where the Russians were most exposed, in both military and strategic terms, was Afghanistan. But now the USA had replaced Britain as the relevant superpower. Still, Britain had a role to play, and there were certain things it could do, and do well, to punch above its weight.

When it came to Afghanistan, I wanted to be part of the punching. Apart from anything else, it would be a means of getting some of our own back for the covert Russian backing of the IRA. But for the time being, I had to be content with a new job as part of a small team developing new tactics and equipment that would help keep us that crucial step ahead in the war against terrorism.

On the seventeenth of April, 1984, we had just started training for the new job at a secret location on the south coast when all our pagers went off. They were showing the emergency code: Immediate Action.

Yvonne Fletcher, a female Metropolitan police officer, had been shot dead outside the Libyan embassy – or 'Peoples' Bureau' – in London. We had to regroup and get to the scene at once. As we were boarding the flight helicopter, I heard the word 'embassy' mentioned, and the cherries came into a line. Bloody hell, I thought. Yahoo! I missed the last one. Let's go.

Advance elements of the Counter-terrorist (CT) team were also arriving by air from Hereford. We jumped into a fleet of waiting cars and set off at high speed for Regent's Park barracks. When we got there, we found hordes of press photographers hanging around, eager to splash our pictures all over the front pages: they had remembered that this was the location used by the Regiment during the Iranian embassy siege. We did a quick about-face, and got out of there, fast, moving to a back-up location just off the A40 to the west of the city: RAF Northolt, otherwise known as the Hole.

The Hole refers to the fact that Northolt is Headquarters, Joint Strike Command, a vast nuclear-proof bunker excavated under Middlesex from which much of our armed response would be directed in time of all-out war.

Our command group set up in one of the aircraft hangars. From the MI5 briefing officer we learned that one week before the shooting the Libyans had brought a shipment of automatic weapons into Britain in the diplomatic bag. These weapons included AK-47 assault rifles, pistols and, probably, grenades. The police had not, as yet, officially requested assistance but we wanted to be there, ready on the spot, if they did. The Libyans had already shown they were ready to open fire on anyone who came near, so there was a fair chance that we would be called in.

While not actually in the CT team at the time I was up to date EMOE (Explosive Methods of Entry), which was why I was there. I was tasked to blow in one of the windows, if the decision were taken to assault the embassy.

We went straight into our 'actions on' planning. We asked every agency we could think of, from the Department of the Environment to MI5, for the architectural drawings of the entire street, as well as precise details of the embassy's door locks, window fastenings, skylights, security and alarm systems, plus any other information they had on the square and its surroundings. The Regiment keeps as many building plans as possible on its computer database, as do the police and the security services. Inside a matter of hours, we knew every inch of that place. We then talked to people who had worked in or visited the embassy building: secretaries, police, caretakers, tradesmen, anyone who had been in there and could remember anything.

Next came the photographs. These had been taken covertly by our own teams: they included shots of the embassy interior. After the Iranian embassy siege, the rule was: 'As much information as possible, by as many agencies as possible.' From the information received, we were able quickly to put together a number of possible 'actions on'. In a curtained-off section of the hangar, we laid out the floor-plans of the Libyan embassy, each floor to its own grid and to scale so that we could fit it all in. We marked out doors, windows, skylights, corridors in tape. Using plywood and hessian screens, we built a mock-up of the entire interior. Then the assault teams got busy, moving through the building, practising what they would do once they were in, going through the options over and over again until they were confident. Then they worked on what they would do to the Libyans once they were inside. In a while, they had it down to second nature.

Some of us had been to the forward control point, and examined the embassy covertly. We familiarized ourselves with the police sniper plans. It still wasn't enough: despite all the information we now had, one thing was clear. To make our best shot when the call came, we needed to carry out an urgent close-target recce. We needed to work out the type of approach to make, our routes in and out; we wanted to use minimum explosives for the greatest effect, and prove our chosen method of entry. You can't work out things like that without getting close.

The next night, the police gave permission for an SAS team to go forward and do the CTR. I was tasked to go. Just after midnight, a police car swept us up to the forward control point, which was high in an office block overlooking the square. News and security cameras were all over the place, so we had to be careful not to get spotted. But in our favour was the fact that the embassy building was towards the end of a long terrace forming one side of the square. This meant that, if we were careful, we could gain undetected access via the rooftops.

We were wearing black police coveralls tucked into black rubber-soled boots over our civilian clothing: if we were compromised, we could say we were Metropolitan Police. Marksmen from SO19 – the Met's Specialist Firearms team – backed up by our own snipers, were assigned to cover us. There were two main sniper positions: one on top of an adjacent building, the other placed at the back of a room overlooking the embassy. If one of the Libyans came to a window when we were examining the outside, the orders were simple: if he's a danger to us, shoot him. The snipers were also acting as our eyes and ears: we had communications equipment on us, and if they saw movement that we could not, they'd alert us. But we wanted no risk of compromise from overheard radio transmissions so the rear man in the team was the only one who had his comms switched on.

We all had personal weapons: I had a Browning 9 mm, in a covert-fit holster, inside the opening in my coveralls.

The police had already positioned ladders at key points on the adjoining roofs, which made it easier for us to move in. We crept along the rooftops until we were on the roof of the embassy. We stopped, to listen and watch. There was no signal from the sniper teams. All was quiet. I had my own window to inspect, with a colleague, Rod. I climbed free down the façade of the building, until I was standing on the sill of the window next to it, and then stepped across, using my arms to hold myself in. Rod came after me.

We were right outside the target window, on the sill. It was a small window, stone-built, with a broad piece of glass in its middle section and narrower side-panels. The Libyans had it curtained off with heavy drapes, which made it impossible to see inside. I leaned forward in the darkness, studying its fixtures, working out where to place the charges, how much explosive we would need, what type of charge. Suddenly I heard someone talking right by my head. I looked across at Rod. He, too, had frozen to the spot. We stood there in the bay, not daring to move. The voice was answered by a second, more muffled than the first but still close by. There were two men, just behind the glass, arguing in Arabic. They were no more than a metre from where we were perched.

I couldn't speak Arabic well enough to follow what was being said – the words were coming thick and fast, the argument sounded fierce, and it was protracted. We breathed out. I signalled to Rod, 'As long as we're quiet, they can't hear us. Let's finish the job.' He gave me the nod. Then I noticed two things: the catch on the inside of the main window, clearly visible, was flimsy. They hadn't bothered much about security up here, possibly because this window was on the third floor and they had wrongly assumed that no uninvited guests would be entering that way. The second thing I saw was that the window opened inwards. We didn't have to blow our way in through this window. If and when the order to attack came, all we had to do was punch through the glass, push back the catch, and we would be straight in among them. From this point of entry, at least, the embassy was wide open.

I hoped we would get the go-ahead, in part for selfish reasons – I had missed the assault on the Iranian embassy by a matter of hours and I was looking forward to making up for the lost opportunity. But my main reason for wanting to get at these men and bring them to justice was much simpler: here was a young female British police officer, murdered in the heart of the nation's capital by diplomatic terrorists. Their diplomatic status shouldn't give them any protection. If the Prime Minister gave us the go-ahead, we wanted to do it.

Frustratingly, even though these people had killed a young woman in cold blood, the call never came. There were complicating factors; what if they were holding hostages in there, one of the female

97

secretaries? They hadn't declared any hostages at this point, but that didn't mean none had been taken. We sat there, waiting, for a further five days. At the end of that time, the murderers, under Metropolitan Police escort, walked free.

This outcome was a serious disappointment. It did nothing to improve my own negative feelings about the role of the SAS in the mid-1980s.

Chapter Twelve

A few days after the stand-off at the Libyan Peoples' Bureau, my spirits got a boost when I was invited to go on a team job to Pakistan. I lost no time in accepting. Team jobs were what was keeping me in the SAS. I started saturation Urdu lessons in the language labs the next day.

The task was to train a Pakistani Army Special Operations Group in the CT role. We were based right up on the border with Afghanistan, in the mountains of the North-West Frontier, an area that was well known to the British Army, thanks to a long and bitter struggle for supremacy with local tribesmen in the nineteenth century.

After five years of war between the Mujahideen and the Russians, this entire area was extremely volatile. Western agencies like the CIA were making every effort to get weapons, money, and supplies in to the Mujahideen. So, too, were friendly Muslim countries like Saudi Arabia. The Russian border patrols were determined to stem this flow, inserting ambush teams in an attempt to cut it. Added to this mix were the refugees and fighters streaming in both directions through the high passes, the Pakistan Army trying to keep some sort of control along its frontier; commercial traffic; and the bandits who had infested the region since time immemorial.

While our task had nothing specifically to do with the war in Afghanistan, the men of the unit we were training talked freely about the fighting. And the Pakistani manservants assigned to our bungalows told us tales of Russian atrocities perpetrated on their families inside Afghanistan.

Sometimes, when we were out on recce, we'd come upon a group of Afghan traders, usually transporting the semi-precious stone called lapis lazuli that is mined deep in the Afghan mountains. Afghanistan is – or was – one of the world's major sources of this stone. Until war broke out, the raw blue stone was cut and polished inside Afghanistan, thereby adding value, but since the Russian invasion, the Afghans had had no option but to smuggle it out across the border uncut, in mule trains, selling it in the back streets of Peshawar for what they could get.

On learning we were from the UK, these men would ask us why the West was not doing more to help the Mujahideen. To that question, I had no answer. I knew the SAS had been put on standby to intervene in Czechoslovakia following the Russian invasion of that country in August 1968. I could not see what was different in the case of Afghanistan, and told these men as much. Again, I felt frustrated.

I could not know, as I learned more about the war taking place a few miles from where we stood, that I would soon be a part of it.

PART TWO

Mountain War

Chapter Thirteen

On the face of it, things were going well for me in the Regiment. I'd been getting the team jobs, which in the SAS means you are considered a serious player; and on returning from the Pakistan job I was promoted to sergeant. But at home things were not so good. I had been away constantly, leaving Margaret alone and pregnant in the bungalow we'd bought in the Herefordshire countryside. Relations between the two of us were uneven: SAS life puts an intolerable strain on even the best marriages. I started thinking about where my priorities should lie. What sort of a life was it, being stuck out somewhere and not knowing whether our child was healthy or not? Or even alive? Coupled with my other reservations about the Regiment's command structure and its future, thoughts like this helped tip the balance: in that year, 1984, I decided to quit the SAS, for the sake of our family life.

I applied for premature voluntary release (PVR). The colonel was astonished. 'You know we were putting you forward for a commission?' he said. I nodded. My father had been commissioned up through the ranks. I was throwing away the chance to do likewise.

'Why do you want to leave?' the colonel asked. I explained that my wife was pregnant, and finding it difficult to cope alone all the time. From the tests we knew that the baby was going to be a girl, and everything was looking good. But in the light of what had happened to our first child, I wanted to be there. Like Margaret, I worried all the time that something might go wrong.

'If that's the problem, Hunter, why don't we give you a job here in Hereford? In Training Wing, say, or in the QM's department? That way you get to stay in camp, and you can go home every night and see your family.' I thought about it for a whole second.

'No,' I told him. 'I joined the Regiment to be operational. I couldn't sit around on the fringes stacking blankets. That would crack me even more than being out.'

'OK,' he said. 'But if things don't work out in Civvy Street, come back and see me. I'll do what I can to get you back in. At or about your present rank.' Now it was my turn to be surprised. This was quite an offer. Normally, rejoining the Regiment meant going through the whole Selection process from scratch, and starting all over again at the bottom as a trooper. I thanked him and left. And, shortly after that, I left the Army.

Chapter Fourteen

I had quit the Regiment in part on the strength of a commercial job offer that had on the face of it sounded very good. But about a week before I was due to start, for no good reason I could see, it was withdrawn. The person who had made the offer was simply untrustworthy. I was under no immediate money pressure, having built up some savings over the years, and Margaret and the baby girl we were expecting were well provided for. But I very much dislike having nothing to do. So I mentioned to the odd mate that I was in the market for interesting work, and waited to see what would happen.

Within the week I had a response.

The call came late in the evening from a man who said his name was 'Mr Williams'. Mentioning the names of two people in the Regiment he'd worked with – both of whom I knew – he asked me if I'd be interested in taking on some training work, 'Along the lines of the work you've been doing recently.' I didn't ask him how he'd got to hear about the team job.

Having checked him out with the mates he'd mentioned, I agreed to meet him at an address in Belgravia.

A doorman behind a wooden desk in the plushly appointed foyer asked to see my ID. When he was satisfied, he lifted a phone on the desk in front of him, and spoke a few words into it. A man came through a door to our right, walked up, and shook me by the hand. He was about five feet ten inches tall, fresh-faced, on the podgy side, dressed casually in light-coloured clothes. To my surprise, he was not wearing a tie, and his straight brown hair was long enough to cover the tops of his ears.

He had a swipe card, which he used to get us back in through the self-locking door. The next door had a keypad alongside it, into which he punched an access code from memory. This door opened onto a long, grey-carpeted corridor. At the end of this, we turned right into a handsome, high-ceilinged briefing room, like a large Regency dining room, with a long, highly polished table in the middle of it surrounded by a dozen or so high-backed, comfortable chairs. It all felt very grand. There was a cut-glass chandelier hanging over the table, and uplighters at intervals around the walls. Through the rear windows I could see a long, well-kept walled garden, with a neat lawn flanked by herbaceous borders, and beyond that the bland back of a neighbouring building.

The room was empty, but almost at once, a second man, slightly taller and plumper, with dark hair brushed back from his forehead came in, shook me by the hand, and said, 'Charles Williams. Very glad to meet you.' The first man left, while Mr Williams and I sat down. A woman appeared next, put down a tray of tea, and then went out.

My new friend had a very clear voice, strong, with a posh accent, posher than his colleague, who was minor public school, as opposed to Eton or Winchester. 'Charles' took a couple of briefing packs out of his briefcase and laid one before each of us on the table. Briefly and succinctly, he laid out the specific mission they now wanted me to consider. It was all very casual, a chat over a cup of tea.

'As you know from your recent experience, the Mujahideen in Afghanistan are in need of a little expert assistance. For the moment, at least, I represent them in this interest.' He paused, and looked at me keenly. 'You know how to fire a Stinger missile – is that correct?'

'Yes. Some of us were trained on the Stinger for the Falklands conflict.' He nodded. 'Very good. Well then, if you're agreeable, I'd like you to set up a little training team. It will mean working with a key group of Mujahideen leaders in a friendly middle-eastern country. They want training across the board in modern infantry tactics, particularly guerrilla tactics, of course. And they need weapons training, above all else on the Stinger missile. Some knowledge of sabotage wouldn't go amiss, either. Think you can handle it?'

I looked back at him for a moment. It was a pretty electrifying offer. 'Yes,' I replied. 'I can handle it.'

'I want you to recruit the staff you will need from among your own contacts, and keep an account of the budget. The operation will begin as of next week. You will be sent further instructions in due course. 'Is this acceptable?'

'Perfectly.' I shook hands again and left. A few days later, I was on my way out to the Middle East.

I found the opportunity I was being given tremendously exciting – not least because it was a chance to have a go at the Russians. I started reading voraciously about the war in Afghanistan. There was quite a lot to learn.

In a round-the-clock operation beginning on Christmas Eve 1979, Russian AN–22 and AN–12 transports airlifted 15,000 men of the élite 105th Guards Air Assault Division into Afghanistan. Two days and 350 Russian Air Force ground-attack sorties later, using pre-positioned trucks and fuel, the Guards fanned out of their Kabul and Bagram bases to take control of the country. At that same moment, four Soviet motorized rifle divisions crossed pontoon bridges flung across the Oxus River on Afghanistan's northern border. With them came the *spetsialnoye naznachenie*, or Spetsnaz Special Forces troops, some in civilian dress, some wearing the uniform of the official Afghanistan government Army, all of them specialists in overt and covert killing.

Linking up with KGB units already in Kabul, a Spetsnaz assault team moved on the presidential palace. Their objective was simple: to kill President Hafizullah Amin, who had done his ruthless best to quash the growing Islamic revolt in the country, and in so doing had served Soviet interests. But when he had had pro-Russian President Taraki murdered, and then expelled the Soviet ambassador, Alexander Puzanov, the Kremlin had decided to invade. They themselves would crush the conservative Afghan tribesmen, who were so bitterly opposed to change, and in so doing they would save face with the Soviet bloc satellite countries, and snuff out the dangerous Islamic flame that was kindling on Russia's southern borders.

As they spread out across the country, the Russian troops were in cheerful mood and their morale was high. They had been briefed that the Afghan people were a poorly armed and backward peasantry, living in a country that was still pre-industrial. These people could have no answer to massive, organized Russian force and the high-tech weaponry that came with it, especially weapons like the Hind D helicopter gunship. The invasion would be like knocking down a row of skittles. Except for an unlucky garrison force, which would inevitably be required to stay and keep the natives in their place, the Russians were certain they would be back home in a matter of months, if not weeks.

Early on Christmas Day, a spearhead Spetsnaz raiding party attacked the Duralamin palace. Here, they ran into a sizeable force of Afghan Army troops, loyal to President Amin, armed with eight ancient T-54 tanks. Outgunned and outnumbered, the Russian Special Forces troops fell back. But no palace guard would hold them up for long. Two entire battalions of the 105th Airborne came up, stormed the palace complex, and overwhelmed the Afghan defences. Once the paratroops had taken control, the Spetsnaz came back in, this time with a team of KGB 'advisers'. After a bitter hand-to-hand struggle in and around the palace, the Russians succeeded in capturing Amin and his immediate circle. They lined the men up against a wall and shot them dead.

The KGB then installed Babrak Kamal, the long-time Afghan Communist Party leader, as Russia's puppet president. Kamal's first action was to invite the Russian divisions already in Afghanistan to 'enter the country and secure it'. But to the everlasting surprise of the Kremlin, the Afghan people, almost as one, refused to accept the invasion. They began to fight back. They were to prove an implacable enemy.

On 13 January 1980, the Mujahideen, or 'Soldiers of Allah', attacked a huge Soviet convoy in the Salang pass, a supply-line choke-point forty kilometres north of Kabul. Together with dozens of troop transports, the convoy was made up of 160 AFVs and APCs, numerous supply trucks, and no fewer than sixty fuel tankers. The guerrillas swept down from the mountain slopes and shot up the long line of vehicles. The Soviet convoy was raked from end to end, set ablaze at a dozen points, and held up for twenty-four hours.

The Afghan War had begun.

Both sides had a lot to learn. The Russians discovered quickly that sending a young, untrained conscript army to fight highly specialized mountain warfare was not a good idea. In fact, the entire Russian Army, designed as it had been for mass armoured assault against the Nato armies on the north German plain, had to be radically stream-lined and adapted. The first thing the Russians abandoned was the tank, as the gun wouldn't elevate high enough for mountain warfare. They also had to learn the art, new to them, of conducting flexible and fast-moving combined operations that allowed local commanders to use their own initiative; and, in particular, the Russians had to understand the value of the helicopter as a modern weapon of war.

The Mujahideen, fragmented as they were into twenty-seven major groups and scores of minor ones, found that fighting the Soviet Army in relatively small and uncoordinated war-bands, armed with little more than rifles, was a quick way of getting dead. From scratch, the guerrillas had to capture, steal or buy weapons of every kind, and then learn how to use them: mortars, recoilless rifles, heavy machine-guns, anti-tank rockets, and, most of all, the AK-47 assault rifle, needed desperately as a replacement for the ancient flintlock muskets still carried by many tribesmen.

Lacking any formal infantry training, the Mujahideen found that they had to play to their strengths, using their expert knowledge of the terrain, their speed and stamina on foot, their all-weather survival skills, and their support in the countryside to maximum advantage. But their most valuable tactic was one they had learned from the Vietnam War: to get in close to the Russians, unseen, hit them hard and fast, and then melt away in every direction. It was a tactic developed by the Viet Cong, who called it, 'grabbing the Americans by the belt-buckle'.

As the war went on, both sides got better at fighting it. In the spring of 1985, the conflict was mired in a steady war of attrition. But the Soviets had modern military technology on their side. And there was one weapon to which the Mujahideen had no answer: the Mil

Mi-24 Hind D helicopter gunship. The Hind D was a flying tank, an airborne artillery park, which, above all else, was making the difference between the two sides. Even high in the mountains, where they would otherwise be safe, the Hind carried the war to the guerrillas. As often as not, it would catch a Mujahideen unit unawares, slaughtering its members to the last man. Its rockets and cannon strafed the Mujahideen's rural support bases, razing entire villages in a single attack. It wasn't the only Russian weapon the rebels feared. There was the AGS-17 automatic grenade launcher, and the new AM2B9 Vailyek 82 mm mortar, which I knew could cover an entire hillside with steel hail in a matter of seconds. In return for information we'd supplied, the rebels had sent us captured examples of these and other Russian weapons, which I had tried on the range. It wasn't all a one-way street.

Western intelligence agencies estimated that the Russians were ahead on points in the war and could win outright, unless there were a significant change in the balance of forces. The West, and in particular the United States, wanted the Russians to lose in Afghanistan. This would teach them the limitations of their own power – a lesson the Americans had learned the hard way in South-east Asia – make the Kremlin look foolish and weak on the international stage, and perhaps even make the Soviet Union more tractable at the conference table. When I met Mujahideen leaders for the first time, Afghanistan was a top priority for the British government, as it was for the White House.

Almost from the moment the Russians invaded Afghanistan, the Mujahideen cross-filtrated Afghanistan from Pakistan and Iran, along frontiers that were thousands of miles long. Russian-paid spies had heavily penetrated their bases inside both these countries, which made any kind of direct contact risky. And even if a Western intelligence agent could get in there was little or no chance of meeting up with the top Mujahideen commanders, who were continually on the move, not least for reasons of personal security. Information came out at third- or even fourth-hand, muddled, confusing, and obscure. In the early years of the war, a lot of mistakes were made in Western attempts to support the Afghan rebels as a result of the 'message-on-

110

a-stick' methods to which Intelligence agencies had of need resorted. It was clear the whole Afghan covert aid and assistance effort needed a much tighter focus. One of the biggest problems of all was that the intelligence agents – and agencies – often didn't understand the language the Mujahideen were talking, the language of war. But guerrilla warfare was my business.

I was very much looking forward to the conversation.

As I saw it, the rebels could only win by making the Russians pay an unacceptable cost for their continued occupation. This meant killing and wounding them in large numbers, sapping their morale and undermining their infrastructure. Defeating the Hinds was only one part of the process we had to initiate. There were other key elements – like sabotage. I relished the idea of helping them do that.

The emphasis on other factors was in no way to underplay the significance of the surface-to-air missile in deciding the outcome of the war. The more I learned, the more I understood this to be true. The Mujahideen had to have a weapon that could defeat the Hind D.

At first, the Americans were reluctant to risk supplying Stingers to the Mujahideen: they thought the risk of these cutting-edge weapons falling into Iranian hands, and being used against their own aircraft, was too great. But by 1985 the prospect of engineering a Russian defeat in Afghanistan outweighed this risk. Only it wasn't quite that easy. Even if we could get the Stingers to the guerrillas, they needed training in how to use them: these were complex, sophisticated weapons, not something anyone could pick up and use without thorough instruction. Which was where I came in.

I put together my training team. We were all allocated pseudonyms, my own being 'Yacoub'. The need for secrecy was absolute. If the Russians got wind of what was going on, they would naturally do everything in their power to stop it. The need-to-know system was enforced to the absolute.

A reception team met us at the airport. They were local troops, acting as our back-up and logistics team while we were in the country. They were told we were conducting a 'specialist training' exercise in the desert. We were training an initial group of sixteen Afghan leaders, all key members of Ahmad Shah Massoud's war-band.

111

We had a month to set things up before this first batch arrived. The first step for the eight of us in the training team was to organize a camp out in the desert, as far away as we could possibly get from prying eyes. We got all the equipment, stores and arms, which, as if by magic, were waiting for us at the airport, loaded everything up, and struck out west until we hit the isolated foothills of the nearest mountain range. We were looking for the most desolate, God-forsaken *wadi* in the whole of the desert. About 200 kilometres out into the sand, we found what we were looking for: a deep, wide, re-entrant in the desert floor that was all but invisible from most directions unless you knew it was there. Here we built our base camp, and began to make ready. For the next few days, we were busy just unpacking the stores. Apart from the Stingers, most of the weaponry was genuine People's Republic of China manufacture, and all of it, bar the missiles, carried Chinese markings.

We spent the next few days familiarizing ourselves with these weapons out in the sands.

Meanwhile, the Mujahideen leaders were slipping through the high mountain passes on foot, dodging the Russian patrols, and crossing into Pakistan south of Peshawar. As we drove them out into the desert, I think only one of the sixteen rebel commanders knew exactly which country he was in.

For the next six weeks, we trained the Mujahideen commanders across the board, from scratch, in the use of light and medium infantry weapons: the AK-47 rifle, the RPD machine-gun, the DshK 12.7 mm Triple-A gun, the American shoulder-fired '66' anti-tank rocket and the small, mobile Chinese-made multiple-launch rocket systems (MLRS). When the Mujahideen were proficient in these weapons, we moved on to the use of explosives for sabotage. We also gave them a basic grounding in modern infantry tactics. But the single most important piece of kit we had way out there in the middle of nowhere, in the baking heat, with nothing but the desert wind for company, was the Stinger simulator. This was a first-rate piece of American equipment. With it, the Mujahideen could practise firing missiles all day long. And we made them practise the firing drills until they could fire the Stingers in their sleep. If this was the weapon of all weapons that could win them the Afghan War, we wanted to make sure they knew how to use it.

As always in the 'empty' desert, we weren't entirely alone. From time to time some of the local tribesmen would wander up to our position, or we might get a goat-herd, or a camel-driver, straying too near. When this happened, we'd fire a few rounds into the air, which generally got rid of them. Then, about five days into the training, a lone man approached us in a smart-looking four-wheel drive. As he drew close, the guard fired a few warning shots in the air to dissuade him. He ignored them, and kept coming. The guard fired some more rounds, this time closer to the stranger's vehicle, but still he didn't stop. As he came up near the entrance to the *wadi* I grabbed an AK-47 and fired a long burst that sent the sand flying up around his front offside tyre. This time, he got the message, turned about and raced away.

I found the Mujahideen tireless, eager to learn – and completely ignorant about modern infantry warfare. In a way, this was a good thing: it meant we were working on a clean sheet. But their inexperience could be a positive danger – and not only to themselves. One morning, early, I was leading them through a sweep and attack on a mock target we'd established out in the desert. I'd had them position one of the 12.7 mms up on a low rise, the idea being that this would give covering fire from the left flank while the main body moved forward, hit the target, wheeled to the right of it and went by. It was a simple plan of attack, as attacks go, but you have to start somewhere. One problem, I discovered, with untrained troops speaking a foreign language, was how to control the main attacking force while co-ordinating the covering fire.

I was leading the main assault force. Up on a sand dune to our right and front was the cover group man on the 12.7 mm. At the pre-arranged moment, I lifted my arm. 'Go!' The main body pepper-potted forward, advancing on the enemy. On cue, the cover man opened fire. He had been told that as we drew into his line of fire he was to switch right and fend off a simulated counter-attack from our rear. We kept advancing, he kept firing – into the target we were about to overrun.

'Switch right!' shouted the gun commander. 'Switch right!'

Nothing happened. The gunner continued firing dead ahead, straight into the arc we were entering. I waved my arms at him furiously. 'Switch right!' I yelled again. 'Switch right!' In about three seconds, if he didn't train that gun-barrel somewhere else, we'd be rehearsing a real-life 'green on green', not a sweep and attack training exercise. The shells kept coming right at us. Someone was going to end up dead.

To make matters worse, the weapon had a rogue barrel on it. I could see the tracer swirling as it came out, instead of going in a nice straight trajectory. Rounds were spraying everywhere, thudding into the sand around us, humming by in the air with a low *zuss, zuss* sound. We had to stop this man. I stared up at him. 'Check fire!' I signalled frantically. No reaction. I waved and shouted again. Up there on the hill with our demon gunner was a loader and the gun commander. They tried to force him off the gun, but he wouldn't have it: he was confused, he thought he was doing a good job.

The gun was right on us. Everyone was ducking and diving for the non-existent cover. Seeing this, the loader hit the gunner a huge thump in the ear, sending rounds spinning skywards. Finally he switched, but left, stitching more rounds into our ranks. Whacking the gun-aimer round the head is not a generally accepted method of controlling fire. How we didn't lose anyone, I'll never know.

At the end of their six weeks' intensive training, and after a few more little misunderstandings of this kind, our sixteen Mujahideen had honed up their infantry skills and understood the workings of the Stinger. They were ready to go back to the mountains – and the Russians. But before that happened, I had some questions to ask them. For me, this was a golden opportunity. I had access to a group of key Mujahideen commanders. Here was a chance to talk through strategy, tactics and targets with them.

I had become friendly with one of the commanders in particular. In the evenings, round the fire, we'd sit and talk about what was happening in Afghanistan. 'What we are doing here', he said, 'is good. But we need more – we need our men to be trained inside my own country. We are few, and we do not have the technology they have. We must train all our men in the ways of the modern war.'

I sympathized with this man. If I'd grown up a Catholic in

114

Northern Ireland, I'd most likely have viewed the British Army as an occupying force and taken the fight to its soldiers on the streets. But I liked to think that I'd have the guts to do it man-to-man, and face-to-face, and not in the skulking way the IRA so often went about it, killing innocent civilians in the process.

Over the course of our talks, the commander described several Russian targets he wanted to attack in and around the Panjsheer Valley. I got him to make up sand models of these objectives, describe them to me in detail, and then explained to him the best way of attacking them. So that he would not forget, I put together a series of what in the Regiment we called 'planning-packs' for him. Planning-packs contain all the technical, intelligence and operational detail necessary to the effective destruction of a given target. They cover everything in the target area from a detailed breakdown of the local topography to the shape and size of the explosive charge that will best destroy the objective.

The planning-pack system was nothing new, being one we'd already used in the SAS for years, targeting Sovbloc assets in the event of a hot war – there were literally hundreds of Sovbloc factories, command bunkers, railway marshalling yards, missile sites, and the like on file in Hereford for our use.

At last, the training came to an end, and we broke camp. We took them back to the airport in total darkness. Still with no idea of where they were going, they boarded a new aircraft, which took them back to the North-West Frontier.

All the time I was out there in that sweltering *wadi*, I worried about Margaret and Natalie, the baby who'd been born just before I left. After what had happened with Andrew I lived in daily expectation of hearing the worst, dreading anything negative in the letters that were my only news, taking even the mention of a cold as a warning of imminent and total disaster. Half-way through the training period I managed to get back to the city for two days, and talk to Margaret on the telephone. It was a huge relief to hear her say they were both doing well, although a part of me still didn't believe it. I got home at the end of that job to find a beautiful, bouncing baby girl on Margaret's knee. Our daughter was – and is – perfect.

115

After two short weeks at home, during which time I completed a remedial nappy-changing course to Margaret's satisfaction, I had an urgent call from Charles's office. As soon as I heard his voice at the other end of the line, I knew my days of wedded bliss were over. 'Yacoub,' he said, 'the Mujahideen leaders you trained have been in touch. They think the world of you. In fact, they'd like you to do another little job. Could you come up to my office on Monday?'

I replaced the phone, and looked down at the baby sleeping in her crib.

Afghanistan, I thought. It has to be Afghanistan.

And I wondered if I'd live to see her grow tall and strong.

Chapter Fifteen

When I arrived at the office in Belgravia, there was a new man sitting with Charles. He looked like an Afghan. He wasted no time in telling me the Mujahideen I'd worked with wanted me to go in and train them in Afghanistan.

I held up my hand. 'Training them in the desert is one thing,' I said. 'But Afghanistan's a combat zone. If I go in there, it won't be as a mercenary.'

He said, 'I'm sorry to hear that.' He thought I was turning the invitation down flat. I went on. 'Don't be sorry. I'll go in to Afghanistan. But I'll do it on my own terms, because I want to do it. And for no other reason. Is that understood?'

'Yes.'

'What exactly would you want me to do?'

'We'd like you to take in six Stinger missiles and a million dollars in gold coins. You will rendezvous with a specified Mujahideen group at an agreed time and place, deliver the consignment directly into their hands, and then remain in country for a period of up to three months. During that time, your brief is to help them in the war as and how you can, not least, if this proves possible, by giving more training on the Stinger missile. We'd also like you to make an intelligence assessment of the war. As you know, a great deal of the feedback we're getting from the Mujahideen is confused or misleading. The information trail isn't clear enough. We'd like you to compile a first-hand account of what's happening and what's really needed.'

I thought about it. As tall orders went, it was a skyscraper. As the implications of what I was taking on sunk in, I found myself wondering if I'd made the right decision. I wanted to help the Mujahideen in their war against the Russians. But I still had a family to consider. We'd trained the Mujahideen: the next step, logically, was to get in and follow that up. 'But the job is not', said Charles, stepping in when his colleague had finished speaking, 'to get in there and start a fight with the Russians. In fact, we'd like you to avoid any direct contact with the Russians.'

We talked the matter over, in a discussion that became general.

The gold was intended mainly for the Afghan fighters to buy weapons with – from China, or even Iran – something that could not be done directly. It was also for paying people off, be it other resistance groups, government forces, or even disaffected Russians. The Stingers, if I could get them in and use them, would be the first in a series of shipments designed to change the balance of the war.

At the end of the briefing, they asked me if I had any questions. 'Ask anything you like,' said Charles encouragingly, 'we'll do our best to answer it.'

'Only the main one: any ideas how I explain what I'm doing in Afghanistan if the Russians catch me?'

'We've spent some time on that one,' he said. 'After all, we're not in the business of losing you, are we?'

I had to hope not. But sitting there, in this peaceful, well-appointed room, I couldn't suppress a shudder of unease.

'You're dead,' he said simply. 'And no matter what you say or do, at this end we won't even acknowledge you.'

We looked at one another for a moment.

'What's my cover?'

'You're a back-packer,' the other man said facetiously. That got the first laugh.

'Yes,' I said. 'Hello Ivan. Would you like to look inside my pack? Oh, six Stinger missiles and a million dollars in Krugerrands – well there's a thing. How did they get in there?'

The afternoon wore on. At the end of it, we all knew the score – there was no satisfactory cover. In the end, we had to settle for the one they'd already concocted: freelance photojournalist. I knew that almost all the journalists who'd gone into Afghanistan hadn't come out again. And although, by and large, their bodies had not been found, we all knew what had happened to them. But the photographer story, though weak, was better than nothing at all.

'And once they've removed my fingernails, and a few other bits? Found out I'm not actually working for *Newsweek*?'

They both looked blank. There really was nothing.

But I had a private idea. It might make the Russians shoot me on the spot, rather than dragging it out: I could tell them I *was* a mercenary, hired by the Mujahideen. That ought to do the trick.

'Will you do it?' asked the Mujahideen contact.

I nodded. 'I'll do it,' I said.

The two men came up and shook my hand. Charles said, 'There's just one other thing – I know we're already asking a lot, and it's not something you should risk your life for.'

I waited. 'It's the Hind D – we need to know about its armour. We know it contains titanium – but if we had the precise composition it would help what we do here . . .'

'You could work out how to defeat it?'

'Precisely.'

'I'll see what I can do.'

Within the week, I was on my way to Afghanistan. The first leg of the journey was by civilian airliner to Karachi. From there I caught a scheduled internal Pakistan Airlines flight to Islamabad, completing the first bit of the INFIL by road. Two very well-presented gentlemen gave me an up-to-date Afghanistan country brief. I read it, committed the important bits to memory, then set about 'sanitizing' myself: checking I'd removed anything and everything personal, rings, watch, photographs, mementoes, clothing labels, the lot. By the end of that process, all I had left on me was a Beretta 9 mm pistol, and a leather satchel containing the Nikons and the other photographic gear. I had nothing on me that could be traced, no maps, no comms, no ID and US dollars only. If they searched me, I'd have only what a professional photographer might have – except for one thing: in order not to compromise any of the real photo news agencies, I had no press card.

119

When it came to the INFIL itself, even I wasn't allowed to know details of the route, the idea being that if I got caught it could be used again. The less I knew about the operation on the Pakistan side, the less likely I'd be to compromise anyone or anything under torture.

That evening I met the Pakistani guide who would lead me through the mountains on the Pakistan side to a spot, about twenty kilometres from the Afghanistan border, where the gold and the Stingers would be waiting.

The first threat we had to face was the bandits who infested the mountains that lay between us. The bandit threat was taken seriously: until we reached the Afghan border, I'd have three bodyguards.

That evening, we clambered on board two superannuated trucks, so clapped-out and painted over you'd never have known they were really, underneath it all, very sound. They looked typical of the local transport and much less liable to attract attention than, say, new, high-powered four-wheel-drive vehicles, which might be reported across the border by Russian informants.

As darkness fell, we set off for the Afghanistan border.

At that time, the Pakistan Army was trying hard to swat the bandits preying along its north-west frontier, as well as keep an eye on the steady flow of Afghan refugees coming out along the main passes. Bumping along, I couldn't help wondering what exactly my 'body-guards' were for: to protect me, or to make sure I didn't make off with the loot? When you're packing a million dollars in gold coins and a clutch of Stinger SAMs, they like to keep a bit of an eye on you. The north-west frontier is, after all, a particularly easy place in which to disappear.

We travelled throughout the night. Bundled into the back of this old vehicle, I had little idea of speed or direction. We could have been anywhere. The metalled road became a track, which grew rougher and narrower, and then began to climb steeply. The mountains we were heading into ranged in height between four thousand and six thousand metres. Ears popping, we crawled ever higher, the air growing steadily thinner and colder. In the early hours of the next morning, we reached our first rendezvous, a broken-down old house near a stream, on the outskirts of a town. As the engine cut out, I heard a loud braying in the darkness. This was where I picked up the mules, and the men who would be leading them.

I clambered stiffly out to meet my new companions. They smelt strong in the still night air. There were ten of them, strange-looking, barrel-chested animals, thin in the leg yet as tough as old boots, with A-shaped wooden carrying frames strapped on their broad backs. Their handlers were short and bandy, with broad faces and narrow, slanting eyes. At first, I didn't fully understand who they were, but from the way they were dressed I took them to be Mujahideen.

The six Stinger missiles were waiting there in long wooden crates. We lashed them on to the first three mules, two each, distributing the gold and the rest of the supplies among the remaining animals. The Krugerrands were in six thick waterproofed cotton-canvas bags, each too heavy for a man on his own to lift.

We began to walk.

The new moon overhead gave us little light, but the handlers made no concessions, either to the darkness or to the steepness of the climb. At first I couldn't see any sign of a trail, but they seemed to know exactly where they were going. I found myself breathing hard in the thin air, but whatever the terrain, up, down or flat, however rough underfoot, they kept up the same horrendous pace. I was fit, but the mule-handlers really shifted over the rough ground, mostly scree and shale, going hard and fast. My mind went back to the Brecons, and the relentless days of Selection. I had the same feeling of pushing myself to the limit, of drawing down inside myself for the inner reserves.

Towards dawn, we stopped. They made hot sweet tea on open fires, and handed out rice and some vegetable mixture, mostly onions with unleavened bread. I ate and drank hungrily, cross-legged on the ground.

We unloaded the mules to lie up during the day. About midday one of the men handed me a large linen package. Inside was a set of traditional Afghan dress: long baggy trousers, a loose shirt with huge long tails dangling down from it, leggings and a thick, heavy waist-coat, with small pockets inside and out, beautifully woven from wool, cotton and leather mixed. The length of your shirt-tail is important in

Afghanistan: it tells the rest of the world which tribe you are from. I was travelling with the tribe of the Extremely Long Shirt-tails.

Seeing my bemusement, they gathered round, helped me to get the stuff on, adjusted the shirt and the baggy pants, then placed a small round cotton cap on my head and, as a final touch, wound a coloured triangular cotton headdress over that. Next came the waistcoat. Finally, they draped a blanket over my shoulders. It was good extra protection against any rough weather, and at night you wrapped yourself up in it, then lay on the ground to sleep. They wore open-toed sandals made out of recycled tyre rubber, and there was a pair of these for me, together with the leggings they wore to stave off the cold in the mountains at night, but for the time being I kept my own boots on in case I had to run in them. Once we had unloaded all the gear and posted sentries, we slept, until the sun blazing down into my eyes woke me.

In the late afternoon we were up and off again. While it had been freezing cold during the night, now it was roasting hot, no whisper of a breeze to cool the iron day. We were contouring the side of a mountain that rose almost sheer on our left, with higher mountains still to the north, on our right-hand side. A plunging re-entrant sep-arated the peaks. The heavy waistcoat made me sweat as we went on, up and up and up. Here the air was the cleanest you could ever breathe, untainted by pollution. Once the sun had burned off the early haze, you could see for miles and miles out over the tremen-dous, spectacular scenery – soaring, snow-capped peaks and plunging ravines cut by rushing streams, row upon row of these gigantic mountains marching away into the distance as if they would never end, as if a child had drawn them. It was high summer and there were flowers, whose scent I could smell long before I saw them, every-where among the rocks beside the track. Birds of prey hung over the crags, Afghan griffons, vultures hovering for carrion prey. The water in the tiny springs that blossomed in among the rocks was incredibly pure and sweet. Everything in this high land was clean and beautiful, like the beginning of the world.

All that day, our guides kept up the same cracking pace. I learned the hard way that if I stopped for a natural function, they wouldn't wait for me – I'd have to run like mad to catch up with them. Wherever possible, I tried to copy their customs, kneeling down to pee, as they did, and eating only with the right hand, never the left, which they used for wiping themselves. Every single one of them was armed with an AK-47 assault rifle, which they kept hidden under their clothes. All the time, as we moved, we scanned the countryside for bandits on the lookout for little convoys like our own.

A lead scout stayed out about 500 metres ahead of us at all times, scouring the track for any signs of trouble, but they didn't bother with a rearguard, as I would have done. I found myself watching the rear, not just in case of an attack but trying to memorize the features of the landscape in case I had to make a run for it.

This first day was the only time we travelled during daylight. Five times the mule-handlers stopped for a few minutes to pray. I was glad of the prayer-stops: they were the only time I got to rest. I understood now that these men were not fighting Mujahideen, but professional mule-drivers, sherpas hired for the trip. They did this kind of thing all the time, for a living, which made me feel slightly better about my fitness. But as we steamed ever onwards and up, I began getting fit in a new way, sucking down the thin air in long breaths, filling my lungs steadily and slowly, and then the long exhale. Slowly, I was getting acclimatized, the hard way, to the thin air and the heat, and to the tabbing – which was Green Jackets pace, but uphill. Normally you'd allow two weeks for acclimatization.

That evening we camped again. Thinking to make myself useful, I offered to help prepare the food. They refused. They were friendly people, laid-back, always smiling, but I understood they saw me as an infidel, whose touch would sully their meat.

That evening, we were supposed to rendezvous with some Mujahideen fighters at another camp. When they failed to appear, we packed up again and continued towards the border. I knew we had to be very near, now, within a few kilometres of Soviet-occupied Afghanistan. That thought gave me pause: I was one day out from the Russians. Maybe less.

Rounding the shoulder of a cliff, there was a sudden scurrying up ahead in the darkness, and everyone went to ground. Two of the mule-handlers pulled all the animals into the side of the rock face to my left, the others took out their AKs. I got down with the others in the rocks and drew the Beretta. There was a low whisper from the darkness ahead. It was the new Mujahideen group. Since they had no challenge and response procedure, the two groups had come close to opening fire on one other, each side thinking the other must be bandits.

There were six or seven newcomers, physically quite unlike the sherpas. These men were much taller, hawk-faced warrior types, with a proud, upright bearing and the gimlet eyes I'd seen in the photographs. They were wearing black-and-white chequered headdresses, the badge of their particular fighting tribe, and green and white armbands inscribed with verses from the Koran. Instead of hiding their weapons, they carried them openly, the crossed bandoleers on their chests heavy with rounds. It was impossible to tell who, if anyone, was in charge: they ranged in age from about fourteen to sixty, and wore no sign of rank. They welcomed us gravely in the silvery half-light. We moved up the track to a broken-down homestead, one room of which still had an intact roof. They ushered me into this room, and left me there on my own, ignoring my pleas to be treated like everyone else.

I'd reached the point of no return. From here on, I was in Mujahideen hands. They had brought in a fresh set of mules, and we transferred everything across to them. Money changed hands, payment for the mule-handlers. When this was done they turned back towards home.

Tired to the bone, I slid into my solitary room and slept like a dead man. But that night, around one in the morning, someone shook me roughly awake. 'Quickly, quickly,' he hissed.

I saw with a shock of alarm that the camp was deserted. I reached for the pistol, beside my face. The fire had died away to orange embers that were still giving off a faint glow, but no one was round it. Empty blankets lay on the ground – everyone was under cover among the rocks. The mules, penned in a small stone corral, were disturbed and restless, stamping and snorting in the darkness. Silence, after that, and the spit of the dying fire.

I brought up the pistol. As always, I had a round ready up the spout. I thumbed off the safety, staring into the night, using my peripheral vision, and listening hard. Nothing moved. Suddenly, two shots rang out. The contact was no more than a hundred metres out. They were right on us. Then there was silence again. I waited. At last, one of the sentries came in: a bandit group had come up in the night to try their luck. Maybe they had spotted our fire or been given information about our trucks. After the warning shots, they had melted back into the night.

Although the attack had been thwarted, the Mujahideen were spooked by it: we were right on the border, now, and they were worried a Russian patrol might have heard the shooting. We loaded everything on to the mules fast and got out of there, tabbing harder than ever under the cold stars and the ghostly sliver of moon. We moved so fast I found myself stumbling and sliding on the slippery scree. At first light, we stopped in a small natural bowl in the mountains, made a brew and rested there all that day. Now that I could see the Mujahideen better, I realized one of them was unarmed. I asked about this, and was amazed to be told he was a conscientious objector: he would help in any way he could to defeat the Russians, but he wouldn't kill. The others respected his beliefs. There was no question of his being anything but their equal.

'Tonight,' the man with the best English told me, 'we cross the border.' He explained how the Russians discouraged Mujahideen convoys like our own coming in from Pakistan: at last light, they dropped off commandos by helicopter, inserting them at random along the minor passes, leaving them concealed in the rocks, heavily camouflaged, waiting and watching through the night, hoping to rip apart a passing resistance mule-train. Like our own, for example. He said they were all afraid of meeting one of these ambush teams. I was bloody worried: it would be just like getting jumped by an SAS covert reaction team.

The path narrowed again that night, dwindling to little more than a goat track, but still climbing, ever upwards, towards a pass I could just make out now against the skyline. The pace was so fast, as we put distance between ourselves and the bandit attack, that I reached the stage where fatigue started taking over, and I forgot to be frightened of the Russian commandos, the bandits, or anything else. It came down to one foot in front of the other and making myself take the next step. At the top, the track levelled off, and I saw open ground ahead of us. We'd reached the summit of the mountain, 4,755 metres in height. A few minutes later, the point man came back down the convoy to speak to me. 'Now,' he said, 'we are in Afghanistan.' It had taken us three nights and an afternoon of the hardest walking I'd done since Wales.

That morning, we stopped in an old village built of stone, apparently abandoned and desolate, but in reality occupied, with well-disguised defensive positions scattered among the ruins. The Mujahideen had deliberately left it looking deserted and broken-down so that the Russians would not think it worth bombing again. The Hinds and the fighter-bombers flattened anything that looked even vaguely inhabitable, repeating the treatment at the first sign of rehabilitation. I settled down as best I could in the corner of a ruin, wrapped the blanket round my head and went to sleep.

At about midday I started awake to the roar of fast jets. I crawled out and looked blearily up at the brilliant blue sky. There, high overhead, were two little silver aircraft, trailing white plumes of vapour. They were Mig-23s. It was my first sight of the Russians in Afghanistan.

We walked on for two more nights, heading north, dropping down all the time, moving even faster on the descent, if that were possible, than we had on the way up, until on the morning of my fifth day in Afghanistan we arrived in another village. It, too, had been badly hit by the Soviets. Most of the buildings were in ruins, there were deep, wide bomb craters all around, and huge black newish-looking scorch marks on those walls that were still standing. Towards the end of 1983, the Russians had started using new types of ordnance, including 500 kilogram cluster bombs and 500 kilogram fuel-air explosives. They had also devised a container bomb, made up of a high-explosive (HE) core charge around which they packed steel nails, embedded in a thick, black tar-like incendiary material, which burned and stuck on contact with vehicles, buildings – or skin. These were set to explode above the ground, so that fire and shrapnel rained down on anyone caught beneath.

Dotted across the hillside above the broken houses were graves, with faded flags on sticks fluttering over them, red and green. As in the first village, I saw no sign of any women or children.

A little stream ran along the village edge, with irrigation ditches stretching away into the fields on its far side. Again, the Mujahideen had left the damage in this new place just as it was, setting up a base camp along the length of a shallow depression at its southern end, concealed behind a dilapidated wall from any casual aerial inspection. In stone-built emplacements around this natural trough they had set up several Triple-A guns on their tripods, Chinese-made 12.7 mm DshKs. I was sorry to see that none of the men I'd trained were part of this particular group.

Having greeted their mates, the Mujahideen unloaded the gold and the Stingers. I never saw the money again.

We stayed in this camp all that day and throughout the next night, resting. The Mujahideen chatted and lazed and, whenever they got the chance, they all smoked, a pungent-smelling rough-cut tobacco rolled up in thick grey or black paper. Thanks to the Russians, none of them lived long enough to worry about cancer.

Chapter Sixteen

I was part of a small battle group of about twenty men, the usual size of a Mujahideen fighting patrol in this area. Although a few more fighters came in over the time we were in this camp, none was Stinger trained – or anything trained. I had to start training them from scratch. Everything was very low-key while we were hanging about, the most exciting thing being the arrival on the second day of a change of clothes, which became a routine occurrence. As they grew used to my being there, the Afghanis didn't try to restrict my movements as they had before, although there were now some women moving about on the fringes of the ruined village, heavily veiled – I wondered if that was because of me – absorbed in looking after their small children, cooking and cleaning.

Towards the end of that second day we moved again, still heading roughly north-north-west, arriving after about five hours of hard marching at a third semi-ruined hamlet. Here I was introduced to a man called Khamed, with a big hooked nose like the beak of a hawk. He was obviously a leader. By now, I had worked out the Mujahideen hierarchy from two things: the better the weapon someone carried, the higher up the command chain he was; if he carried a radio, he was very important. Our leader had a new-looking Soviet AK-74 5.45 mm, and a walkie-talkie.

I was having big trouble distinguishing between the Mujahideen. In the first place, a lot of them bore some resemblance to one another, for the very reason that they were close relatives. And I'm not very good at remembering names, especially names like Ahmed and Abdullah when they occur more than once in the same group, as they did here. Then there was the universal beard. All the younger men were desperately trying to grow their beards to show how mature they were. The longer the beard, the more august the figure. The Mujahideen with the longest beard of all was the mullah of the group, leading the others in prayer five times a day. All this facial hair didn't help with recognition.

I looked at the man nearest me. He was shorter than the others and, uncharacteristically for one of the Mujahideen, round and fat, with a bit of a pot belly and curly hair. He had a scar running up through one of his eyebrows, which gave him a permanent expression of slight surprise. He didn't have long hairy feet, but he waddled a bit when he walked, and he was always smiling, very happy-go-lucky. Suddenly, I let out a bit of a chuckle. *The Lord of the Rings* is one of my favourite books. He reminded me of Bilbo Baggins. I tried it out on him, and the nickname stuck. Bilbo was the first among the Mujahideen with whom I became friendly. At about forty, he was older than most of the others and relatively unfit. I discovered later he was rarely used in front-line fighting. But as he had a few words of English, he had been detailed off to look after me, not as a manservant but as a kind of minder, checking now and again to see that I was all right, had what I needed in the way of food and clothing. While we were waiting, I showed him how to use one of the Nikons.

Bilbo had a cousin, also on the short side, but younger, slimmer, with much more get-up-and-go, impatient to get on with the business of killing Russians, and with more of a warrior look about him: Frodo, I thought straight away. It might sound whimsical now but at the time it was a way of sorting out all these strange-looking people. Next there was a small, skinny-looking bloke, with sharp, piercing eyes, and a sly, weasel's face I distrusted on sight. Sméagol, I thought, to the life. I worked my way through the members of the group as I came to know them, giving them nicknames from Tolkien.

The group's commander I called Aragorn. In the book Aragorn was the rugged, ugly-looking character, but he was also knowledge-able, he had his pride and his honour, he was going to lead the men to victory. This man was like that, muscly and slightly stooping, with

129

a great hook of a nose set in his long face. He had the quiet charisma of a good leader, but as time went by I saw he was as much of a diplomat as a fighter, spending a great deal of his time negotiating on behalf of his own ultimate boss, Ahmad Shah Massoud, in the endless jockeying for position that went on between the different warlords and their followers.

After the food, which was rice with goat or mountain sheep (usually I couldn't tell the difference), we had a brew of their tarry black tea. Aragorn beckoned me over. Along with the gold and the missiles, I had brought in more of the planning-packs, with target profiles requested from the London office by this group. He ripped open one of these now and laid out all the maps, sketches and photographs on the beaten-earth floor of a roofless hut. He pointed at the aerial reconnaissance shots with a skinny brown finger. 'Bridge,' he kept saying. 'Bridge.' I recognized it as one of the bridges they most wanted to blow up to block a well-used Russian convoy route south of the Panjsher. I'd helped to prepare that very pack. He wanted me to talk him through it.

The difficulty we had was in communication: his English was almost non-existent. I managed to get the gist of my meaning across to him using pidgin Pashto, mixed with the odd bit of Urdu. Sign language was pretty useful, too. As we were both military-minded, a lot of the symbols and gestures I used clearly meant something to him, and I was further helped in that the names on the maps and the written indications on the planning-packs were in Pashto. All the time, as we talked, I was watching him, as I watched the others, learning from their body language how to tread, when I could come forward and suggest something, take a lead, when to step back. When I had finished explaining the way I would go about attacking the bridge he looked at me quizzically, as if he had only half understood. He had thin eyebrows over that great hook nose, and they were right up in the top of his forehead.

'Do you want me to look at the ground?' I asked, using gestures as well as speech. 'I can tell you a lot more about this job if I can see the target first.'

'Maybe.' He nodded noncommittally. 'Maybe.'

By now, I thought I knew that this meant 'absolutely not'.

But I was wrong. That evening, the Mujahideen came up to me in a group. Would I go along on the reconnaissance the next day? Too right I would. That was one of the main reasons I was there. Just before we turned in, they gave me an AK-47, complete with six magazines of ammunition, which made me feel much more a part of things. I took it as the beginning of a certain acceptance. I was also glad to have it for my own protection, now that we were here, miles inside Afghanistan. If the Russians caught me with a Mujahideen war-band and a shipment of Stinger missiles, I was definitely for the drop. Might as well be armed and take some of them with me.

On the fourth day we rose again before dawn and tabbed a fair few miles to the north-west. We climbed to the crest of a ridge, from which, to the left and between the plunging re-entrants, I could see the beginning of the Kabul plain, stretching out to meet us from the south and east of the city. At this spot we met up with a second Mujahideen battle group, whose members looked as though they had just come out of a bad scrap: they had various injuries, mostly superficial shrapnel wounds, with grubby blood-streaked bandages wrapped around them. Like ourselves, these men were armed to the teeth, mostly with AK-47s and Chinese-made Mark II RPG-7s. Every mother's son seemed to be packing extra rockets on his back for the RPG launchers, the elongated diamond-shaped warheads sticking up out of the stitched canvas carrying-tubes. They all had a good clutch of Chinese-made hand grenades draped off their leather cross-belts. I noticed that the fighter I'd nicknamed Frodo had a beautiful Dragunov sniper rifle, Mother Russia's best production. I'd come to know him well, by now: he was young, and not afraid of opening up to me a bit. He told me how he'd taken the weapon from a dead Soviet paratrooper, one of a pursuit group they had ambushed a few weeks before.

We were moving in daylight now, making no attempt at conceal-ment, which surprised me. In company with this second group, we dropped down a spur off the main ridge we had just traversed. This gave out on to a plateau about one and a half kilometres wide, which we crossed fast, almost running over the open ground. One thing the

131

Russians had to learn from the Mujahideen was speed of movement, especially in these mountains, where wheeled vehicles were largely useless. At the far end of this open space, I looked down. Right below us was a metalled road.

Then I saw the bridge.

It was just a bridge, made of reinforced concrete, slung slapdash across the torrent. But it was the same bridge I had helped my Afghan friend build a model of out in the desert, as we planned its destruction. That seemed a long, long time ago, as if it had happened in a different life. I had a strong sense of *déjà vu*.

This was our target. This was the first attack I would be part of in Afghanistan. I wanted it to succeed.

The arched concrete single-span bridge carried the Russian supply road across a fast-moving narrow river. The road skirted the base of the mountain directly in front of us, running in towards our position from its north-eastern shoulder, on our right, and then looping round to the south, directly below where we were now standing, until it curved sharply up to the north-west again and, of course, to our left, once it had crossed the bridge. The river followed the road as far as the bridge, then flowed on east where the road turned sharply north and towards Kabul.

The bridge was lying on an axis roughly WNW-ESE. By its western end was a large pillar of overhanging rock. Blowing bridges isn't always as easy as it looks in the movies. They can have an irritating way of hanging together, despite a lot of explosives. Blocking it could be just as effective, and easier to accomplish. Now, seeing the structure for the first time, I was certain that the overhang was the key to cutting the road. It would take a lot more explosives than the Mujahideen had with them to blow all that reinforced concrete to pieces. But if we mined that rock tower, the chances were that we would block the pass for weeks to come. And once it was blocked, the Russians would have the problem of how to repair the damage and protect the engineering company from hit-and-run attacks while they were doing so.

The Mujahideen commander stood up just then, in full view, as if there were no Russians for a hundred kilometres. I motioned urgently to him to get down but he grinned at me, pointing and moving around. In the end, I gave up trying to be tactical, and we both walked along the edge of the plateau, gesturing and talking about the target below.

'How do you want to initiate the explosives?' I asked. 'By remote [i.e. radio] control? Or command-wire?'

'Remote,' he said. This was good news – it was by far the safer option. Ideally, we should have had pressure pads, as well as the remote initiation, so that if one system failed the other would cut in. But in this situation, where it was difficult not to leave sign, the pressure pads were out: an RPG would have to do if the remote failed.

'Is it enough just to block the road?' I asked. 'Or do you want the explosion to form part of an ambush?'

'Ambush!' he replied, with a gleam in his eye. 'Ambush!'

I agreed with him. If we were going to have a crack at the Russians, we might as well sort them out in good style.

I started pointing out where we should place the primary charge, at the base of the rock mound, then the secondary devices, in the spots where I reckoned the Russians would try to take cover after the main explosion. We talked about where he could position his men, so as to lay down harassing fire during the attack and to mop up afterwards. We moved carefully along the cliff edge, talking the whole thing through until we were sure we understood one another, but being careful not to leave any sign that could be seen from the road. Before the light went, we began pulling back to our base camp. They had had intelligence that a convoy was on its way from Kabul.

The attack was scheduled for the next day.

The next morning, at dawn, I got up to find that another eight men had turned up in the night, bringing all sorts of extra kit with them: detonators and detonator cord, unexploded mines, RPG rounds and lots and lots of Chinese-made plastic explosive. This was in a poor state from long storage in the dry mountain air, crusty round the edges and difficult to work. The Russians had laid a lot of mines, and these new men had a fair old selection: anti-tank mines, made of steel painted a light-green with yellow stencils on them; smaller 'butterfly' anti-personnel mines, so-called because when you stepped on them they sprang up into the air, and exploded in a lethal hail. The anti-tank mines surprised me because at this stage of the war there was little chance of a tank threat.

The butterfly mines the Russians scattered widely and in great numbers, often by means of a Hip helicopter fitted with a tail chute. The Hips would fly a certain pattern, scattering the mines either among the rocks, where they were naturally concealed, or on sandy ground, where they would sink in and the wind would cover them. Whatever the Russians did with the mines, the Mujahideen were accomplished at defusing and re-using them. After breakfast (more rice), with all this lethal material laid out as if for inspection around them, the Mujahideen sat down on the ground, chatting and smoking as usual, and set about making portable bombs.

They stuffed the plastic explosive into the recovered mine-cases, bundling these up with sections of unexploded bomb, active mines, live shells and live RPG rounds, until they had about twenty devices. They did this with absolutely no regard for their personal safety. I retired to a safe distance. Home-made explosives have a way of going off when you least want them to.

I sat watching them from my crag. These people had nothing, as we have, in material terms, but they had an overwhelming faith, an absolute certainty that theirs was a just cause, and the only cause, and that to die in battle was the greatest honour Allah could confer on them. I had to admire this. They were warriors to a man. The only thing they seemed even slightly to fear was getting captured and falling into the hands of the KGB, or its Afghan government equivalent, the KHAD. The Russians, they told me, liked to begin their interrogations by cutting off a prisoner's fingers, slowly, one by one. What the KHAD would do didn't bear talking about. But, in return, the Mujahideen could be just as brutally cruel, if not more so – as I was shortly to find out. They had a torture called 'lifting the shirt', which involved partially flaying their prisoners and then leaving them to the flies and the sun. They reserved this one for the Russian Airborne and Special Forces troops.

That afternoon, the Migs came back. The Mujahideen heard the jets before I did – they seemed to be tuned in to the sound. They all got up and started running around, shouting '*Dushman! Dushman!*' (enemy). There were six aircraft, about five kilometres to the north of us, clearly visible, lazily circling the next village. Staring at their silhouettes, I reckoned they were Su-25 'Frogfoot' ground-attack aircraft, the Russian equivalent of the American A-10. But, to the Mujahideen, all Russian aircraft were Migs.

As we watched, the first pair dropped their noses, wings flashing silver, like fish bellies, as they rolled into the dive. They disappeared down behind a ridge, then swooped back up into view. As they pulled up hard from the attack we heard the noise of their bombs exploding on the houses below, like thunder rolling up along the valley towards us. The pilots were super-confident, just circling calmly before putting in their attacks. They dropped their bombs in pairs, one right behind the other, going round for a second run after they had inspected the results of the first. Their only concession to safety was the brilliant hot infra-red decoy flares they popped out continuously on the way down, in case, from somewhere, the Mujahideen had suddenly got hold of some heat-seeking missiles.

They had now.

Then I saw another reason why the pilots felt safe. Much lower down, hugging the sides of the hill above the village, was a pair of Hind D attack helicopters, in the hover, hosing down the houses and the surrounding land with their rockets and cannon fire, suppressing any possible reply from the ground. When the noise of the bombs stopped for a few seconds, we could hear the heavy *whop, whop, whop,* of their rotors, even at that distance, through the clear air. That and the sinister *zzzp! zzzp!* of their rotary cannon.

The Mujahideen around me stood and watched the attack in complete silence. In a minute or two long columns of smoke began to drift lazily skyward from the shattered village. Later, Bilbo told me that many of the men there with me had relatives in that place. What he didn't say was that he had relatives there too. They said nothing, either at the time of the attack or afterwards: they simply looked their hatred. As we ate that evening, and immediately afterwards during their prayer time, the Russian artillery started up, peppering the newly destroyed village and the surrounding hills. The Russians,

135

Aragorn said, liked to hit them with their artillery while they were praying: it was a favourite tactic. Looking at those hard-set faces, it struck me as just a little bit counter-productive.

That night we moved back to the southern edge of the flat pan that led across to the bridge, carrying the newly manufactured bombs between us in long wooden cradles. The devices were in all shapes and sizes, a regular motley collection of home-made death. The biggest I saw was the centre section of a Russian 500 kilogram bomb, missing its tail fins and its nose-cone, but with much of its explosive charge intact. I stayed well away from that one. The four men who would be carrying it down to the bridge next day had my best wishes.

At the bottom of the ridge we came to a curious hollow feature, cut into the base of the mountain where it joined the plateau but extending back in underneath the flat ground. Once we were down in this space we were out of sight. It was a great LUP, completely protected from the air, and very hard to see from the ground, even when you knew it was there.

While we rested I took stock. I had been in Afghanistan for ten days. I had a tan on my face from the wind and the sun, I was dressed like a Mujahideen and, like them, I was usually covered in dust. I even smelt like one of them. There was no way I'd be let off the hook if the Russians got me. We ate, late in the evening, for the first time that day, wolfing down the flat dry bread and the handfuls of cold rice. We had no fire, for obvious reasons, but we had a glimmer of yellow light in our half-cave from a couple of ancient kerosene lamps.

Next morning, just after daybreak, we moved back down to the cliff edge overlooking the bridge. The planning-pack appeared again. Casually, I squatted down next to Aragorn, and we talked it through, both of us pointing at the photographs and the concrete structure down below to make ourselves clear. Gradually I convinced him not to go for the bridge itself but for the overhang.

While we planned the details, the rest of the Mujahideen were busy carrying the charges down the little goat-tracks running into the ravine. I got to my feet. 'Hang on!' I shouted. 'You're going to leave sign like that! They'll spot your tracks – especially from the air.' They just grinned at me and carried on. Their training, in any formal military sense, was non-existent: it amounted to 'Come along and learn what you can.' In general, the more experienced your commander the longer you lived. It was as simple as that. Because of this, the Mujahideen suffered tremendous losses in the early years of the war. But they were learning – and they were getting better all the time.

They packed the main bunch of charges around the base of the rock pillar, more or less where I had advised them to, then placed some of the other bombs close to the road where I estimated the convoy would stop. I watched as one man stuck a big lump of plastic explosive on the outside of the biggest bomb wedged under the rock tower, and then shoved a detonator into it – just the one. As tactfully as possible, I explained that as one detonator might fail it was always best practice to put in two, with separate tails of cord leading to the initiation device. I also tried to show them how to link the explosives up in a 'ring-main', in such a way that each charge fired the next in line. At last they understood me and set each separate charge with a tail of detonator-cord running back from the detonator, each of these tails clipped on to a single piece of cord linking all the charges together in a circle – the ring-main. Since det-cord ignites at over 10,000 metres per second, there would be just one enormous explosion. And if either end of the det-cord circle was broken, the charge would still reach the explosives from the other end: again, dual initiation.

They wouldn't let me wire up the explosives, even though I knew more about it than they did. But I could respect that: this was their country, and their war. When they had completed the ring-main, I showed them how to run a command wire, consisting of two lengths of det-cord taped together, back up to where we were hiding, with two detonators on the end of the cords connected to the remote box for a dual initiation.

The time for the convoy's expected arrival was near. Aragorn, myself and a couple of the others were the central command element, up on the cliff, where we'd have a grandstand view of the action. We put two flanking groups about 150 metres out on either side of us, one to rake the front of the convoy once the charge had gone off, one to do the same at the rear. The men got down among the rocks. In a

moment they were invisible, the natural hues of their clothes blending with their surroundings.

The two cut-off groups had the RPDs – old-style 7.62 mm
machine-guns, with twin fifty-round belts coiled inside their drum
magazines. Like the AK-47, these weapons were robust, simple in
design, and rarely failed. I saw a sniper with the Dragunov attached to
the eastern cut-off squad – young Frodo again. Frodo and Sméagol
also had Chinese-made RPGs, one of them, I was glad to note, a
Mark II with the telescopic sights. There was no back cover; everyone was in on the attack. No messing.

Everything was set.

Where I would have stayed hidden at all times, the Mujahideen got
up, now and again, and had a good squint around for signs of the
enemy. All day long we sat there. No convoy. Come dusk, it was
back to the LUP under the ridge, the cold rice and the smoky
kerosene lamps. Next morning, at dawn, we were back again. The
Mujahideen would wait for as long as it took. They had all the time
in the world.

At about midday, I heard a low rumbling from the east.

The convoy was coming.

I watched as it crawled into view around the eastern shoulder of
the hill. I could feel my heart knocking at my ribs. There were two
BRDM-2s in the lead, followed by five open trucks laden with supplies. There was a third APC, a BTR-80, bringing up the rear.

This was it.

The vehicles were well spaced out as they approached, but as they
came down the slope towards the narrow bridge they had to brake,
causing them to bunch up. In reckoning the placement of the cut-off
groups and the secondary charges, I'd allowed for this bunching but I
was relieved to see it happening.

I could see two uniformed soldiers keeping a lookout, one sticking
half out of a hatch in the lead APC, watching the road ahead, the
second in the turret of the BTR at the rear of the convoy, watching
the road behind. It was impossible to tell at this distance whether they
were Afghan government or Russian troops. Then, from the corner
of my eye, I saw some of the Mujahideen leaping about to my left, in

138

plain view on the skyline. My heart sank. If they didn't keep down and out of sight, they were going to compromise the whole thing. If the lookouts on the convoy had been more alert, they would have spotted us.

They weren't, and they didn't.

The first BRDM-2 was crossing the bridge. I looked across at Aragorn. He had his hands on the remote box but he hadn't triggered. He was waiting for the next APC to come under the lee of the rock. 'Fire it!' I muttered between my teeth. 'Fire the thing!' His thumb went down on the clacker. There was the most God-almighty blast. The rock pillar disintegrated. The secondary devices went off at the same time, in a deafening roar of sound. Huge lumps of rock flew up into the air, then crashed back down on to the road. Even though we were more than 30 metres above the explosion small shards of rock and stones showered down on us. I saw a thick cloud of dust and smoke blooming from the shattered rock plug, towering up through the air towards me.

The centre of the convoy ground to a halt. At the same time, forgetting all about tactics, the Mujahideen stood up among the boulders on either side of the road and let fly with everything they had. I saw the backblasts from their RPGs going off. The RPD machine-guns from the flanking cut-offs were firing in long bursts, plucking gouts of dust and soil up from the ground as they stitched towards the convoy, the big 7.62 mm rounds making flat metallic thwacks as they hammered into the trucks. Another RPG rocket grenade went off, the warhead missing and exploding among the rocks. I could hardly think, the noise was fantastic. Underneath everything else, I could hear Frodo thumping away with the Dragunov, like someone pounding on a bass drum. I looked down at the scene. It was like the Third World War. The smoke column from the bridge was already well up above the level of the cliff-top. We might as well have set off a small nuclear device.

Any second now, I thought, they'll call up air support.

Then I saw the BTR-80 at the rear of the convoy start reversing madly back up the slope, hoping to get back around the eastern side of the mountain and away. We didn't want him to escape. If he hadn't already radioed for help as soon as he got round into safety he would do so. And we had no idea how close the Russians were.

I had been told not to get involved in any direct contacts in Afghanistan, especially not with the Russians. But there I was, right up alongside Aragorn, armed and capable, and I wasn't going to get any credibility hanging back now.

I pepper-potted fast down the slope to my right, zigzagging on a diagonal, dropping in behind a large rock. The driver's hatch on the BTR was open. It would be a chance in a million if I got one in, but it had to be worth a try. Remembering that the AK-47 kicked high and to the right, I started squeezing off rounds, firing deliberate aimed shots, double taps low and just to the left of the hatch. Between taps I was watching where my strike landed, then correcting aim. I missed. The BTR-80 kept going, heading for the shoulder of the hill. Fuck! It was getting away. The tyres. I knew the tyres were non-deflating, designed to run for thirty or forty kilometres even with a bullet through them. But if I could get enough rounds in through one there was a chance of blowing it apart, putting the driver off or causing the vehicle to skid. I put in a few more bursts, but none of my shots made any difference. The APC was around the shoulder of the hill and away.

Peering through the thickening smoke and dust I realized with a shock that only part of the main device the Mujahideen had made had detonated. The explosion had only partially blocked the road. The two APCs at the front of the convoy were dodging through the bigger lumps of fallen rock, rushing to escape. Unless we stopped them. They had abandoned the trucks they were supposed to be pro-tecting, it was every man for himself. Once round the shoulder of the mountain they, too, would be safe.

Now that I'd joined in the contact, my blood was up. I switched fire on to the fleeing APCs, letting rip with the remainder of my magazine. I hit the rear one with a long burst of about fifteen rounds, again going for the tyres. Sméagol had the same idea, stop them at all costs, but his rocket missed, skipping off the ground in between the two vehicles and ballooning high up into the sky.

The second APC was nearly around the road block. Sméagol fired a second rocket. Direct hit. There was a flash on its side and a few seconds later the hatches blew open, great sheets of flame and smoke pouring out. One down. Meantime the first APC was over the bridge and away, but where he would go and how soon he could get help was anybody's guess. This was not a controlled engagement. Double-fuck.

But the rocks and the firepower had stopped the wagons dead in the centre of the pass. I changed magazines and blasted more fire down into them. The lead truck and two bodies beside it were burning fiercely. The second wagon was slewed sideways across the road – it, too, was on fire. The other three trucks were smoking, riddled with hits, rocking with the impacts as the Mujahideen on both sides kept up the relentless fire, machine-gun and RPG rounds pouring into the stricken vehicles, the whole valley bottom filling up with fresh clouds of smoke and dust. For a second I saw more men lying dead or injured on the far side of the vehicles. Aragorn gave a signal and the Mujahideen began rushing down the slope firing into the mayhem below. They meant to finish the job.

All the time I was thinking we should be out of there. If they had got a message out, any gunships out on patrol would be on the scene within minutes. I checked my ammunition. I'd loosed off three whole magazines, not two. Which left me with the same amount again, ninety rounds, plus my pistol with three full mags. Enough for a fighting retreat. If only. The rebels had other ideas. As the smoke swirled, I watched them run right up to the trucks and pour machine-gun fire into the cabs. One of the drivers was still burning on the ground next to his blazing vehicle. An RPG round had decapitated a second man in DRA uniform near to him. The Mujahideen swarmed into the back of the two trucks that were still not fully alight, and dragged out the more portable stuff before it caught fire. Then they rushed round picking up all the weapons and ammunition they could find, and torching anything that wasn't already fully ablaze. Finally, they went to the bodies on the ground, systematically riddling them with bullets, even those that were obviously dead.

Then I heard shouting from the tailgate of the fourth wagon. Four of the Mujahideen were punching and pulling at something.

They'd captured two prisoners.

141

The Mujahideen regrouped, falling back up the slope towards us. Aragorn pointed to the last truck and Frodo and Sméagol fired their rockets together. It went up, in a huge, blinding explosion. A long sheet of orange flame raced right along the length of the convoy, billowing up through the air to where I was crouched.

It was over.

After the exhilaration of the attack, something like collective panic set in. The Mujahideen were realizing what I had been feeling for some time, that we'd been on the scene much too long. The Hinds. We charged, running as hard as we could across that flat open rock pan. The four Mujahideen with the prisoners jabbed at them with their rifle-butts, forcing them to run with us. As we pelted towards the LUP I shot a glance at them. They were white Russians, little more than boys of eighteen or nineteen. To my eyes, they didn't have the look of fighting soldiers, more like clerks or storekeepers, or just possibly mechanics, strictly rear-echelon types. They were baby-faced, spotty youths. They were wearing well-worn drab-grey overalls, no regimental flashes or badges, not even name-tapes, which for Russians was highly unusual. This told me they were conscripts, from a second-rate unit, nothing special.

One was quite tall, about six foot, with a single lance-corporal's insignia. The other man, shorter and broader, was a private. They both had head-lice haircuts, shaved down to the bone.

They were terrified.

The private was badly burned: large clumps of his hair were crisped to the scalp, the skin on his face and forearms was blistered and bright red where it wasn't black with soot. In places, his clothing had caught fire. He was also bleeding from at least one shrapnel or bullet wound – a big dark-red patch stained the top of his camouflage trousers. The other was relatively unscathed, with just the odd cut or bruise, nothing serious. I knew that if this pair were really lucky, the Mujahideen would keep them, unharmed, to trade for important prisoners of their own. Otherwise, depending on how much time they had, they would either kill these boys outright – or torture them to death.

These Russians weren't lucky.

The burned one was in bad shape: he could hardly stand, let alone

142

run, he had a man on either side of him dragging him along. The taller one kept trying to hang back, but they clubbed him forward with the AK-47s. I could see what he was thinking, in his desperate state – get to the rear of the group and then leg it as hard as he could in the other direction, hope the Mujahideen wouldn't follow him, but they made sure they kept him penned in. We kept running. We had to get back across that kilometre and more of open ground to the rock channel and cover. If the Hinds caught us out in the open like this, we were dead meat. I saw the others glancing back fearfully over their shoulders as we ran. All of us were wide-eyed, we were all expecting the worst. As we sprinted for the rocks, I found myself gasping for breath. I was completely dehydrated: the dust and the gunsmoke, the contact, and now this panic run in the heat for the ridge – all without water. We had it with us, but we didn't have time to stop and drink it. Stopping now was out of the question. That kilometre or so felt like a hundred.

I reached the cutting first with Aragorn and Frodo, who could move his little legs when he needed to. Aragorn climbed up along the spur for some way, looping us back round on to our tracks, then stopped and watched back from the high ground for any sign of pursuit. When there was none, we slipped down into our strange series of deep natural undercuts, almost like pipes, at the base of the cliff face. So far no triple-fuck. Here, for the first time since the attack, I felt reasonably safe.

Unlike the Russians.

Once we'd got our breath back in this LUP, and made sure there were still no signs of pursuit, we set out at a good clip for base camp. After a couple more hours of travelling, we stopped. The Mujahideen whacked the prisoners to the ground, got round them, and started: kicking, laying into them with their rifle-butts, a long, continuous, intense beating. They weren't trying to get any information – they had no language in common with these boys – they just wanted to make them suffer. They succeeded.

I had known from the start they were going to torture these two boys to death.

Except for the odd grunt of pain when a really heavy blow landed the Russians made no sound. The four men who had made the capture did most of the work. Sméagol was orchestrating the beating, his narrow face pinched to a furious point as he took out his hatred on the squirming men. They concentrated mainly on the badly injured private. In his case, they didn't have much time – he was slipping into shock, his eyes taking on the dead, glazed-over look I'd seen in the past, on another young boy's face when he was dying.

The other prisoner was much more aware of what was going on – only too aware. They forced him to kneel on the ground and watch as they beat his mate. For a short time he stayed there. But then, when he thought they were all busy, he half stood, stumbling off to one side in a clumsy attempt to get away.

It was a terrible mistake. At once they were on him in a pack, beating him as hard as they could with their feet and the rifle-butts. He fell on his back, curling up like a baby to protect himself, wrapping his arms tight around his head under the rain of blows. I knew how he felt.

In a while they stopped, staring down at him. They started talking at top speed, discussing the boy, but so fast that I couldn't follow their meaning. There was no need for any translation. They meant to do something worse. Four of them got round him, pulling his arms and legs apart until he was stretched straight out. Two more sat down on his shoulders and kidneys. A third man sat on his backside, pulled the Russian's right leg up between his own, and held it so that the foot stuck straight up. Sméagol came forward. There was a flash as a knife came into his hand. With swift, slashing strokes, he sliced away the Russian's boot, the blade cutting deep into the flesh of the foot. The boy was kicking and thrashing, trying to look round, he knew something bad was coming. The Mujahideen held him still.

When the foot was exposed the man holding it grabbed the prisoner's toes, pulling back as hard as he could on them, at the same time forcing the heel up and out. Sméagol stepped forward. He brought up the knife, rammed its point through the ankle behind the Achilles tendon, hooked back on the blade, and twisted it. The tendon snapped like a piano wire, the white strings of it flopping apart where it was cut. The Russian let out a scream, a terrible high-pitched howling that went on and on, the sound I had heard when Chris had the paling go in through his thigh, the sound the pigs made up on Dindor Hill when the farmers slaughtered them, only this scream was a thousand times worse.

To stop him making that terrible noise, they hammered him in the face with their rifle-butts, slamming away until he fell silent.

I had frozen. I was trying not to look, and at the same time I was transfixed by the horror of what was happening not five metres in front of me. The Russian's foot was hanging off. The Mujahideen themselves were quiet, intent on what they were doing. Aragorn shouted something. The four men who had done the disabling walked across to the other, badly burned, Russian. The rest of the group had propped him up with his back against a rock. He was now fully in shock: his expression told me he didn't know much about what was going on.

Lucky for him.

They got hold of him and pulled him upright, splaying him backwards across the boulder so that his stomach was fully exposed. Another man came forward with his knife and cut away the prisoner's clothing. I could see a bad shrapnel or bullet wound in the skin beneath his right ribs, still oozing blood. Two of the other Mujahideen stepped across to the man with the severed tendon. He was bone-white and shaking uncontrollably, curled up, staring at his useless foot in disbelief. They yanked him up by the hair, forcing his head back and holding it so that he had no choice but to watch what would happen next. When he was sure that the lance-corporal was paying attention, the Mujahideen man plunged the point of his dagger deep into the private's side, dragging the blade across and down with both hands. A huge cut opened up. The conscript's stomach bag slit apart and all his entrails fell out. The smell hit me and I gagged. The watching Russian retched, once, and then began to scream again. In another second, the pain of his disembowelling hit the man on the rock, and he, too, started to scream.

You can never forget a sound like that.

I could stand no more, I had to move, get out of there. I started to turn.

But a flashing movement in the corner of my eye made me glance back. The Mujahideen was sawing at the throat of the man he had just disembowelled. Almost immediately, another fighter put a pistol to the Russian's head and fired a single shot. I couldn't understand this, there was a risk that the Russians might hear, if any were in pursuit, and they would exact a terrible revenge. I wondered what was the point of killing the boy like that. What lesson were they hoping to teach the other?

They left the dead man opened up on the rock.

We started moving again, making ground until we were just outside our base village. I was keeping well back, I didn't want to see or hear more. Most of all, I didn't want to make eye-contact again with the remaining Russian. Every time he looked up he tried to catch my gaze. In spite of my clothing he had spotted me as another European: to his mind, I was his only chance. But I couldn't help him. There was no way in the world I could stop what was going on. To this day I can't forget the way he looked at me – that desperate, dumb appeal.

Always, when they were on the move, the Mujahideen would stop, from time to time, to listen out for aircraft. Their ears were the only early-warning system they had. When we stopped they dropped the Russian in the dust, listened for a minute, then stood around him, muttering. I could tell they were fed up with having to pull him along. I hoped they were going to make an end of it. As Sméagol came up with the knife, I could feel myself shrinking inside, my own guts curling up at the sight of that blade and that murderous face. God only knew what horror the boy was feeling.

As he saw Sméagol coming, he tried to wriggle back, but they caught him, this time holding him fast around the head and neck. Sméagol stood in front of him, waving the knife in his face, taunting him. He looked like a snake about to strike. Suddenly, he lunged forward, sticking the knife point repeatedly into the skin all around the prisoner's eyes. Deep gashes appeared in the skin of his forehead and cheeks. Then Sméagol moved the knife down to the arms and chest, drawing the edge of the blade slowly through the flesh so that the blood welled up out of the cuts. I turned away for the second time, standing with my back to them and pretending not to care. I tried to talk to Bilbo, fiddling with my AK-47, but for some reason the words wouldn't come. Then I heard another scream, the same ear-splitting pig-scream he'd made when they'd severed his ankle, and I saw they'd cut the other one in the same way.

Still it wasn't enough for them. They got on top of him, pinning him again so that he was utterly unable to move. Pushing the eyelids apart with his finger and thumb, Sméagol stuck the point of his knife into the Russian's left eye. With a flick of his wrist he hooked out the eyeball, then stood back, leaving it hanging from its stalk. He was about to do the same to the other eye when Aragorn laid a hand on his arm. They had another short chat. Our commander wanted the Russian's remaining eye left intact, not out of mercy, or because enough was enough, but so that he'd see and understand exactly what they were going to do to him next.

I couldn't imagine what there was left they could do. And I didn't want to. I thought – hoped – they'd finish him now. I went down into the camp, and sat on my own, staring up at the clean beauty of the mountains, with my mind full of another man's screams.

Later, unasked, Bilbo came up and told me what they had done to the Russian. They had wanted the wild animals to get him so they had dragged him a good bit further up the mountain away from the camp, to a flat spot near a low rock where they'd smashed all his fingers with their rifle-butts. After that, they'd slashed open his stomach, the cut just wide and deep enough to start his stomach con-tents bulging, so that he'd reek of his own blood and guts but live on for another six to twelve hours. Then, to stop him screaming, they had cut out his tongue. I hoped he had choked on his own blood – at least that was quicker. They'd left him like that, face down on the rock, with his eyeball hanging down and his insides coming out, for the rats, the wild dogs and the mountain foxes, balanced carefully so that he could see them coming for him.

And that's how he died.

In the camp, meanwhile, I could see that the Mujahideen were well pleased about the contact at the bridge: they had suffered no serious casualties, picked up some useful weaponry and supplies, and destroyed an APC and several supply trucks. But the great thing was they had killed at least seven white Russians. They kept going over the details of the attack, telling and retelling it, exactly as I had done after contacts many times before with mates in the Regiment. As well as celebrating victory, it's a way of dealing with stress, fear, and with the excess adrenaline that's still pumping through you long after the contact's over.

As for the men they had tortured to death, Bilbo tried to explain to me that it meant nothing to the Mujahideen, it was part of the furniture of war. It was true that while they were at it, there had been no screams of enjoyment, no jeering or laughing. They hadn't done it for the sadistic pleasure of watching two men suffer. But for me, that was one of the worst things: the cold-blooded, measured, deliberate way they had gone about it. I had trained the Mujahideen in the desert so I had had some idea before I went into Afghanistan of what they were like. I had heard their stories about flaying alive Russian prisoners. But when it happened I wasn't prepared for it. To understand something like that, you had to be a part of their culture.

They had their own logic for treating their Russian prisoners in that way. They hated the Russians for killing their women and children in the relentless air attacks. And it set an example to their own men, dissuading them from going over to the Afghan government forces. But, mainly, they did it out of hatred, for revenge, and to break the enemy's morale. They wanted the Russians out of their country. They would do anything to achieve that. Fear was their most potent weapon, and the Mujahideen had to make the Russians pay too high a cost.

Chapter Seventeen

At dawn we split into two groups. The smaller group, ten-strong, was heading back to the ravine where we had ambushed the convoy, to harass any Russian follow-up. I thought this was a bad idea. I tried to point out as tactfully but as insistently as I could that if the Russians came back they would do so in massive force, with top cover in the shape of ground-attack aircraft and possibly Hinds. The attack group went off regardless. The rest of us stayed put up at the base camp, waiting until the marauding group came back from the gorge some twenty-four hours later.

They had taken a severe mauling. Of the ten men who had set out, only three had come back alive, two of whom were badly injured. The Russians had been waiting for them. They had outflanked our team, shredding them with enfilading fire, and then moved in to finish them off. The three who had escaped had been lucky to get away. One of the survivors had a bad arm wound: a 7.62 mm round had gone in, glanced off the big arm bone and blown his triceps apart, exiting the other side. There was a great gaping hole where his muscle had been. I set about swabbing it clean as best I could with the disinfectant from my medical kit, and bandaged him up. They had no trained medics, and very little in the way of what we would call medicine: they relied on herbal remedies, supplemented by the odd painkiller captured from the enemy. There was no morphine, no plasma or blood, no chance of putting in a drip for a life-threatening injury, or any of that. With a serious gunshot wound, there was every chance of a fatal complication. If a man was lucky, he might get to a missionary station with a Western medical-aid team, or across the border into Pakistan.

Food was in short supply and hygiene virtually non-existent. Even without the additional risk factor of the war, the average male life expectancy up there was about the same as it had been in England at the turn of the century: not much above the mid-forties.

It had been a wild raid, but despite having fought on their side I was still the outsider. We talked it over with the three survivors, and I could see that they thought that while going back to the scene of a recent attack might have been incredibly brave it was also suicidal.

The next morning a small party of new men came up to replace those who had been killed. I had a brief word with Aragorn. The main reason for my being in Afghanistan was to train teams on the Stingers. I had been in the country for two weeks, and it was time to get on with it. He nodded, and gave orders to unpack one of the missiles. At first, Aragorn said he wanted everyone trained on the system, twenty or more men. I shook my head. I had learned that this just wasn't realistic, particularly now that I was on my own. The Stinger was complicated and, like many shoulder-fired weapons, it was easy to score an own-goal with it. It was more than a matter of simply acquiring the target, pointing and firing. Safety in handling was essential. I could see he wasn't very pleased.

'Look,' I said, 'I can't train twenty, but what I can do is get six of your men up to a useful standard. This will give you three fully operational two-man teams. For a group of this size, that's not bad.' After a moment's reflection, he said, with his thin smile, 'OK, train six good.'

But I had a problem. Who to select for the training? Aragorn had no more idea than I did which of his men might be cut out for the job. There was only one way to find out: get them all to try a bit of dry-firing. He agreed we should carry out an aptitude test, then explained to his men what I wanted to do.

First, with the whole group seated in a semi-circle around me, I tried to explain how the weapon worked. It was now almost dark, and I had a sudden idea: why not use the fire? Leaning forward, I put out my left hand flat. 'This is the Mig,' I said. I used my right hand to represent the missile. 'Rocket,' I said. 'Rocket.' They nodded. I picked up the launcher, and mimed firing, pulling the trigger; I brought my right hand up from the mouth of the missile tube, and started its track up towards the 'Mig'. At the same time, I started sniffing, tapping my nose and nodding down at the fire. Shit, I thought suddenly, I must look like old Nose-wanker Brown down in Belize. I pointed at the missile hand, moved it in towards the fire, sniffed, tapped my nose and then made the 'missile' track back up towards the imaginary aircraft. 'Fire,' I said in Pashto. 'The Mig makes fire out the back. The rocket goes for that.'

They got it first time. I didn't bother explaining about the cryogenic coolant in the seeker head. I thought it might be a bit over the top.

The next morning I assembled the Stinger, clipping the pre-sealed launcher tube with the missile proper on to the re-usable gripstock. I went very slowly, talking them through the process step by step, not because I thought they were stupid but because this was all entirely new to them. I explained that each missile came in a sealed tube. It was a one-shot weapon. From switch on, you had ninety seconds of battery life in which to make the shot, that was it. First you had to get the target with the naked eye. Once visual, you clicked the trigger. This switched on the battery, started the passive IR seeker head cooling, and made the optical sight come live. You tracked the target with the optical sight, while the seeker head searched the sky for a heat source. The missile started growling. When the head saw the target's heat-signature, it changed its audio signal from a low growl to a high-pitched buzzing. Now the head was in 'lock-to-launch' state: it was seeing only 1 to 2 degrees of sky, the bit with the heat in it. If it all still looked good, you made the second trigger click – and she fired.

Simple, really. Try explaining it in broken Pahsto/Urdu/sign language to pre-industrial tribesmen.

One by one I let them come up and look through the sight, which I made active for very short periods. It meant we would use up one missile battery, but they had to learn.

I also tried to explain that after firing the missile they mustn't discard the gripstock, to which the launcher tube was fitted, as it was re-usable; and I encouraged them to keep the gripstock and the missiles together at all times. They had a tendency to take things apart, squirrelling away the component pieces of a weapon in widely scattered hidey-holes. This meant that, whatever happened, the Russians wouldn't get hold of a complete Stinger system. But if they were to use it effectively, the Stinger need to be complete and readily available for firing at all times. The Russian aircraft weren't going to hang about while they went off to fetch the missile bits: Migs were targets of opportunity. I tested the batteries and the firing circuit. Everything was working. Time to begin selection.

I had chosen a big flat rock overlooking a long V-shaped re-entrant for the aptitude tests. From there, we should have early sight of any enemy activity, in the air or on the ground, and we could make ourselves scarce, pronto. One after another, the Mujahideen stepped up to this firing platform. And one after another, I saw I had the same problem we had had in the desert. They knew these mountains, and how to live off them, much better than I ever would. They could move through them at speed, disappear into them like ghosts, and outfight the Russian Army's best, given equal terms. But anything much more complex than an AK-47 and they were stumped. Most of them fumbled uselessly with the Stinger, unable to focus through the sight properly, fiddling about with the switches on the control head as though they had no fingers and ten thumbs. I watched them bugger about with the weapon. As each man gave up, defeated by this mysterious piece of Western technology, I took back the missile and shook my head at Aragorn.

Then two men stepped up together, both younger, one clearly the father of the boy who was glued to his side. The boy was ten or eleven, bright-looking, with a shock of black hair and the gleam of a keen intelligence in his eyes. He had a spindly frame, but he was wiry with it, and he had a way of jumping about, as though he were everywhere and nowhere at the same time. I handed the Stinger to his father. Immediately I could see that this man was far less afraid of the weapon than the others, far more confident about handling it. He gave a grunt of surprise as the pin-sharp picture through the optical sight swam up into his vision, and then a slow hiss of pleasure. Seeing that he was holding the weapon correctly, I went through the initial firing drills with him, slowly and thoroughly, getting him to repeat each step as I explained it. His son was standing nearby, watching us like a hawk. That child, I thought, understands what I'm saying better than anyone. Whenever his father faltered, the boy would correct him with a few muttered words, and we'd go on. It was a pity I couldn't just train the boy, but he was under combat age even for those mountains and, at about 10 kilograms launch-weight the Stinger was too heavy for his thin frame. Then I saw that two of the fingers of his left hand were missing. I asked him what had happened. 'Mine,' he said gravely, waving his arms up in the air to mime a big explosion. He pulled aside his shirt, showing me a huge scar running up his left side.

The other man tried next. He, too, was far better with the Stinger than any of the others except the boy's father. I looked at the two men. They were of similar appearance, with the same classic hawk face and intense, beady stare. I nodded at Aragorn. Here was our first two-man Stinger team. These were the men I would start training up. But if I were going to work with them I needed to call them something. I asked them their names, and in both cases got back an unintelligible stream of Pashto. I decided to call the father Hawk, and his companion, who was slightly darker, Raven. And since I was handing out wacky bird nicknames, I'd call the boy, whom up until then I'd been calling Bonzo, my father's name for me as a boy, Sparrow. I made the bird team practise some more in the afternoon, but as soon as I saw signs that they had had enough, I wrapped it up. Better to keep them hungry for more than to leave them fed up.

I went back to Aragorn. There were things he needed to learn about using the Stinger, too. In fact, as the team commander, his knowledge would be critical. 'When you use the Stinger for the first time,' I told him, 'it must be with the best chance you can get of a kill. And only then. Right now, the Russian pilots are confident: they think there is no threat. But as soon as you fire one of the Stingers, they'll all get to hear of it and the whole game will change. They'll fly higher, spend less time over the target, they'll put out flares all the time, maybe they'll fit missile warning receivers in their aircraft if they haven't already done so. So the first time with the Stinger must be a certain kill.' I drew the index finger of my right hand across my throat. 'Maximum impact.'

He grinned and nodded enthusiastically. 'Maximum impact.'

'So we need a game plan.'

'Yes,' he said. 'I will think.'

The next day I selected four more men from the remaining bunch for Stinger training, and we began work. And it was work. I started again with the Hawk and the Raven, on the grounds that if they could get the hang of it, they could help me explain things to their four mates. But even these two had difficulty coming to grips with some of the concepts, in particular the concept of backblast. The Stinger missile is a recoilless weapon. This means that when you fire it, there is an enormous backblast as the solid fuel in the missile ignites. Anything – or anyone – standing in the danger arc behind the launch tube will get fried alive when it ignites.

Then again, I couldn't get anyone to understand they had to keep still and *wait* for the aircraft to enter the safe parameters of their chosen firing position. I told them over and over that if the man firing made a sudden swing with a missile like that on his shoulder, then he was going to kill or very badly injure a friend nearby. But it was very frustrating. The concept of firing angles, and the absolute need to keep within them, was beyond my pupils. It was hard, too, to make anyone see the missile's great potential danger to the person firing it. If the Stinger is fired at too high an angle the backblast can rebound off the ground and blow up the person firing it – quite literally. The same thing can happen if you try firing it on a forward slope: the backblast will smash up off the gradient and give you a very unpleasant time, not to say burn off your arse.

All the time I was lecturing and demonstrating, the Sparrow was listening and watching, then scampering about the man with the missile, worrying at him until he got it right. In the end, it was the Sparrow who saved me. The boy's quick comprehension, and his father's willingness to listen to his son, meant that by the end of the afternoon at least two of them understood what I was getting at. Next day, we were back up on our firing platform with the scenic view again. Still no progress with the other five. I was going through the firing sequence with one man, who was mucking about with the Stinger like a Sister of Mercy testing condoms, when I caught the Sparrow looking at me. He looked at the man with the missile, looked back at me, and rolled his eyes heavenwards. I nodded. It was like that.

'OK,' I said to the boy. 'You explain. You tell him what to do – you understand it better than anyone.'

And he did just that. I talked the kid through it, step by step, while he relayed the instructions to the older men. A great kid – me and the Sparrow against the Red hordes.

When I thought this core team of six was reasonably up to scratch on the system, I sat them all down with Aragorn for a talk on tactics. It was one thing knowing how to fire the Stinger: picking the right target at the right time was another matter altogether. I explained that although the missile would engage an oncoming aircraft and have a fair chance of bringing it down, its chances of a kill were much, much higher if they fired it up the exhaust plume of a target that was going away. The heat-signature was that much greater, and the pilot was much less likely to look out and see the missile coming. But the point I stressed above all others was the need to cause catastrophic damage with this missile *every time* – and, above all, with the first two or three they fired. As far as I knew, the only Stinger missiles in Afghanistan were the six I had risked my neck bringing in. As I had already told Aragorn, they *had* to get maximum impact from every single one. This meant firing only on the most optimal targets. What did I mean by 'optimal'? One example I gave them of this was a transport that had just taken off from Kabul airport, heavily laden with troops or equipment, in a steep climb, with its engines at max revs chucking out a nice fat exhaust plume. Now, that was optimal. An aircraft that was coming in to land might look vulnerable but its engines were generally idling or at low revs, its exhaust plume was relatively small, and there was always the chance that the pilot, if he were skilled, might just succeed in crash-landing the plane even if it had sustained severe damage.

The idea of hitting a Mig-23 or a Sukhoi SU-27 was attractive to

155

people who had lost their women and children in the continual bombings. But they had to think about what would best sicken the Russians' morale. And here I was indebted to my father, who had once told me that what the SAS feared in Malaya was not getting killed out in the jungle fighting the Communists but getting shot down when they were on the plane coming home. Seeing men get killed while they were looking forward to the good times, at the very time you thought they were safe – now *that* was a morale-sickener.

Each Stinger attack, we therefore agreed, had to be carefully worked out for a precise target. As well as choosing their targets with care, the teams had to get in close enough to give the Stinger its best chance of killing. The missile had an effective range of about five kilometres, but it was better to get well inside that distance.

Once we had finished going through all this in exhaustive detail, and when I thought they had understood it, they were all ready to go out there and then and let fly at the Russians. 'No,' I said. 'It needs to be like any other attack – say, with an RPG. The Stinger team has to be protected so that if anybody does bump you they bump a cordon first. You need your scouts, front and rear, you need your flanking parties – all the stuff we talked about. At all costs, you save the weapon system – and the men trained to use it.' I grinned. 'I might not be back. Also the Stinger team must be able to concentrate on firing. They can't be looking over their shoulders when the target pops up.'

A small group of them went off into a huddle with Aragorn. I sat back and left them to it. In a minute, he came up to me on his own.

'We want to go and do an attack,' he said. 'After tomorrow.'

'In two days?'

'Yes. You will come?'

'I will come. Where?'

'Near Kabul. Many aircraft.'

'True,' I replied. 'And many Russians.'

Taking to heart my little speech about engaging optimal targets, they had set their sights on getting up near the perimeter fence of the Russian military airfield at Kabul and going for the transport full of homegoing troops. The heartlessness of this appealed to them. There was only one thing wrong with this plan: the defences around the city. The Russians had three concentric rings of defence around Kabul, the inner ring manned by their best-quality troops. Besides these cordons of self-reinforcing fixed points, there were frequent random mobile sweeps right round the perimeter: on the ground with APCs and foot patrols, in the air with the Hind D helicopter gunship. Taking a Stinger into that den of lions was about as hairy as it got. But, then, in a way I'd asked for it. And I wasn't in Afghanistan to sit around the camp-fire singing Scout songs.

'OK,' I said. 'How do I fit in?'

Aragorn thought about that one for a long time. 'I don't know,' he said, stroking his beard. He wanted my expertise, but he was worried about my appearance. I was worried about it, too. To get near Kabul with a couple of Stingers, they would have to use motorized transport, as well as moving on foot − it was more than fifty kilometres away. Then there was the problem of getting up close. By posing as innocent farmers sympathetic to the government, some Mujahideen fighting or sabotage patrols had sometimes managed to penetrate the Kabul cordons, hit, and run. But with a white man in their midst, they had no chance if the DRA or the Russians stopped them at a vehicle checkpoint. I could see that he was hesitating, doubtful about the wisdom of taking me, unsure whether the benefits of doing so outweighed the enormous risk.

'Look,' I told him, 'this will be your first Stinger attack. You want to have every chance of getting it right. Especially getting the tone.' He nodded. 'Well, won't it help if there's someone there who can say when the lock-on is good? Be sure when to fire?'

'Yes.' He disappeared again for another conference. Later that night, when I was stretched out ready for sleep, he came back. 'Tomorrow you can go with them, Yacoub, and may Allah protect you.'

'Amen to that,' I said. It was the first time Aragorn had used my Muslim name and invoked the Muslim faith to offer me protection.

It gave me a strange comfort.

157

Chapter Eighteen

We packed up the next morning and set off towards Kabul. Not for the airport itself – overnight, they had thought better of that, with me there – instead, we were headed for a low range of hills to the east of the city, populated with villages hostile to the government, which came under frequent air attack. The Mujahideen thought it was time the Russians learned a little lesson there. It was a target-rich environment – on both sides of the equation. We were a twelve-man team, which included all six men I'd trained in firing the Stinger, two of Aragorn's trusted deputies, the Sparrow, a couple of other men and myself.

We headed north and west towards the Kabul plain in broad daylight for a few hours. It was clear to me that, although we were moving by day, they had proved the route in advance, scouting ahead to make sure it was Russian-free. Come the evening we stopped, splitting down into two sections. As we ate, a couple of battered old Nissan pick-ups bounced up out of the gloom, no lights, springs squeaking, engines grumbling. This was unusual. The Mujahideen had virtually no transport; in fact, these were the first wheeled vehicles I had seen since arriving in the country that weren't Russian. It showed how much weight they were placing on the attack. All the weapons, including our personal ones, disappeared with four of the men in one of these ancient trucks. The rest of us packed into the remaining one, which was dark-grey, painted with several coats for good measure. Three of the Mujahideen got in the front, the rest of us climbed in the back. Unarmed except for the Beretta, I was looking forward with eager anticipation to the moment when we were stopped at a VCP manned by Russian troops – and they spotted me.

We bundled along in the darkness, bucketing over a track composed of hard-packed earth but in quite good nick, headlights off, looping up and around into the countryside every now and again, watching and waiting with the engine off, then rumbling back down to the road. We travelled like this for five or six hours. We stopped at about three in the morning and slept for a couple of hours, then it was up again at first light and on. At about noon we met up with the detached element of our group and got our weapons back. As usual, there were no rendezvous procedures, they just rolled up in the distance and we somehow knew it was the good guys coming back. They had brought up one of the Stinger systems, including two missile tubes and a control unit, and a number of RPGs in case we ran into any armour.

Now, still in daylight, we began climbing again, as a two-vehicle convoy. Towards evening, we found ourselves in a range of low, rounded foothills, featureless, barren and covered in scree. There was no sign of Kabul, no sign of a village, and we certainly weren't near any airfield. To me, it didn't look like a promising patch. But they reckoned the Migs came over there, regular as clockwork, and I had no choice but to believe them.

The next morning I had a good look round. 'If they do fly up across this range,' I said, 'I can't see how we can get a Mig into a narrow band – I mean, get an angle for a firing solution.'

'No,' said the deputy commander, Khamed, with a smile, 'you are right. But we are going to move again, more to the south. You will see, Yacoub. Only wait.'

They had set up a trap for the Russian pilots. Without telling me, they had staged an attack on a supply route in a valley to the south of our position; the attack, still in progress, was purpose-designed to lure in the Migs. This was good news: it meant that the Mujahideen had taken on board what I had told them about ensuring a good target. They had kept me completely in the dark about this plan because I was their biggest risk of compromise if we were caught.

I had no idea by what route the weapons had travelled, or how the two groups had made a precise rendezvous at a certain time and in a certain place. I only understood in retrospect how the elements of the whole scheme fitted together, and how well it had all been worked out. Not for the first time I reflected that the Soviets had a fight on their hands.

We began moving again, this time tactically and on foot, with a lead scout and the overall commander up front, two two-man flanking groups, and a rearguard, around the rest of us with the SAMs. We got to the next rendezvous around noon, had a brew and some food, then climbed up on to the flattish shoulder of a rounded hill. This was where they meant to ambush the Russians. The commander put out a defensive cordon, and we sat there for the rest of that day, waiting for the Migs to come along. We were still waiting the next morning. But then, at about eight o'clock, the Sparrow, who had the best ears, raised his finger and pointed to the north. 'Mig!' he called. 'Mig!'

A second later I, too, heard the low rolling roar in the sky. We watched. There were three, Mig-23s, tracking north-west to south-east across us, from left to right. I saw at once that they would pass in front of our position. The only question in my mind was how close they would come. We could see three in the sky, but I had a strong feeling there would be another lurking somewhere nearby – aircraft tend to move around in pairs, leader and wingman. I went over to the Stinger team. The Hawk and the Raven had already got busy on the missile. The Hawk was the trigger man. As I came up he was raising it to his right shoulder.

'Right,' I told him, 'turn the unit on. Start tracking. Let the aircraft come to you. Don't raise the missile too high. Don't let anyone get in behind it. Remember what I told you about the backblast.'

He peered through the optical sight, trying to pick up one of the Migs. 'Wait!' I said. 'They're high – at least two thousand metres. And they're still about four clicks off. It's too far. Wait.' As I spoke, two of the Migs detached, dropping lower and vectoring slightly nearer our position. They were bombed up. The third Flogger stayed high – he was out of it. I saw the Hawk tense slightly. He had acquired one of the descending pair.

'OK,' I said. 'Easy now. Wait.' I was trying to keep him calm, but in reality I was just as excited as he was. If we got one of these fuckers it was going to prove the point of my being there. At the same time I was worried. The Mig he was tracking kept on changing height: the launcher was going up and down like a yo-yo as the Hawk followed the fighter-bomber's random jinks. What was the pilot doing? Avoidance manoeuvring? Was that routine? If so, why wasn't the other one doing it? It seemed strange. The other Mig of the pair was ploughing straight on, slightly off to one side. Then we got tone – the high-pitched beep that told us the unit was seeking. The whole group went still, waiting for the growl of the lock-on. The second we got that, the Hawk would fire. The second we fired the three other Migs would see the missile's vapour trail. And they would be down to do a bit of investigating – with their 23 mm cannon and their cluster bombs. But there was nothing I could do about that: we didn't have a second team.

The target started to turn away, presenting its three-quarter aspect to us. This was good – but at the same time it was still at least four clicks away, and beginning to climb sharply. Not so good. Worse still, there was no growl, no steady tone that would indicate lock-on. Lost target, I thought, and in the same moment the Hawk's index finger curled around the trigger. The Mig was still climbing, still going away from us at high speed. There was still no lock-on. I stepped forward, grabbed his finger, pulled it off the trigger and reapplied the safe.

They all looked at me, their faces a picture of mixed disappointment and surprise.

'It's no good,' I said. 'You had no lock-on.' I mimed with my fingers and my nose again. 'The missile smelt something, but it wasn't sure. There was no lock-on tone. We have to be sure. It's not worth wasting a shot.' We could have fired on the Mig, the Stinger's head is self-seeking, but first time out I was determined to get that kill.

Once they had got over their disappointment, the Mujahideen sat down among the rocks, prepared to wait for a better firing solution. We didn't have to wait long. A few minutes later, the Migs came roaring back low and fast in front of us. They took us completely unawares. I'd been right – there were four of them now, they had regrouped somewhere, preparing for an attack run. They dropped

161

behind a hill to our left front, and at once we heard the sound of bombs going in, the rolling thunder of the explosions hitting a target we couldn't see. They came in low and very fast, one behind the other, using the folds of the land to maximum advantage, hitting hard then peeling off behind a hill. The way they attacked reminded me strongly of the Argentine attacks over San Carlos Water during the Falklands War. I knew they were bombing the decoy Mujahideen group that had been put in as bait. We could only watch and hope that the decoy team weren't catching too many hits.

We were hoping the Migs might come back over our position as they set up for a second run, but instead we saw them swoop back up into view on the far side of their target, re-form, and roar off away to the north. Pity, I thought.

Later on, when we talked about it, the Mujahideen admitted that they had known exactly where the decoy group would be. 'Knowing that,' I said, 'I could have selected us a much better killing ground. When you're springing that kind of trap, you can get the Stinger team in a much better position than we had just now. You can get right in there, much closer. There's no way they're going to see you from the air – no way. We could have guaranteed a kill.' I understood their reluctance to give me any information before the event. Even though it had resulted in a failed mission, keeping me in the dark was good basic ground security. And, luckily, there had been no loss of life in the other group.

Having grasped the lesson that we needed to be closer still for a missile kill we packed up, walking back out of the hills until we came to an LUP where our drivers had hidden the pick-ups. Everybody piled in around the weapons, and we trundled off. But where before we had moved tactically and with extreme caution, now here we were, all fourteen of us, travelling at speed in bright daylight, in convoy and with all the kit. You never could tell with the Mujahideen – they were completely unpredictable. It was as dangerous on the way out of a mission as it was on the way in, if not more so, but to them it made no difference. Maybe that's why the Russians found them so hard to fight. We drove all that day, stopped to eat in the evening, then set off again once it was dark. We were doing about

thirty kilometres per hour, so we must have covered a fair
ground that night. I didn't know, but had to assume, that the ar
were now going into was still part of Ahmad Shah Massoud's sp.
of influence. Towards dawn we stopped at a crossroads, and de-
bussed. Once again, the drivers took the vehicles off to a separate
hiding-place. Hefting all the weaponry, we tabbed quickly away
from the road, which was making me nervous, then up a steep, rock-
covered slope to a level, roughly circular area below the crest of the
nearest ridge. This place was surrounded by sharp crags, broken stones
and boulders, giving us much better cover than the previous ambush
site. Looking round, I had a bad feeling we might need it. We were
still within two kilometres of the crossroads that we had just quit; and
to the west, directly ahead, there was a new road, about five kilometres distant at the far end of a re-entrant. I borrowed Khamed's
ancient field-glasses.

The route was teeming with Russian military traffic.

We sat up there for the rest of that morning, watching the military
convoys lumbering by on the road, the trucks heavily protected by
armoured vehicles. On the still hot air we could hear them occasionally, a low distant grumble.

Fair enough, I'd said we had to get close in to the Russians. I
hadn't said we had to sit right on top of them.

'We must be careful,' said Khamed, stating the enormously obvious. 'There is a checkpoint over there – and there', he pointed to
another peak topped by a small fort, 'is a Russian observation post.'
He gave me his best wolf's grin. 'We are near Kabul.'

Like me, the Mujahideen were much more nervous in this new
position, very alert and aware, watching and listening the whole time.
They had good reason to be worried. If the Russians spotted us they
would have a Hind or a Frogfoot out of Kabul airport down our
throats in no time – if an armoured patrol didn't catch us first. I had
no sooner finished thinking this than everyone around me dropped
down flat among the rocks. They were flat on their bellies with their
heads right down, almost cowering, something I had never seen them
do before. I dropped down with them, face in the dry soil. I felt the
quick crawl of fear. My hearing, even then, wasn't all it should have

been – too much close exposure to gunfire. Then I heard it: a heavy, low-pitched rumbling with a counterpoint of high-pitched squeaks. The sound of tracked armour coming right at us. I strained my ears: two vehicles, minimum, possibly more.

Shit.

I put my face back. The sound was getting closer, approaching our position.

Russians.

Lifting my head the tiniest fraction and peering between a crack in the rocks, I saw two BMDs, airborne infantry fighting vehicles (AIFV). Triple-fuck. They were a light sand colour, with paler, light-buff camouflage patches, white unit numbers and Cyrillic letters stencilled on their sides. They were two hundred metres away, moving slowly along the road we had travelled in the pick-ups. When they reached the crossroads, they ground to a halt. A hatch clanged back and there was the sound of men moving. No orders had been given: they were airborne troops, professionals. And they had BMDs.

Which was about as bad as it got.

The BMD was a tracked, airborne-dedicated, fire-support vehicle, with a quick-firing 73 mm smooth-bore gun, a 7.62 mm co-axial machine-gun mounted alongside that, an anti-tank missile launcher, and two more 7.62 mm machine-guns fixed at its front corners. Despite being tracked, it was fast. And along with its crew of three it could carry six fully-armed paratroopers. We were about to find out that each of these AIFVs had its full complement. Twelve men.

The Hawk and the Sparrow were with the Stinger next to me. I glanced across at them. They were both lying on one cheek. Both had their eyes closed. I could see that the Hawk's lips were opening and closing, soundlessly, as though he were praying. The Sparrow opened his eyes then and stared back. He looked as frightened as I felt.

We were in deep shit.

Through the tiny crack in the rocks, I watched the Russians going into all-round defence on the vehicles, their movements smooth and well drilled. A couple of them weren't defending: they were moving, bending down and looking at the ground, scanning the area all

164

around the crossroads. Fuck! I thought. The tracks! That's why they're here. We hadn't bothered covering our tracks. Why hadn't I insisted we do so?

Double-fuck.

I put my head back down very, very slowly. We were totally and utterly outgunned. All we could do was lie there and listen, and hope against hope that they wouldn't find us. I heard the slow servo whine of a turret traversing as one of the gunners kept a wary eye out for movement among the rocks. Then the sound of the engines died away to nothing. I lay there, sweating in the hot silence. What about our own sign? I wondered. We'd thrown out a hook around the base of the hill before moving up it. That was something. And the pick-ups had driven off, leaving more tracks that the Russians should see – and follow. But twelve of us, carrying heavy weapons over that ground? In single file? What sort of sign had we left? A fucking ploughed furrow, unless we were dead lucky. How rocky was the ground we'd covered after leaving the road? How obvious to the trained eye was our LUP? The questions buzzed in my brain as I lay there, skin cooking in the heat but ice cold inside, praying the Russians would find the tyre-marks of the Nissans leading away and take off after them. If our drivers were spotted at least they could make a run for it. We were caught like rats in a trap.

I shifted slightly, moving with extreme care and slowness, trying to inch my weapon up closer to hand so that I could pour some fire down their Soviet throats. Surprise was our only chance. As I lay there, sweat dropping off my nose into the dust, I was working out the options, theirs and ours, working out which way they would come if they did hit our sign. And what they would do. At the heart of our group, I should have a few seconds' warning from the defensive cordon we had put out. But supposing they stood off, keeping us bottled up, and radioed for back-up? That's what I would have done. Then we were truly stuffed.

What if a fighting patrol came at us? What was my own best course of action then? Our cordon would fire first. The first thing was to get two RPG rounds in through the sides of those BMDs, try to stop them sending for back-up. Who was on the RPGs? Did they realize that? If I had to, if I didn't hear the rockets go, I'd get on one of the RPGs and do it myself. Grenades. Grenades would be useful. Most of our guys had grenades. I didn't.

But, in my heart, I knew that even if we won a firefight up here on the rise it wouldn't save us. The second the first shot was fired the BMDs would close up like clams. Then their commanders would whistle up reinforcements, shelling us with the 73 mms to keep us pinned down. We would never disable them both in time with the RPGs. And then, when the back-up troops arrived, they would be on us like wolves.

I heard movement in the rocks below. They had seen our sign. They were coming. I could hear the odd loose stone slipping, and once the *chink* of something metal against stone, but they were good, these Russians, very, very quiet. I had the AK-47 up beside me now, fingers around the stock. Ready as I'd ever be. If I could hear them from where I was, they must be almost on top of our cordon. A lifetime went by, seconds, minutes, hours and days. There was another tiny sound among the rocks.

Then, in a great surge of relief, I heard the sound of engines, revving hard. They were going! Or was it a feint? Khamed came up, crawling slowly on his belly, elbows out, cradling his rifle in the crook of his arms.

'They have gone,' he said quietly.

'It may be a trick,' I whispered back. 'Lie still and tell your men to do the same.' We lay there for the best part of an hour. There was no sound. At the end of that time I turned to him. 'OK, they may have moved off – a little way. But whatever you do, don't let anyone here move until it's dark. If I were the Russian commander I'd be sitting somewhere close by, under cover, watching this position through my field-glasses. I'd have cut-offs all around, and I'd have other people closing to help.'

We stayed there all that night. Because we'd come unprepared for a night in the hills we had no blankets, nothing at all except the clothes we stood up in, and we couldn't make a fire. There was no food, and just a few flasks of water. No one smoked, no one coughed. We lay there and shivered on that barren crag for twelve hours.

Just before dawn, the Raven came up. He had been out on the edge of the defensive cordon. He said that two of the Russian paratroops had come within five metres of where he'd been lying. Sure they were about to stumble right on top of him, he had come within a hair's breadth of sitting up and opening fire. At the last instant, miraculously, they had turned away.

Before daybreak we came down off the slope, in single file, laden with weaponry. We had no choice but to follow in the wake of the Russians – they had gone straight towards our vehicle LUP. Everyone's eyes were wide open, staring. Even the Sparrow was tip-toeing along, casting fearful glances at the sky and the rocks around. I fully expected to arrive at the LUP to be met by a pair of burned-out pick-ups and a small army of Russian airborne troops.

As it was, we had been lucky – maybe the Russians had lost the tracks of our own vehicles among others, or maybe they had been called somewhere else. At any rate, we found the Nissans intact – but with their drivers just as spooked as ourselves: they, too, had come within a whisker of discovery.

By now we had had enough. I didn't have to tell the Mujahideen they had been seriously burned – compromised. We got into those trucks and we got out of there, travelling all that day and all through the next night until we arrived back at our base camp. When they had finished telling Aragorn the gist of what had happened to us, he came up. 'I agree we need to get the Stinger team closer. This will be done. We must look and move like farmers to get near Kabul. But you, Yacoub, you cannot be part of such a thing. Instead, you can help us plan the attack.'

'It will be a pleasure,' I told him.

Next day, as luck would have it, one of the fighters I had trained before turned up. He was the first of that group I had come across in five weeks in and around the Panjsher valley. After more than a month in Afghanistan, it was a relief to have someone there who could interpret properly for me from English into Pashto. 'Now,' Aragorn said to me, 'tell us how we are going to use the Stingers at Kabul.' He took out the planning-pack I'd helped prepare for an attack on Kabul's military airport. We went through it in detail,

167

spending most of the day on it, drawing out a mock-up of the airfield in the thin dust, going over and over the strengths, types and disposition of the defending forces, as well as the terrain and the physical barriers they would face, discussing all the possible ways of getting in – and out. I worked out ranges and arcs of fire, calculating how close a two-man team would be able – and need – to get with a missile and still have a dog's chance of escaping. One thing was a big help: the Mujahideen knew exactly where all the Russian defensive points were around the airfield, as well as the troop strengths at each point and their precise equipment. Their intelligence was consistently good on detail. The plan I devised meant going right around to the other side of the capital, the side from which the Russians would be least expecting it, and penetrating the defences there. The extra time needed for this was of no matter – the operation wasn't time-critical. I paid particular attention to the escape routes: I wanted my Stinger teams to come out alive, if at all possible. By the end of the session we had worked out several possible options, both for the INFIL and the EXFIL.

I still thought it was a one-way trip.

The Hawk and the Raven had volunteered for the job. I had to agree they were the best available. The Sparrow, for once, would have to stay with the rest of us: there was no way he could go with his father. I made sure they understood that the Russian aircraft would always take off into wind, so they must get themselves into a good position under the flight path at the upwind end of the runway. I worked out that the aircraft would still be low enough, and well within range, at the point where they normally turned away from the peaks – between three and four kilometres out from the military field. This meant the Stinger team would still have to penetrate two of Kabul's three defensive rings. And, of course, once they had fired, assuming they got in, they would be in extreme danger. When we had finished planning I went through the missile drills again and again with the two men, until I was sure they had got it down pat.

The next morning, early, the Hawk and the Raven left, with eight of the other men. I never saw or heard of any of them again.

About two weeks later, on 1 July, a Russian Antonov AN-26

168

transport aircraft with a full company of troops on board was shot down as it took off from Kabul airport. To my own knowledge, it was the first confirmed Stinger kill of the Afghan War.

Chapter Nineteen

When they were sick or wounded, many of the fighters relied for their cures on the itinerant soothsayers we came across in the hills. These mountain nomads made their living by combining various roles: fortune-teller, wise man and medicine man. They used semi-precious stones, polished by constant handling until they were round and smooth and shiny like beads, to tell the future. Once they had been paid, they tossed these pebbles high into the air, let them fall into the dust and read as omens the patterns into which they fell.

Walking the next day with Bilbo, I met one of these strange hermits just outside the camp. He was squatting by the side of the road, his black old eyes gazing out at us from his leathery brown face. He was stick-thin, wizened, ageless. He muttered something.

'He wants to tell your fortune,' Bilbo said. 'Give him some money – just a little – and he will do it.' I reached into my pocket and took out a US dollar bill. 'It should be silver,' I joked.

'No,' Bilbo said. 'It will be all right.' The old man stowed away the money inside the folds of his ragged clothing. Then he opened the drawstring of a little leather bag around his neck, and poured out his fortune stones. He gave me the stones to handle for a minute, telling me to turn them in my hands; then he took them from me, rolled them around in his cupped palms and flung them high into the air. They dropped into the dust by the side of the road. When he had studied the pattern for a long time, he looked up at me. 'You're OK,' he announced, in a Pashto dialect, which Bilbo translated. 'You'll live to be an old man of forty-five!'

He grinned at me, showing broken and blackened teeth, as if I should be happy at this prediction. At the time, being a mere lad of thirty-two, I didn't mind. Now I've only got two years left to go.

About three days later more reinforcements arrived. Aragorn said there was a push on: they had decided to attack an outpost manned by the DRA near Kabul. I listened while he outlined the plan.

'It means coming down out of the mountains, into the open, close to the Russian defences?'

'Yes.'

'A big risk.'

'Yes. Very big.'

Very big indeed. In setting up the triple cordon, the occupying forces had depopulated a thirty-kilometre zone around the capital. Anyone moving in that area without permission was liable to be killed on sight. He gave no indication that they wanted me to come. I thought about offering to do so, then decided it was better to wait.

In the dead of night, I woke to find Aragorn shaking me. In his broken English, he was saying, 'Will you come with us?'

'Of course.' I looked into his eyes, black stones in the moonlight. There was a new warmth in the way he'd asked the question. I lifted the AK-47 beside me so that he could see it in my hand. He gave a quick nod of satisfaction. 'We go. Come.'

In the darkness we all made ready, a round up the spout and locked. Then we set off, in single file. All that night we marched, heading south-south-west, by the stars, not north, as I had expected. The next day, we went to ground, resting under cover. Around noon, some local men brought in a sheep, the organized back-up without which every army would starve. The Mujahideen cooked it whole for hours in a dugout dirt oven, with onions and spices. We ate it just before dusk, with some thick sour yoghurt to drink, followed by strong green tea. The meat was delicious: I realized that I hadn't eaten this well – or this much – in weeks. Food was so short now. The blanket Russian scorched-earth policy had systematically destroyed all farms and orchards, razing anything that even looked like it might be growing. Eating so little, the weight had fallen away

171

from me, so that I was getting leaner and lither, more like the Mujahideen.

Before we set out that night, I inspected everyone casually, glancing at weapons and dress. If someone had a grenade hanging a bit loose, I'd touch it, usually without saying anything, or just mutter something indistinguishable and move on. By the time I looked back at the man, he would have corrected the problem. Same with jewellery, earrings and bracelets or watches − if I saw the slightest reflection, I'd touch my ear, to show him what I could see, or rub my wrist, and the offending article would vanish into a waistcoat. I had gained the confidence, by now, to check the Mujahideen routinely in this way before an attack. They didn't mind me doing it as long as they didn't lose face with the rest. To them, face was everything.

One thing I didn't like was the habit they had of taping two rifle magazines together, one in the weapon the right way up, the other mag reversed. This looked very cool, very TV-news guerrilla chic, but it was a really, really bad idea. Nine times out of ten the mag that was upside down collected all kinds of crap in it so that when it was most needed, in the heat of a contact, you'd get a stoppage. Followed immediately by a one-way ticket to paradise. I tried to get them to tape the magazines together, same way up, but with a spacer between as we did on the CT team at home. In the SAS, we'd had specially made aluminium spacer clips. Up there in the mountains it was a matter of bodging something up.

With all the new faces that had joined us, the assault force was about twenty-eight, roughly platoon strength. Along with their AK-47s, most of the men had either RPG-7 rocket launchers, for attacking armour and hard-points, or RPD machine-guns. We were all weighed down with great belts of ammunition and spare rockets. I was intrigued to find that one man had a disposable anti-tank weapon, a Russian-made shoulder-fired equivalent of our own 'fire-and-chuck' '66' anti-tank rocket. Apart from the RPG-7, it was the first dedicated modern anti-armour weapon I'd seen in Afghanistan.

As we advanced on that second night we passed through a series of broken and blackened villages, one shattered hamlet after another, riddled by rockets and gunfire, blasted by bombs. Some of these places were hostile to us: the people there had had enough of the Russian battering, they just wanted to be left in peace. If that meant denying their own fighters food and shelter, so be it. From time to time, I made out the hulks of wrecked T–62 tanks by the side of the track, rusting in the darkness, more evidence of the bitter fighting in that area. More than once, I saw the tail fins of an unexploded bomb sticking up out of the ground.

At about three in the morning we came to a new village that was still relatively intact. We skirmished forward slowly between the darkened, silent homes until we were spread out at its furthest edge. For once, the Mujahideen had put out a back guard: they were going about the attack well. We came out of the edge of the village, sliding in among the last scattered outbuildings, and there was the target in front of us, a stone fort set on top of a small hillock at the far end of a broad, shallow re-entrant, squat and black against the skyline, with no lights showing, no sign of any life. From Aragorn's brief, I knew this strongpoint was relatively isolated while strategically important, part of the Russian policy to dominate the countryside. It looked like a good position to win.

Looking round, I saw the Mujahideen were all bunched up together in a mass for the attack. Khamed was nearby. I whispered to him that this bunching wasn't such a good idea – more men would be killed if a mortar round or a burst of fire smacked in among them. He nodded and gave some whispered instructions. The fighters spread out along a line. While I had Khamed's ear, I suggested he position two cut-off groups to cover each side of the main gate. This was in case the garrison came out to counter-attack. Again, I was thinking what I would do in the fort commander's place. Khamed grunted further orders.

We began moving forwards silently. We kept to the dead ground as far as possible, using the *wadis* and the folds of the land to get in closer. I saw a movement, then, from one of the parapets, and stopped. If we could see them in the moonlight, they could certainly see us. Talk about grabbing by the belt-buckle.

We stopped about a hundred metres out. Now that we were in close, I could see that the walls were made of mud brick, very thick, about four metres in height, with watch-towers about twice that height at the four corners. On the inside you could bet they had reinforced the walls with sandbags and rock to stop the RPGs. We were coming up on the left-hand front corner of the complex. The main gate, to our right, was wide enough to get an armoured vehicle through. I was surprised that there were no searchlights. The Mujahideen said they were sure that the ground we were treading was free of mines. I hoped fervently that this was true.

We were ready. Someone fired a shot. At once the night erupted into flame noise. I stood up and took aim at one of the black patches in the dark wall ahead of me, hoping it was a window or a port. I fired three short bursts, watching my strikes go in. There was an ear-splitting roar all around me of rockets firing, the RPDs hammering, my own and the other AK-47s barking away. Through all the noise I heard yelling. I stopped firing. Aragorn was shouting at the defenders, telling them they had to surrender and come out. The officer in charge had other ideas: he was bellowing that if any of his men even tried to surrender they would be shot.

A flare from the fort soared up into the night sky and bloomed, followed at once by a second, flooding the whole scene with a ghostly yellow-white light. Immediately the firing started up again. Looking across, I saw that our left-hand cut-off group was in a contact. There was a big firefight going on over there, with shouts and screams adding to the confusion. As I stood squinting over the sights, one of the huge iron-bound wooden doors in the main gate swung open, and a mass of ground troops came pouring out. They weren't going to sit inside that place and get shot at, they meant to carry the attack. It was exactly what I would have done – and what I'd feared. They were well organized, spread out and pepper-potting, running hard, pausing, then firing. They were headed right for the dozen or so of us in the command group, having correctly identified this as the main body of the attack. I could hear and feel their fire thudding and thumping into the ground all around me, as well as the crack-thumps overhead. They were already on target, not firing high as inexperienced troops tend to do at night.

Our left cut-off group was pouring fire down on this flying

column, and getting a whole lot back. The troops kept coming right at us. I had that slippery, sliding feeling you get inside when an attack's going wrong. From their combat skills, I was pretty sure these were Russians, and not the feeble DRA opposition we had been expecting.

We were the Indians, running round and round outside, loosing off our fire-arrows, taunting the cowboys holed up inside. They were supposed to cower, acknowledging our great strength. But this lot hadn't read the script: they weren't demoralized Afghan Army conscripts. Sometimes, when a fresh garrison of DRA troops was taking over a garrison, the Russians would make a point of coming in with them, to train them and instil some discipline. It was my guess we had bumped the changeover detail: we had two garrisons for the price of one, plus the Russians. For certain we were heavily outnumbered.

One of our side fired another flare. By its light I saw fire going in at the cut-off group to my right, but not from the fort, from the darkness beyond them. This was more bad news: that had to be a Russian roving patrol, lurking on the outside, waiting for just such an attack. I had heads up, deciding which way to make my move. The enemy force on our left was closer, only fifty or sixty metres away now, still skirmishing towards us. I moved back and to the left, fast, got down on one knee, and brought up the AK-47.

I made out the lead Russians, dark shapes running: they had become people behind their tracer and the muzzle-flash. Three or four were leading the main pack, firing and running in short bursts, sprinting from left to right. I tracked them with the sights. It all came back to me — moving target, left to right, running pace, at fifty metres aim at the leading edge, it's an AK-47 on automatic, keep it low and left. I squeezed off a burst of four or five rounds. The bullets smashed into him, flinging him up and away from me. His arms flew out wide in the shape of a star and he was down. I put down a second burst of fire with the same point of aim. The next man in the group ran straight into it – he, too, went down boneless. Seeing this, the others broke track, swerving left and right and going to ground. As soon as they were down they began firing in my direction.

More and more Russian and DRA troops were streaming out of

the fort now. Their fire was getting more and more accurate. They had 12.7 mm going from the walls – I could feel the disturbed air around me as the heavy-calibre rounds flew past. Gunfire was whistling down the main street of the village at my back, smacking into the house walls *thwack! thwack! thwack!* Right after that I heard more shouting, Aragorn yelling the same command over and over. I didn't need to be told what he was yelling – get out of there, and get out fast. They were too many, we were too few. We had made our little point. In a few seconds more they would be on us and among us. Then we'd die.

We skirmished back. At the critical moment, Frodo fired his RPG, slamming a rocket right into the gates just as more troops were pouring out. There was an enormous blast. Great chunks of wood and bits of gatehouse shot up into the sky, lit from below by the flash of the explosion. Everyone was firing on full automatic now, including me, hardly aiming, everything was gone to shit, we'd come down to the Wild West. The hammer clicked dry and I slammed on a fresh magazine. I was running and turning, dropping on to one knee, blazing a few rounds back at the enemy to check their rush, then it was up and run and turn again and fire. Rounds were slapping into the surrounding buildings all the time, humming past our heads as the Russians and their friends got their counter together.

They were moving and firing professionally, supporting one another in good style. Night turned to day and then back again as the flares lit the sky and then died. Three Mujahideen came haring past, running for their lives. When I saw that, I let loose a long final rip of automatic fire, turned and ran like a maniac after them. This wasn't the Alamo, I wasn't Davy Crockett. We found the rest of the group spread out behind the buildings in the centre of the village, they covered for us as we ran up to join them. Aragorn and Khamed were shouting orders, and the Mujahideen started firing back with real purpose. Then, as a unit, under control, we did a fighting withdrawal, sniping back at the pursuing pack to make them keep their heads down. Once we were clear of the outskirts we swung to the south, stopped firing, and began running fast into the night. A few desultory shots rang out after us, then died away.

Except for the padding of our feet and the rasping of our breath, there was silence.

When we were sure there was no follow-on, we did a quick head-count: three dead, five wounded. It could have been worse. Marching hard into the night, we headed back up into the mountains.

Chapter Twenty

After this contact we rested for a day then set out on another mission. The Mujahideen didn't believe in standing still: they had a war to win. After two days of hard marching, we came to a well-established ambush point on a high plateau thirty or forty kilometres or so south of Kabul, only a few clicks back from the outermost Russian defensive line. There was a mountain right behind this position to the south-east, and a relatively low ridge of rock, about thirty metres in height, to its front.

The further slope of this ridge dropped sharply away to the plain – and a convoy route – directly below. A platoon of about thirty Mujahideen fighters was deployed up here, armed with a battery of four Chinese-made 82 mm mortars, staggered two and two near the base of the ridge. Half a dozen 12.7 mm tripod-mounted Triple-A guns were standing around ready in case of any air attack. There were a few foxholes scattered about, but not nearly enough.

There was a Soviet outpost a few kilometres to our west, supplied from time to time by convoys that came through on the road below. The Mujahideen had intelligence that a convoy was due, and this was confirmed by the intermittent artillery fire that fell among the peaks around us all day. Before they sent out one of their convoys, the Russians would often shell along and around its route, or scatter mines from the Hips, concentrating on likely ambush points, hoping to get lucky and knock out a hidden ambush group. But far from suppressing the Mujahideen, this activity served only to announce upcoming convoys and invite attack.

The Mujahideen were hoping to catch the convoy at last light, nothing fancy, it was a basic hit-and-run operation. Using the ridge in front of the camp as dead ground, they were going to lob mortar shells up over the top of it and down on to the vehicles as they went past: we're talking indirect firing. As so often, I thought the lack of any thorough planning was dangerous. I went up and had a chat with the commander of the group we had now joined. He told me they had been training with the mortars, not using live rounds but dry firing. As far as he was concerned, the Russians had no idea we were there, no way of knowing we were there, and by the time they had reacted, we would be gone. He assured me that the ridge would disguise our location from the Russian DF equipment. I retorted that the Russians would spot where the mortar fire was coming from at once – it was obvious. And they would retaliate. Hard. Never mind, said our leader, his men would do it anyway. They had good cover and caches for men and weapons close by.

There was another slight problem: the Mujahideen hadn't dared fire the mortars to bed them in, as this would have given away the position. This meant that when it came to the attack their fire would be effectively unaimed. But with four of the 82 mms firing at once, and someone up on the crest of the ridge correcting fire, there was a chance they might get lucky and hit one or two of the trucks.

I walked around the position. The more I looked at it, the less I liked it. There were traces of old cooking fires on the ground, which told me – and any Russian aerial reconnaissance – that they had used this location before. It was the vulnerability to air attack that bothered me. To the front and sides we were highly visible from the air. The Mujahideen thought we were in dead ground, invisible because of the ridge, so they had made no attempt at camouflage. This was a big mistake. Even a cursory Soviet reconnaissance flight was going to spot us. In short, I thought the whole operation was extremely risky. But I was there, and I could hardly walk away.

At its southern boundary, where it joined the mountain behind, the plateau was cut by run-off channels and sink-holes created by the melt-water pouring down from the peaks in the spring. I had noticed these strange twisting runnels on our way across to the mortar battery.

I didn't know it then, but they were going to save my life.

The morning went past and became afternoon. The air was pure and hot, with a strong sun beating down. It was the dog hour, between four and five. I was squatting on the ground with Bilbo, Frodo and the Sparrow. Since his father had gone, the boy spent some of his time with me. I had been teaching him the odd word of English. None of us was saying much, lost in our own thoughts, in my case of Margaret and Natalie. It was ten weeks now since I had had any news.

We never heard the gunships coming. They had used the landscape expertly, keeping low on the attack run, then climbing straight up the edge of the plateau to our right, using the rock face to deflect their noise.

They had succeeded brilliantly. We were done for.

As the first Hind reared up above the cliff edge, the sound crashed over me: *whop, whop, whop, whop.* I stood up, not wanting to believe what my ears and eyes were telling me. Then a second gunship loomed up behind the first.

'Run!' my brain was yelling at me. 'Run!'

I ran.

With a cold roar, the first wave of rockets came down. I felt the hot blast of the explosions on my back. I ran as if the wind had picked me up, ran without thinking, survive, that was all.

Live.

It was every man for himself.

They were going for the mortars first, and the *dushkas*, but there were men falling all around, the air gunners shooting movement, picking people off as they ran. *Zzzzp! Zzzzp!* There was the chain-saw noise of their cannon now, mixed with the thunder of the rotors and the continual *whump* of the exploding rockets. I didn't even have the time to know my fear.

I saw a run-off trench ahead and threw myself into it, diving headlong, burrowing down into it, frantic to escape those enormous armour-piercing shells. A gunner had seen my run. The ground jumped around me, the shells spewing up a kind of dark froth as they chewed the dirt and rock. My eyes filled with dust so that I couldn't see, but it hardly mattered: at any moment, one of those tank-stopping rounds would smash me apart, and that was the end.

The shaking moved away. There was still the roaring thunder of the rockets and the guns, but for some insane reason I put my head up. I saw Frodo, then, with Sméagol hard on his heels. They ran up to a DshK right in front of a Hind. Grabbing hold of it, they let rip. Lazily, the long questing stalk of the cannon slewed round, roared out and blew them apart.

Something clicked in me, maybe the feeling that I would die whatever I did, and I brought up the AK.

All my rounds hit the Hind, it was so near I couldn't miss. None had any effect. The gunner noticed the incoming fire and switched round. The rotary cannon was pointing at me. For the first time, I had a conscious thought: What if I die here? Who'll care? Will they even know? I didn't want to die and lie in an unmarked grave. I wanted to be buried within sight of my old school, St Martin's, with the people I'd known lying on either side of me.

The world turned to dust and stone.

I was deafened, yet the noise seemed to fill my head, it filled everything there was. The earth around me shuddered and bucked. It wouldn't protect me – I had to move. For a second or two, the earthquake of shells went somewhere else, and I was up and running for the hard rock at the base of the mountain. There was a big plug of rock here, and I got in behind it, curling up around and into it, wedging myself right in so that I was one with the stone. Shells splatted and ricocheted everywhere, sending rock splinters that cut into my back and neck.

If he fires a rocket now, if he's got one left . . .

Then the miracle. Silence.

I lay there for a long time, curled up around this rock, unable to believe that the killing had gone away. The fear came to me, the conscious fear of what had been, what might still be, and I began to shake. It took me a long time to calm down enough to get to my feet.

I looked back across the open ground. It was a scene of utter devastation. Where once there had been a platoon of men, with

181

mortars and Triple-A, now there was nothing but debris and dust, strange lumps that were still smoking, that might have been weapons or men and were probably both. I began walking. My feet didn't feel like my own feet as they touched the ground, there was another person walking inside my empty shell. I heard something and looked back. One of the Mujahideen was behind me, treading in my footsteps in case of mines. Still trembling, I sat down on a rock for a minute, and put my head between my legs. I couldn't really accept what had happened, although the evidence was all around. When I thought I was more in control, I looked back around the open space. By now most of the dust had either drifted away or settled. Still there was no movement. Then I saw a man lever himself painfully out of a hole in the ground, one of the foxholes they had had ready, and after him another man. Then, nothing. I counted the figures sitting dazed in the sun. Thirty-two Mujahideen had been up there before the Hinds attacked, not including myself. There were only six of us left alive.

This time, the Russians had got their own back. We all had superficial injuries: cuts from the flying shards of rock, abrasions, bruises, minor breaks, but we were the luckiest men alive, among the very, very few who can say they have survived a Hind attack.

We spread out to look for the wounded.

We found two men who were seriously injured: one lacked the lower halves of his legs, the other had a huge open head wound. We did what we could for them, but we all knew they were going to die.

Cautiously, watching the sky and listening at all times, ready to run at the slightest sound, we searched back over the position. The mortars and the *dushkas* had been blown to scrap. In most cases, there wasn't even a tangle of metal to show where they had been, no more than the odd heat-fused lump. We moved like zombies, shell-shocked, among the wrecked humanity and weapons. It was carnage. There was no one else left alive, no one to rescue. There were these strange balls of matter: earth, flesh, metal, all mangled up together. Most of the human remains were almost unrecognizable, bodies blown to ribbons by the rockets and shells. A sweet-sour smell of blood and broken flesh rose above everything, stronger even than the stink of the Russian cordite.

The Sparrow, Frodo, Bilbo: a few minutes before I had been sitting with them, soaking in the sun. 'They can't be dead,' I kept telling myself. 'They're alive, they must be alive.'

I felt like yelling their names.

Up on the mortar line, I saw bits of a familiar body. It was Sméagol. His arms had been blown off and he had been partially decapitated. His head was hanging off at a grotesque angle. He had tortured his last Russian prisoner. I had been wrong about him. He had had the face of a weasel, but he had been as brave as a lion during the attack, getting up and running for one of the DshKs – and he had paid the price for it. An expression of utter terror was frozen on his face. I put out my hand and closed his eyes. Another man had been scattered by the remains of a 12.7 mm. He had taken a direct hit from a rocket. It had cut him in half. He looked oddly at peace, there was even the hint of a smile on his face.

All the time I was searching, I had this hope inside me about the Sparrow. I tried to think back. Last time I had seen him, just before the Hinds, he had been sitting on the ground near the mortar lines. I had this wild, insane feeling of hope that he had run. I walked round and round, going over the same ground again and again, but I couldn't find any sign of him. The Sparrow was just a kid: he had to be alive. Could he have scrambled up the ridge? Surely he'd have come back down by now, seeing we were there. I went back along the remains of the mortar line, for the third or fourth time, quartering the ground for sign.

This time I found a stub of wrist-bone sticking up through the broken ground.

I crouched down. The bone was wire thin, a child's bone, the ends of it splintered and raw.

It was the Sparrow.

He was buried under a layer of loose soil. I could just see the outline of his body. It was as if someone had already dug his grave and put him in it, face down. Only that splinter of white bone showed he was lying underneath the rough mound. The rest of him was completely covered. Kneeling down beside him I gently brushed the earth away from his face. Although I already knew the answer, I reached forward and touched the side of his neck. He was dead.

I remembered him teaching his father how to use the Stinger.

Close by, I found Frodo and Bilbo. Like the child, they had been blasted by the cannon and then ploughed under, dying in the same long burst of fire. All three had been close to me when the Hinds had come in. Why hadn't they run with me? Why hadn't I told them where to run? I felt as if I had betrayed and deserted my friends. I closed my mind to it and the shutters came down.

The odd corpse was still intact. They were lying in the most bizarre positions, flung by the rockets and the guns. One man was laid out on his back with his arms straight down by his sides, as if at attention; another was lying with his arms neatly folded across his chest. But most of the Mujahideen had been blown up then dumped down any old how. Most of them I knew, although not as well as the four I had already found dead. Another was buried in the earth head first, his legs sticking straight up in the air. It might have been comic, if it hadn't been a vision straight from hell. I stood by him, staring down. Of all of the ways a man could die, this was the one I feared most. I imagined him diving in the hole, then the rocket striking down and the earth caving in on top of him. I could feel him in there like that, stuck fast, buried alive with the choking dirt in his mouth and nose, I saw him kicking and thrashing in the slow panic of his suffocation. I couldn't get the vision out of my head. For months, even years later, I would awake in the dead of night, sweating with fear, and be back on that plateau, looking down at that man who had been buried alive.

So many dead, so many faces I had known cut down by the gunships, gone in a matter of seconds. As the reality sank in, and I began to understand, I felt overwhelming guilt, in that I had survived and they hadn't. I kept asking myself the same questions. Why hadn't I made the others run with me? Why hadn't I told them where to go? What had stopped me going for the Triple-A?

There hadn't been many flies before but suddenly there were thousands, drawn by the smell, buzzing and crawling over the mess, swarming over the broken remains in disgusting black colonies. I moved back, and sat down facing away from my friends. I heard a few single pistol shots. I didn't have to ask to know what those meant. I hoped, in the same situation, my mates would do the same for me.

That night, under the waxing moon, the Mujahideen buried their dead. A fresh group of fighters came in to help. There was no ceremony. Once the clearance patrols had made sure it was safe all around, they began picking up the body-parts and putting them into sacks. I was very glad when they refused my offer of help.

For the Mujahideen, it is a great honour to die in battle, a passport straight to Allah, the one true God. They buried their dead fighters right there, as close as possible to where they had fallen, wrapped in their sackcloth, in the tatters of clothing still sticking to them. There were no prayers, no cleansing rituals, only long sticks pushed into the fresh-dug graves, tied with green flags they left fluttering in the quick wind.

The next morning, just after dawn, when we were already far from the scene, we heard the Migs going in, to make sure of the position they had already smashed.

The Russians always liked to make sure.

Chapter Twenty-one

After fourteen weeks in Afghanistan, it was time to get out. I had done what I'd come to do, delivered the Stingers and the gold, trained them on the missile, helped them all I could. I had gathered some of the information that was required, and arranged for Russian equipment to follow me out so that it could be analysed. If I stayed any longer, I'd be killed, it was only a question of time. It had been the job of a lifetime and, now that was it upon me, I was sorry to be leaving. The odds were against them, everything was against them, but that didn't matter. They had their faith, and they were going to stay there and fight regardless. I respected them for that.

We gathered in the village I had first come into, the place where I had first met all the men who were now with their God. They had died and opened the door to heaven for their families, the ones who would come after, for this was what they believed. Aragorn and a few faces I recognized were there to see me off.

All the rest were dead.

The Mujahideen had this extraordinary mountain mail system. Each group commander had a different ink-stamp with his personal device cut into it, which he used with his own colour ink to verify messages. Every village had its own courier, and delivery rarely, if ever, failed. Using this, Aragorn sent word that I was coming out.

They made me a feast to say farewell – a roast lamb with mountain herbs, done in the earth oven, tender and succulent. Being strict Muslims, they never drank, but they were merry without it, and me with them: they didn't sing exactly, but they did chant. Later,

186

Aragorn asked, 'Why doesn't the West do more to help?' I shrugged. There was nothing I could say.

Like the Mujahideen, I had little to give, but before we turned in, Aragorn came up. He took me by the arm. 'Come back', he said gravely, 'when the war is over. You shall have land here, and live well.'

'I thank you for the offer, but I can't come back, not to stay. But if I ever can, I'll come back to see you when the war is won.'

I still hope to keep that promise one day.

Then I remembered the Beretta pistol. I wouldn't need that any more where I was going. I reached round, pulled it out and presented it to him.

'Take this,' I said, 'with my thanks.'

'Thank you,' he said. 'But it is we who should thank you, Yacoub. For you have done much.' I turned and walked away. I did not look back, I knew that for them it was already as if I had never been. They lost people all the time.

Only I would never forget.

That evening, with an escort party of five men, I started back out the same way we had come in. This time, with no mules to slow us down, the journey through the high passes flew by, faster even than on the way in. I was combat fit now, as fit as I would ever be in my whole life, hardly noticing the massive climb. I remembered that I was no longer one of the Mujahideen: it was time to change back into my Western clothes. I dug them out of the bottom of my pack, and put them on. They were mine, all right, but I felt like a stranger in them. I had grown used to the freedom and comfort of the baggy Afghan dress, and the European shirt and jeans felt tight, restrictive. The boots, in particular, felt weird, uncomfortable after the open rubber sandals I had worn over the preceding weeks.

In three months I had turned into a mountain man, with long matted hair and a wild scraggy beard. I hardly recognized myself; would I scare Natalie the way my dad scared me?

But it wasn't just clothing. I had to hand back something else: the battered old AK-47 Aragorn had given me after my first week. Parting with that weapon was like losing a limb. I had lived with it, and almost died with it.

At the last second, as I turned to go, one of my escort reached down into his pack and took out an AK-74, the new Russian 5.45 mm assault rifle.

'This is for you.'

It was as if they had known. I took the gleaming weapon. With weapons in such short supply up there, this was an amazing gift. For that reason alone I took it.

'Thank you,' I said. 'Thank you with all my heart.'

'Allah go with you,' said the man.

'And with you all,' I replied.

There was nothing left to say.

I turned, at last, heading back down the track. Somewhere, down there in the darkness at the bottom of the gorge, a vehicle was waiting to take me home.

When I got back to London, I met my Afghan contact again. He was anxious to debrief me about what had happened over there. He wanted everything, first, the basics – what had happened and when? I replied in enormous detail, more than I can now recall, as it was all still fresh in my mind. What were my thoughts and feelings on the performance of Russian forces, on the DRA troops, and on the Mujahideen? What did I make of the political balance between the various Mujahideen groups in the area where I had operated? Was Massoud's group worth supporting further? I gave him a big 'Yes' to that one. Was it worth sending in more Stingers, more money? Very much so. Would the missiles and the gold be well used? Yes, without a doubt. What were the Mujahideen like to work with? They were among the most serious and committed soldiers I had ever worked with, I said, and that included the SAS. What had happened up on the plateau? That was a good one. After the attack, and for weeks afterwards, I thought we had been set up, betrayed by one of the Mujahideen and then ambushed. Looking back now, I think the Hind pilots just got lucky. If it had been an ambush, then for certain they would have sent in the Migs at the time to finish the job, not later.

This debrief served its purpose: my friend, and other people like

188

him, continued to support Massoud, as well as some of the other key Mujahideen groups, sending in a great many more Stingers during the subsequent years. I don't know how they got in. I only know that I didn't take them. But by the time the war ended, in 1989, that missile had downed more than 270 Russian aircraft, and helped to make sure the Russians lost the war in Afghanistan.

Chapter Twenty-two

Afghanistan had been one of the great adventures of my life. I'd been extremely lucky to survive it. But without any payment for so many months, I was anxious now to get back into regular work. And I was lucky enough to find a job straight away, as Commercial Manager, Special Projects, for a firm that supplied specialized outboard engines to outfits like the Regiment, HM Coastguard, the SBS and the RNLI. Margaret, Natalie and I moved up to Oxfordshire, near Banbury, and at first things went well. My immediate boss, Robert, was a skilful and dedicated man, who led the company into new fields of excellence, taking me along with him, and who understood why I had left the SAS. I also met a man who was to become a firm and loyal friend: Stuart Henderson, one of the company's directors. Stuart was my guide into a world I knew little about, the world of commerce and closing deals. Both men remained friends and mentors a long time after I left the company.

Things went well. Margaret was pregnant again and happy, Natalie was thriving, but inevitably, as I grew into the job and took on ever more responsibility, I began to travel, looking to expand our export markets in new countries as we needed to do. Very soon, I was spending long periods away from home.

The day came when the baby was due. Margaret went into hospital. We went through the labour together, both very anxious. A short while later, the baby was born. 'A fine boy!' the nurse said. I looked down at Alex, as we had decided to call him. Something wasn't right. I said nothing to Margaret, but the world went black. A few days later, they confirmed that he was very disabled – and unlikely to live. He was too sick even to be moved from that hospital. Neither of us could deal with this all over again, it was unbearable. All the time that was left to us before he was taken away, we went in to see him, to hope, but he was lost to us.

The firm was good to me – they did what they could in the circumstances. But it was all too much. There's no way you can survive something like that for the second time.

One day I went back to Hereford for the funeral of a friend killed on a night free-fall jump. As I stood there, under the brooding face of the clock-tower, I found myself thinking, 'What am I doing here, on this side of the fence? That's where I belong, over there with my mates. The whole thing's still going on. It's still going on, and I want to be a part of it. I began to resent being out of the SAS.'

Taking the colonel at his word, I went back to see him in Hereford. He stood by what he had said. The Regiment accepted me back in at the same rank: sergeant. But I had lost all my seniority at that rank, and any chance of a commission was now gone. And, he reminded me, I would have to undergo the usual exhaustive positive vetting procedure all over again, accounting for all my time away. I went through all this, and came out the other side, and rejoined without too much difficulty.

Some time later, Margaret and I were divorced.

Towards the end of 1988 I was invited to take over as Operations Officer, Northern Ireland. Two operational SAS commanders are stationed over the water permanently, both, under normal circumstances, of staff-sergeant rank. I was still only a sergeant, but the Regiment will not tolerate anyone in that position unless he can prove himself capable of doing the job. It is a hard one, entailing planning, co-ordinating and briefing highly complex operations, and getting out as necessary into the field. The ops desk officer has an enormous responsibility: any mistake can result in men losing their lives.

Considering the fact that I'd not long been back in the SAS, and my rank, it was a first-choice posting. It would be my seventh tour of the Province. We did two months' excellent build-up training – by now, the Regiment's reputation had climbed back as high as it had ever been in Northern Ireland, not least for its increasing success in fighting not only the IRA but the extremists on the other side without giving them propaganda victories. We had become ever more careful about the way we conducted operations. We had learned that the Regiment had to use its guile in the war as well as its stealth and its force.

One of the first people I met up with again during the build-up phase was Ian Phoenix, the RUC Special Branch sergeant whom I had first met in the forests of Armagh with our bogus 'informer'. Like myself, Ian had moved on in life, he was now a chief superintendent, and second-in-command of RUC Special Branch.

His first task was to bring me and the troop up to date on current operational practice in Northern Ireland. He set out clearly how we would be working in support of the RUC, and explained the Regiment's interface with his own department, the TCG. He went on to describe how we fitted in with the other security agencies, not just the regular police and the Army but with DMSU (Divisional Mobile Support Units, thirty to forty men, one unit to each police division, trained in riot control, advanced firearms, and OP techniques); HMSU (Headquarters Mobile Support Units, assigned to the RUC's two main rural regions, trained in advanced firearms, operating mainly in plain clothes, but like modern US-style SWAT teams, to some extent overlapping the functions of the SAS); and the SSUs (Special Support Units, which were the RUC's own answer to the SAS, trained by us to act like us). Last but not least, there was E4A, the RUC's answer to 14 Int & SY. Things had moved on.

You can see at once from this structure that the RUC had gone a long way towards taking over the functions of the British Army, and where it hadn't already done this it was developing the capability to do so. This was in line with the policy of Police Primacy, which by now had taken firm hold. Having seen some of the SSU recruits we had trained at Hereford, I had my doubts about the wisdom of the RUC's using them as if they were the SAS. By and large, they were sound men, but we had learned the hard way that CT operations across the water, as anywhere in the world, were almost always highly complex. Good as they were, these men came from a police not an Army background.

The Phoenix went over recent major operations, those that were current and those he knew were scheduled for the future. He reminded us all very firmly of the prominence of the law, and that we would do a lot better for our cause if we operated within it at all times. He was always very hot on this. Having seen the public-relations and political disasters that could ensue when we didn't obey the rules, I could only agree with what he had to say.

After Ian's brief, there was no doubt in anyone's mind as to what we were trying to achieve: peace. Ian wanted peace in Northern Ireland, as quickly as possible, with a minimum of death or injury on either side. He was an optimist in a dark hour, at a time when the situation looked impossible, and I loved him for that.

The troop would often see Ian in the location we worked from so we all got to know him well in the first few vital weeks. Whenever TCG had something in mind that might involve us, Ian would give us the heads up; if time allowed we met in his small office, sometimes up to twenty people cramming into it, to talk through the op before we were officially tasked. He would give us an outline of the operation, task the various agencies involved, ask if anyone had any questions, then send us away to come up with a plan. Time wasn't always a luxury we had, but if we did Ian would listen to our comments on how we might best be used, and hear them: others listened without hearing. Most of the time he pre-empted what we had to say, such was the depth of his experience. There was never a doubt where Ian stood on a task: it had to be done correctly, within the law, and by the right people for the job.

Of the many ops Ian gave us the most memorable to me, and the one that best showed his character, was when we were covering an IRA arms cache in South Armagh. We had the cache under technical surveillance for two weeks. One night the duty team went forward to eyeball the cache and test the equipment, only to find that it didn't work and they couldn't get it to work.

The following day the team lay up, watching the routes into the cache area, but unable to see it. I was running the ops desk to which the team on the ground was reporting. Ian was at home catching up on lost sleep. The ground team reported a car moving down to the cache, then stopping short of it. It was unusual for this type of vehicle with the driver and passenger smartly dressed to drive down a remote track with nothing at the end of it at that time of day.

I called TCG at once as required and explained the situation to them. I said that if the car was unsighted for more than ten minutes then we should treat it as a target and react to it as such. A minute or two went by, and nothing happened. It was a TCG call, but they could not find the officer in charge, and the officer on the phone would not make a decision. Ten minutes later, there was still no decision from TCG.

The car began to move.

'Get me Ian at home,' I told the operator. 'No, leave that – get on the radio.' I ordered the arrest team to stop and search the car. They moved in. There was nothing in it and the two men inside it had no form. I reported this to TCG. At once the missing officer came on the line, bellowing, 'Why did you stop that car? Who ordered the stop?'

'I did,' I said, and I explained why.

'You've blown weeks of work!'

'Did anyone call Ian Phoenix?' I asked. The Phoenix had final say in a situation like this.

'No. But I'll do that right now.' He slammed down the phone.

I felt like shit. Had I made the wrong call? My own people said the call was right. I heard nothing more that night from TCG. I put the team back into cover hoping that if the IRA got to hear about the arrest they would think that a foot patrol had stopped the car for a routine check.

Next morning, Ian called everyone involved down to a meeting at TCG. We all sat in his office. Suddenly I noticed spare chairs on both sides of me; then I saw that all the TCG people were sitting as far away from me as possible. Ian came in. Some of them looked at me as if to say, 'You've had it now, it was your call.' Ian looked at everyone in turn. Nothing moved; no one drew breath. Fuck it, I thought. I stand by my call.

Ian said, 'About last night. That was the right choice. We can't on any account risk weapons going loose to kill people we're here to protect.'

All of a sudden, the seats around me filled up.

'Nice one, Gaz!'

'Good call.'

'Well, it's a shame no one here last night made it,' Ian barked. They all looked away, unable to meet his gaze.

The Phoenix was a true man, and a good man. In that thirteen months I was working with him, we became good friends.

One thing I'd agreed to do before taking on the NI desk was to join the spotting team at the Red Day Parade in East Berlin at the year's end. This is a regular B squadron task, and that year we watched the Parade dressed as members of the Parachute Regiment. Our objective being to note any and all changes to Warsaw Pact weaponry, uniforms and equipment. East Germany was B squadron's designated sector of activity in times of hot war. (G squadron's designated warfare area was Norway/Northern Flank, while A and D squadrons were to operate in direct support of mainstream Nato forces.) As a member of B squadron, I had made detailed analyses of many targets over the years, including airfields, radar installations, comms and control centres, and major railway marshalling yards. These Red Day Parade surveillance operations were always carried out in close co-operation with Brixmis, the British Cross-border Mission unit.

The next night, I joined them on a deep recce.

We were going into an out-of-bounds area, to investigate modifications that had been made to a bunker complex up against the Polish border. This particular site had been declared redundant and unused by the Sovs under the latest round of arms talks. It looked as if it had been reactivated. There were clear signs that they'd installed new ventilation systems in the roofs. Int had noticed these changes on the satellite photos and wanted to know why they had been made.

Like its American counterpart, Brixmis was a Nato-controlled operation that ran monitoring missions into East Germany. Officially, these missions were designed to make sure that the Warsaw Pact wasn't cheating – for example, by exceeding its quota of tactical nuclear missiles. The Russians and the East Germans had equivalent monitoring units, which ran missions into the Allied sectors. The whole system operated under a detailed, tightly controlled and carefully negotiated set of reciprocal agreements. It was designed to defuse mutual suspicion, and therefore tension, between the occupying powers.

The British teams went over in declared vehicles, with British Mission plates on them, at carefully appointed times, dressed in uniform and unarmed. All Brixmis vehicles were supposed to keep to the agreed zones, allowing the opposition forces to follow them. But dawdling around the prescribed routes with a fleet of minders wasn't going to tell us what was really going on behind the Iron Curtain.

For that, we had to get out into the closed zones.

This was a risky business. Any Allied car caught in an out-of-bounds area was liable to be stopped and its occupants arrested. If it failed to stop, they shot to kill. Not long before my arrival in West Berlin that year, an American major had been shot dead in his vehicle while making a run for it.

Covert Brixmis teams were usually three strong, each member a hand-picked specialist. The Royal Corps of Transport drivers were really good: able to drive fast in the dark down an unknown road, trained in all forms of driving, and excellent mechanics, able to make running repairs to just about any type of vehicle.

There might be a spotter, usually an Army intelligence agent, sometimes a signaller, fluent in colloquial Russian, a comms expert, and a first-class photographer. His job was to gather and compile the raw intelligence. And sometimes there would be a Special Forces presence. Missions were carefully planned and targeted, but a Brixmis team could just get lucky. A convoy might appear suddenly out of nowhere, in the heart of a permitted zone. The drill then was: car off the road, down out of sight, cameras out and start recording: 'BRDM-2, standard fit, 14.5 mm KPVT turret, retractable Sagger housing in up position, six AT-3 missiles showing, never seen that whip aerial at the back like that . . .' Everybody on a given mission was cross-trained to some degree, so they could mutually assist in case of need.

Observation was one thing. Brixmis was actually about theft. It got all its best Warsaw Pact equipment this way.

We went down to the unit's underground garage. Brixmis cars were very like the intercept cars we used in Northern Ireland – big, solid, high-performance vehicles, in this theatre mostly Opels and Range Rovers, tuned for extra speed and acceleration, with low-profile wheels and special tyres. Jock introduced me to Bones, our driver for the night, and Ray Good, the Army intelligence man, who was a staff sergeant.

It was still light as we went through Checkpoint Charlie. At the barrier, the sentry checked our documents and then phoned through to alert the GRU/MFs (Anti-Mission) car teams waiting to pick us up on the other side.

We drove slowly through the Eastern sector of the city. Once inside the target zone, Brixmis cars always moved slowly, rarely above thirty or forty kilometres per hour. There were two reasons for this snail-like progress: to keep the windscreens clear and to make sure we didn't miss anything. If someone was trying to take photographs of an installation or a convoy, he wasn't going to get a very good shot through a smeared mess of dead insects. One speck in the wrong place could ruin an important photograph. If an insect did splat and die, the driver was marked down for a round of drinks. Bones was known for his stinginess. He drove *very* slowly.

We crawled along with the MFs on our tail, not enjoying the scenery. The difference between the East and the Western sector we'd just left was really startling. At the end of the Second World War, the Russians had simply moved their forces straight into the old German Army barracks. Although it had been badly damaged during the battle for the city, mostly by Russian gunfire, the Soviets had done nothing to improve the accommodation for their troops. Many of the buildings still had shell-holes in them dating from around 1945. They looked hard, miserable, uncomfortable places to be stationed, bone-cold in winter, sweltering in summer. I didn't envy the poor bastards quartered in them. As for the civilian population, almost all of them were packed into dreary, blighted, broken-down, leaking tower blocks like very tall rabbit-hutches, with whole families sardined into one-bedroom flats. It really was as grey and horrible as everyone said. I'd seen this before on trips into East Berlin, but it never ceased to amaze me.

The Russians' lack of basic care for their armed forces worked in the West's favour. The younger Russian conscripts, in particular, were often disaffected, and had been known to hand over their assault rifles for a carton or two of Western cigarettes. Later that night we were to be glad of this disaffection.

The big problem for a car team looking to go covert was losing the official East German tail. There were several ways of going about this, but that night we were using the saturation method: we had come over as part of a five-vehicle convoy, the four other cars with us acting as decoys. But the opposition weren't fools: they were on to all five as soon as we crossed. Now it was down to persistence – and sheer luck.

We drove on through the ugly suburbs, hoping our tail car would get bored. It did. We drove into the forbidden zone. When we were well away from prying eyes, in open countryside, we parked up in a little copse, got out our kit, had a brew and some rations, then a short kip. At around two in the morning, we moved off towards the target, having made sure we weren't being followed.

An hour or so later, we were approaching the target. Bones got us as close to the bunkers as he dared, headlights off first, then side-lights as we got closer, which on Brixmis cars knocked out the brake lights. Now in pitch darkness, Bones put on the night-vision goggles (NVGs) and eased us forward to the drop-off point. He stayed with the vehicle, engine off but ready to go. Ray and I crept up to the target, staying well off the road. The countryside in this area was thickly wooded, slightly undulating, crossed by small country roads of the type you find down in Devon. The bunker complex was built into a relatively flat section of land about three hundred metres distant to our left.

Both of us were listening intently for the slightest sound, the slight-est movement of the wrong kind. It was a cloudy night, with very little moonlight breaking through, good conditions for what we were about. When we hit the perimeter fence we stopped. There was no noise, no sign of any perimeter guards, in fact no sign of life at all. Perhaps this site *wasn't* important, maybe it really had been abandoned and was unguarded. We ghosted along the fence, which was in a pretty poor state. There were signs on it at intervals, warning us in Russian and German to keep out. As we moved, we were searching the ground for any signs of recent activity: cigarette butts, bits of spilled loads, anything that might give a clue to what they were up to. There was nothing.

We spotted the first of the bunkers. It was a long, low structure with a flat roof, no windows and solid steel doors surrounded by a wall of earth. It loomed up, black against the skyline, a thick round tower of fortified concrete. Now we were close, the brand new ventilation system was obvious. There was a paved access road leading up to the bunker that would take a tracked vehicle. We crouched in the darkness by the wire for a long time, watching and listening.

Nothing moved. The darkness was complete now, the countryside a grave. The squat bunkers marched away into the night.

Gingerly, I cut the first wire. No audible alarm. I waited a few minutes then cut the next and we slipped through into the base. Our Russian speaker, Ray, went first in case of trouble. We skirted round the bunker. On the side away from the road, we found some wide steps leading down into the darkness. At the top there was a kind of brick bay, for delivery vehicles, and to one side a concrete ramp, for sliding packing cases, leading down into the blackness below. At the bottom of the steps, Ray came up against a set of massive steel doors. He signalled for me to come down and join him. We explored the obstacle, gauging the thickness of the steel and the strength of the lock. It didn't seem to have an alarm on it, which isn't as surprising as it sounds because when it came to guarding things the Russians tended to rely on their overwhelming manpower rather than on expensive electrical equipment. I stayed down there for a minute, working out how best to blow it, if it ever came to that, while Ray went back up to have another scout around for bits of broken packing case or, better still, scraps of labelling, which the Russians often left lying around at sites like this. From this litter, the Rays of this world could often tell what a shipment had contained, where and when it had been made, and a whole lot more besides.

I turned at the foot of the steps, to follow him up. My foot never made it to the first step. A voice barked, '*Shtoy! Kto tam?*'

I don't speak any Russian, but I understood that challenge.

It was a young soldier. He had an AK-74, and its business end was pointing straight at Ray's gut. Everyone froze. We were unarmed, he had an assault rifle. He was a guard, we were spying.

Life stopped.

Then Ray took over. Bursting into a rapid stream of Russian, he brought out a pack of twenty king size Western cigarettes, stuck one in his mouth, and offered them to the guard. The boy looked at the cigarettes, then at Ray. Finally, he reached over and took one.

Ray was still talking. 'My dear chap! Thank goodness we bumped into you! It's not a problem – our car's down on the road – you see, we're lost. We were hoping to find someone.' He chuckled. 'Thought you were a farm. Can you possibly direct us to **** [the nearest town]? Oh, and by the way, have you got a light?' At this point, two things happened. The guard's rifle barrel dropped a fraction. He reached into his greatcoat for a match. He was eyeing up the luxury smokes, about as different, in cigarette terms, as a Rolls Royce is to a Trabant. They were worth about three months of his wages, if sold individually to his mates. He wanted them.

I began moving noisily up the steps, coughing so he'd hear me coming. 'Excuse my friend,' said Ray. 'He was just answering a call of nature.' The weapon twitched on to me, and for a second I feared the worst. The kid had to know I'd been inspecting the doors. But Ray was brilliant, he kept the patter going, not allowing the guard a moment to think, explaining that we were colleagues on a business trip. A minute later, the Russian was standing at ease, with his rifle on its sling across his body, not pointing at us any more, he and Ray chatting away like old friends.

Brixmis personnel always have their pockets filled to the brim with goodies for just such an emergency. I didn't need to be told what to do. Keeping a smile on my face, I reached in slowly, and pulled out four packs of Marlboro cigarettes. I held them casually in my hand, so that he could see them. 'Can you point us in the right direction,' said

Ray, 'in return for a few smokes?' All the time Ray was talking, I was covertly inspecting this soldier, memorizing his insignia so that we'd know which regiment he was from, and possibly, even, which battalion. I handed over the cigarettes, which he took with a quick, nervous smile and a muttered word of thanks – '*Spasibo*'. I nudged Ray. It was clear the kid wanted us out of there. We had been dead lucky coming up against someone so young and untried. If we had met an old hand, he would most likely have shot first and asked questions later. Best not to push our luck.

But the Russian wasn't that naïve. He understood what was going on, but he had been on duty all night with no relief, he was pissed off, and he wanted the Western goods. I didn't know it, but Ray and the sentry had reached an agreement. Ray started backing away from him, pulling me by the arm so that I followed. Watching us all the time, the Russian moved the other way. When we were about thirty metres apart, we stopped.

'OK,' said Ray, 'now turn and run like fuck.' I turned. I ran like fuck. As we ran, the first blasts of the sentry's whistle rang out, shattering the peace of the night.

As we came out through the hole in the wire, Bones flicked the sidelights on and off once so we would know exactly where he was. Although it was freezing, he had been listening and watching with the windows open. Great man. We were in and away in a second, only now we definitely weren't going slowly: Bones was gunning it, Michael Schumacher had nothing on him, he was the wizard of the night in his NVGs. The narrow lanes unwound like a video game, a fainter ribbon against the surrounding dark, we had the lights off in case they put up a helicopter. I glanced back: the base was a blaze of lights. Thumbing the window down, I stuck my head out. There were whistles going, the roar of engines starting. They were coming after us. The Opel bounced round a corner, shimmied, then bit the road, following the pre-planned escape route. They would need a Damon Hill to keep up. And Henry the Navigator to find us. Having neither, we left them for dead.

In about fifty kilometres, we pulled off into a patch of dense cover, lay up all the next day and slipped back into East Berlin that evening.

Back at Brixmis HQ, we delivered our report: as suspected, the base had been reactivated, the bunkers had been refurbished, the place was guarded, they had moved something in there, most likely something they shouldn't have moved in under the arms agreements.

Normally, there was no way we would have risked a compromise: before going in, we would have put in an OP and watched until we knew it was safe. But sometimes, as in this case, an OP was a luxury we couldn't afford, because of the lie of the land, the lack of time. We had taken the higher risk: it was the nature of the business we were in. It had paid off, this time. We'd been lucky – and, as you have to in these situations, we'd made our own luck.

PART THREE

SAS Command

Chapter Twenty-three

Half-way through that Northern Ireland tour I was promoted staff sergeant, which meant that, despite my time away from the Regiment, I was roughly back where I should have been on the ladder of command had I stayed in.

At the end of thirteen months over the water, I came back to Hereford. On the second day of my fortnight's leave I met Tracy, who was thirteen years younger than I was but who had the panache of someone much older. She had acquired this sophistication from her father, who was a self-made, down-to-earth millionaire. They had a newly built house on the western side of town. Tracy was tall and slim, with flowing brown shoulder-length hair that fell in loose curls. For the next two weeks, we had a ball, travelling everywhere together, visiting friends like Stuart and Susan Henderson, with whom Tracy was a smash hit. Within a few months we had fallen in love and pretty soon after that we were engaged. She became my friend and mentor, and she got on with Natalie, who was now eight and shooting up physically and mentally. Tracy had a way of applying common sense and sound judgement to life's knottier problems, but she did this always with compassion and understanding.

But just as it had for my father, duty came before my private life.

On my first day back after leave the OC called in myself and Matt Smith to see him. Matt was a contemporary of mine, a staff sergeant, who had recently moved over from A squadron to run one of B squadron's troops. I had first met him years before, in Northern Ireland. By coincidence, his wife was a friend of Tracy's, so we had spent some time together socializing. He was tall, about six foot two, well educated, well spoken and very good-looking. He was a keen mountaineer and interested in the arts. I knew him to be solid as a rock.

We sat down and the OC began the brief. 'There's a team job come up in Colombia,' he told us. 'It's the drugs war.' Mrs Thatcher had been having talks with President Reagan at Camp David: they had reached the conclusion that the drugs trade represented a 'clear and present danger' to the Western way of life, and that something drastic had to be done about it. Mrs Thatcher thought she had the answer: call in the SAS.

Colombia, the global centre of the hard-drugs trade, is not only a major producer of narcotics but also the world's major distributor. Most of the cocaine grown in South America passes through Cali, Medellin, or Bogotá for on-shipment to the user countries. In typically direct style, Mrs Thatcher had decided that the trade should be countered at source. By the Regiment. But the idea wasn't for the Regiment to go in there guns blazing. By now, our performance in theatres as diverse as Northern Ireland and the Gambia had shown that it could be much more than a simple blunt instrument. It had done countless team jobs for official foreign security agencies throughout the world, training and advising in counter-terrorist techniques. And, on the world scale, the Regiment's new links with the FCO and the SIS were bearing strategic fruit.

The British and US governments wanted us to go in and train up a Colombian national anti-narcotics police. The Americans had tried, and failed, to forge a new drugs-enforcement unit from the Colombian police and it had been agreed that while the US would provide the lion's share of the money, equipment, vehicles, helicopters and arms, the British would train the new force.

'The key thing here', the ops major stressed, 'is that it has to be done softly-softly. As the Drug Enforcement Agency found out to its cost, the Colombians don't like outsiders waltzing in and taking control. We're not going in there to impose a paramilitary force *on* them. The idea is to help them create their own force. Once they have that capability, they can use it – or not – as they see fit.

At the end of his brief, the major handed us a sheaf of notes.

'We've already had an initial reconnaissance team in country,' he said. 'This is their brief. The next step is to get in there and get the training programme updated and completed. Hunter, Smith, I'd like you to lead one of the teams. Are you up for it?' I'd been here before; I accepted without any question.

'One last thing,' he said. 'For the duration of this mission, I'm giving you the rank of acting major. The Colombians take that sort of thing very seriously. It will give you a bit more clout down there.'

The only thing I could think of, as I walked back through the camp, was that in this odd way I'd finally attained the same rank in the SAS as my father.

I went home and told Tracy where I was going. She listened without speaking as I gave her the news, her eyes gradually filling with tears. 'I'm sorry,' was all I could say. 'I think it will be at least three months.'

'It's what they pay you to do,' she said. 'You're a soldier.'

That same day I set about assembling my team. As soon as news got out about the mission, I was badgered: trade was slow in the Regiment then, people wanted to be in on the task. I selected mainly from my own troop, because those were the operators I knew, but I also had one SBS man attached, and I took two men from G squadron who had been on the initial deployment. I needed people I could trust. Among those I selected from my own troop were Dinger and Andy McNab.

The Colombians are fond of saying that they haven't got a drugs problem: they tell you it's the rest of the world, above all the US, that has the problem. But addiction rates in the major Colombian cities are among the highest in the world, and that means substance addiction across the board, not just addiction to cocaine in its numerous forms. There are, for example, an estimated one million alcoholics in the country, while any kind of solvent, and even petrol, inhalation is commonplace.

The Colombian government needed help. The major cartels in Colombia had become a state within a state. The big bosses, like Pablo Escobar and Ernesto Gacha, were becoming more powerful than the elected government. Not long before we arrived in the country, Escobar had been threatened with imprisonment and had offered to pay off Colombia's entire national debt. Cartel leaders were even threatening to stand for legitimate political office – and they had a realistic prospect of winning. Buying the votes they needed to take power was only a matter of money. And if they couldn't buy people they terrorized them: politicians, judges, policemen, as well as those further down the scale.

In some areas, the cartels had put in place social initiatives, building schools and health centres for the people – which the government should have been doing but hadn't, for whatever reason. When his sick child was cured and then given an education by the Cali cartel, the average *campesino* might well think Escobar offered him a better future than *el presidente*. The cartels also took bright young people from working-class families and educated them, paying their university fees and supporting them while they were at college. It was an investment. Those children, effectively bought by drug money, came back to work for the cartels as chemists, lawyers, accountants, or whatever was required.

If the hearts and minds policy didn't work and a community refused to grow coca, cartel gunmen would encourage them to change their minds. Intimidation and violence in the countryside had driven thousands off the land, swelling the shanty-towns of Bogotá, Cali and Medellin.

In 1990, only 1 per cent of Colombia's population was directly involved in the drugs trade – but that meant we were up against some 340,000 people. In the country, where we would mostly be operating, the drugs cartels were frequently at war with each other. On top of that, something like sixty guerrilla groups were at large, some in alliance with the cartels against the administration, others fighting the cartels for land or political influence. Right- and left-wing death squads slaughtered apparently at will. As a result, Colombia was one of the most murderous countries on the planet.

Not a place in which to take any chances.

We landed at night by C-130 on a covert airstrip well away from any population centres. The first thing I did was get the weapons out and make sure everyone was locked and loaded. Along with our longs – M-16s and 203s – we had 66mm anti-tank weapons and several GPMGs.

We boarded our Colombian police transport for the six-hour drive up-country to the dilapidated barracks we would be using as our supposedly covert training camp. I assumed everyone knew where it was – the word 'secrecy' didn't seem to figure in the Colombian vocabulary. As soon as we got there, I set up all-round defence with our own security and patrolling regime. To protect our perimeter, we put out Claymore mines, set our arcs of fire and selected a fall-back point to which we would fight if necessary. We may have been inside an ostensibly friendly barracks, but this was a country at war with itself, and I wanted to make the camp as secure as we possibly could. We were there to do a training job, not put our lives in jeopardy. If we were attacked, we would give a good account of ourselves.

The next morning, we started working with our first batch of recruits. These were policemen nearing retirement, many of whom had done nothing more in their entire careers than direct Bogotá's traffic. (Mind you, that takes *incredible* nerve.)

We had been trying to run Selection pretty much as we did it back home, but we soon saw that this wasn't appropriate. These old boys were willing enough, but we had to match our expectations to the reality of what they could do. Which isn't to say we gave them an easy time. We made them work as hard as they possibly could, tempering it so that they weren't doing too much at once – their attention-span was relatively short, and the work was much more physical than they were accustomed to. We taught them basic weapon drill on their existing firing ranges, then we moved up into the mountains, cutting jungle ranges to teach them close-in jungle warfare. We also covered navigation, and the use of demolitions for sabotage. There were a lot of drug factories out there to burn.

By the end of the first scheduled ten-week training period, our first batch of recruits was up to a high standard – for them. Every one of us in the training team could see, though, that their standard of soldiering needed dramatic improvement before they had any chance in the field against the cartel gunmen. And I didn't want them only to have a chance: I wanted them to live and win.

Our other problem was that the officers, most of whom refused to be trained, took their lead from the base commander, a Colombian major. He was a short, round, pudgy character, with a broad, soft face that managed to look at once weak and arrogant. He was one of those officers whose main interest is in having his base look pretty, and in using his position to score empty points. On more than one occasion, when we wanted to get our men into the gym, he prevented us, on the grounds that he was using it with his wife. Anything we asked for was too difficult for him: as far as he was concerned, the base and its facilities were there to enhance his status and his social life. He was constantly making complaints about the way we trained 'his' men, and in order to show who was really in command, he would go so far as to pull them off the parade-ground right in the middle of a training lecture.

I had a few run-ins with this man, the Spanish for 'Keep your nose out' coming in handy more than once. But it was going to take more than that to get him out of the way.

The initial task finished, I reported back to Hereford with my preliminary assessment. The first thing I suggested in my report was that we take raw eighteen-year-old volunteers straight out of basic police training: people who had respect for their country and wanted to cut some of the cancer out of it. That way, we would lose all the ingrained prejudices and bad operational habits the older men tended to bring to the job; and they would be relatively fresh and enthusiastic, uncorrupted by sloppy police procedures – or something more sinister.

I also insisted that the officers start training. Already I knew that some of that first batch we had trained had been sent out on missions and killed, for the simple reason that the senior officers, having refused all instruction, had no idea how to plan and execute basic operations and would not listen to the junior ranks. This had to be stopped. The Colombians had to take the training seriously – all of them.

I explained, too, about the problem with the base commander. The OC listened carefully to my brief, made some notes – and had the major fired.

Chapter Twenty-four

Having delivered the Colombia report, I went back to running Air Troop. I initiated an intensive training programme, aiming to get our combined and individual skills up to the highest possible standard. We practised anti-terrorist assaults on disused office blocks in London, rappelling down the façades, blowing or smashing in through the windows, and we sharpened up on our techniques for using the lift shafts and the ventilation shafts to achieve surprise.

We also did a fair bit of parachute work, in particular on the then new system known as HAHO, or High Altitude High Opening. HAHO is used in situations where, for example, you might want to do a covert cross-border INFIL. Jumping from the converted Boeing 737 at around twelve thousand metres meant we could drive a steerable rig upwards of thirty or forty kilometres before hitting the deck. Our Stealth equipment and clothing made us virtually impossible to detect on the way in. Useful in certain volatile Central European countries.

Some weeks later, I was called back into the ops office, to be told that the colonel wanted Matt and me, plus four signallers, to do a follow-up assessment in Colombia. The signallers were coming with us because the Colombians had made it quite clear that they didn't want the assessment done. They were happy to have the SAS training programme continue, but that was it. Any scrutiny, they considered, would constitute a breach of sovereignty. To get around this, we offered them a big carrot, in the shape of some excellent new field communications packs. The idea was for us to get out there and

211

talk our way around the relevant sites using the comms gear as an incentive.

I was looking forward to the trip. I wanted to see how the training was shaping, not least for reasons of professional pride. In Hereford, things were still pretty quiet, although there had been a warning call about tension in the Gulf. By the end of December 1990 it looked increasingly as though that tension in the Gulf was shaping for war.

By coincidence, G squadron was due to take over as duty CT squadron. This would have freed B squadron for action. But when the air war against Iraq started on 17 January 1991, the G squadron team were still out in Oman doing desert-warfare training. HQ thought it made more sense for them to hop across into Saudi Arabia and pitch straight in as and when required. Although I didn't want B squadron to be left behind, and miss all the action, someone still had to provide the CT team in the UK. Which left us holding the baby.

To make matters even more complicated, I was scheduled to fly to Colombia with Matt at the end of the month. I handed over responsibility for running the CT team to my second-in-command, Sergeant Andy McNab. But as things deteriorated in the Gulf, I became worried. If it came to outright war, there was a chance the whole Regiment, including B squadron, would be sent there without either Matt or me. But we were B squadron's most senior NCOs: how could the squadron operate effectively at war without its operational management? The idea was ridiculous – and potentially dangerous. I went in to see the ops major. When he'd heard me out, he said, 'I appreciate your professional concerns, Hunter, but for the moment, you're booked on a Spanish course in London with Staff Sergeant Smith. Starts Monday next, details to follow. Let's talk after that.'

I was going on a Spanish course while the squadron made ready for war.

As the huge Allied effort built up, things changed at Hereford from minute to minute. Both A and D squadrons were sent out. G squadron came back and took over the CT team as scheduled. This left B squadron in reserve at Hereford. Wrestling with the Spanish subjunctive in London, Matt and I were still totally out of the Gulf picture. The next thing I heard on the grapevine was that, just as I had feared, elements of B squadron were also being sent to the Gulf: four men here, half a dozen there, always in dribs and drabs, to 'reinforce' the squadrons already in theatre.

This was my squadron they were sending to war, these were the men I had trained and led. Why wasn't I going with them? There was no way this could be right. If the men under our direct command were going to go out and fight, we had to be there leading them. There is no point in having a command structure if you throw it all away at the time when it's most needed. I started calling the ops desk. The major was busy. I got his clerk. This was a warrant officer, not someone I knew well, or wanted to know – he was one of the few remaining people in the Regiment wearing dead men's shoes. He'd been parked on the desk to keep him from doing any operational harm, and he was in his element. 'We're not at war yet, you know,' he said.

'No,' I replied, 'but we soon will be. And I want to be there with my command.'

'As things stand, Hunter, you and Smith are down for Colombia. I suggest you get on with your Spanish lessons.'

Back in London, Matt and I talked it over.

'We've got to make them see sense,' I said. 'If the lads are going out to fight, we've got to be out there with them. Right?'

'Dead right. Let's get back down there.'

We caught the next train. That same evening we went in to see the ops major. He was out. The clerk told us again we were down for Colombia, end of story. Next morning, another batch of men from B squadron left for the Gulf. Just about the only people left in camp were G squadron, the ops desk staff – and us two. Then I heard that B squadron's headquarters element, of which we were supposedly a key part, had suddenly deployed.

This was getting beyond a joke.

There was only one thing for it now: go directly to the top. I asked to see the squadron OC. He was still there, but he, too, was getting ready to go. Like the ops major, he listened while I said my piece. 'I

213

agree with you,' he said. 'It looks as though the Iraqis mean to fight. In which case you should both be with your troops. I'll see what I can do.' The words were hardly out of his mouth before he was on a plane bound for the Gulf.

The next day, I stormed into the ops office, uninvited, and marched up to the desk. 'Listen,' I said, 'this is bollocks. My troop's going into action. I'm their staff sergeant. My job is with them. Simple, really, isn't it?'

'No,' replied the WO. 'It's not that simple. I've told you till I'm blue in the face, and the answer's still the same. The priority for you is Colombia. And that's where you're going.'

'The priority's Colombia? We're talking about war here! The priority's my fucking troop!'

That same afternoon, I had an unofficial phone call from the Gulf: the Regiment had been asked to provide a CT team in the Gulf to counter the threat of terrorism. At this I went straight back into ops. 'Look,' I said, 'let's be reasonable, shall we? They're forming a CT team out there. Matt and I have just finished our six-month tour running the CT side here in the UK. G squadron can't go and do it – they're needed for CT here. So don't tell me we're not needed in the Gulf. I'm getting on a plane and I'm going out.'

As I turned, the warrant officer called me back. 'Listen,' he said, 'either you fucking shut up and do as you're told, or you'll be RTU'd right here and now.'

I stared into his eyes. 'This I don't believe,' I said. 'You're threatening me with platform four because I want to lead my troop? Because I want to do my job?' I turned on my heel and walked out. The only thing I could do now was make an appointment to see the ops major.

Unfortunately the major, when I saw him, said pretty much the same thing. 'You're going to have to wind your neck in on this, and just do it.'

'Why?'

'Look, Hunter, I can see how you feel, but the FCO puts a lot of weight on this Colombia job. The Prime Minister wants it done. Your orders are cut. I didn't make them, and I don't necessarily agree with them. But as long as they stand and there's no one here with the authority to change them, I've got no option but to ask you to carry them out. It's either that or it's platform four. OK?'

It was not OK, even though he'd put it well.

That same day, while the ops desk were busy telling me I'd get the bullet if I didn't withdraw my neck, I got another call from the Gulf. This one was a long tale of woe: the squadron was going to be deployed on poorly thought-out missions; the intelligence was inadequate; they were having to scrabble around for vehicles, kit, clothing, food and even ammunition, especially 40 mm grenade bombs and anti-personnel mines. And, as if all that wasn't enough, they didn't even have any decent maps of Iraq – the spooks had photocopied bits of the *Times* atlas, or one-in-half-a-million scale air navigation charts. As the troop staff sergeant, it was precisely my job to sort all these things out – and they'd bloody well get sorted out, pronto, if they'd only allow me to go and do it.

No dice.

On 22 January 1991, an eight-man patrol from B squadron with the code-name Bravo Two-Zero, led by my second-in-command Andy McNab, crossed behind enemy lines. Their mission was to destroy the communications landlines in the northern main supply route (MSR) through which the Iraqi command directed the mobile Scud-launchers, and to destroy the Scud TELs. They went into the northern desert in the worst winter out there in living memory, ill-equipped and very poorly briefed. They were followed by Bravos One-Zero and Three-Zero, virtually my entire command.

A few days later, the movement order for Colombia came through. At RAF Lyncham, there was the customary long delay. While I was waiting, I rang Tracy. I hadn't told her where I was going, for reasons of operational security. 'Someone keeps trying to call you from the Middle East,' she said. 'They want to know if you're going in after Andy.'

'Andy? You mean Andy McNab? What are you talking about?'

'One of the patrols has gone missing. Bravo Two-Zero. Is that what you're doing? Are you going out there to get them back?'

'No,' I replied slowly. 'No, I'm not. I don't know anything about it.'

I listened with mounting fury: one, because Tracy knew what had happened before I did; and two, because I wasn't out there leading my men.

I knew enough, though, to understand that things were going badly wrong. Inside me, something turned over and sank. I felt guilt and a cold anger. Fucking hell, I thought. The ground war hasn't even started yet and they've been sent out into the desert with God knows what planning, on a fearsome mission, and they're in the shit.

'Listen, Tracy,' I said, 'this is really important. Do you know if there are any dead?'

'No. All I've heard is that they're missing.'

The story of Bravo Two-Zero has been well told, and it's a very good one – except for the fact that three men died on it. I wouldn't want to claim that if I had been out there it would have made any difference. There is no way of telling. But at the very least I would have been on the ground, and even if I'd been on another patrol, I would have made sure they were better briefed and properly equipped before they set out.

On our way out to Bogotá, we landed for fuel in Dulles airport, just outside Washington DC. The regiment's US Military Liaison Officer (MILO) came on board. He was a young captain. Matt and I went straight up to him. 'Have you heard any news about Bravo Two-Zero?'

'Yes,' he said, 'I have – and from what I hear there's a big problem. You know the men involved?'

'We're supposed to be out there commanding them. Only they sent us to Colombia.'

'OK, then, brace yourself. They think all those men are missing, probably dead. All except for one guy, Chris Ryan. He's managed to walk out. One hell of a walk, by first accounts.'

I stood there staring at him, trying to make sense of what he was telling me. All missing? All those good men dead, except Chris? At first, I couldn't take it in. I just kept thinking, What the fucking hell is going on out there? The rage and frustration burned me up. I sat back down heavily in the aircraft seat. The MILO's words kept going round and round in my head. A quarter of my troop was missing or dead.

I heard someone speaking, from a long way off, and looked up. The MILO was still there. 'And that's not all. One of A squadron's patrols was hit – the SSM [squadron sergeant-major] has been killed and the rest are missing.' I looked across and met Matt's eyes. Like me, he was dumbstruck. Will, A squadron's SSM, was his closest friend. They'd done Selection together, and Will had been best man at Matt's wedding. We sat there, shocked to the core, silent for the rest of the flight.

The next morning, myself, Matt, and the four signallers landed in Bogotá. During the night, I'd had some time to think. There was nothing we could do to help in the Gulf. We had to concentrate on the job in hand. I reminded myself it was an important, high-profile task, and we were being given free rein to do it – a sign of confidence in us, and trust. If it hadn't been for the war we would have classed ourselves lucky. If I concentrated hard enough, it might just help to dull the pain I was feeling about events in the north-western desert.

Chapter Twenty-five

We landed at Bogotá airport in broad daylight, against all the standard operating procedures, and were met, in the usual discreet Colombian style, by a wagonload of armed police, who roared off through the streets of the city with us in the back of the vehicle. Worse still, we soon heard that our arrival in the city was all over the Colombian press.

'Why don't you just stick a fucking great flag on the top of the jeep, with our names on it?' I asked the police captain, who was supposedly in charge.

'*Que, Señor?*' he replied, looking puzzled.

They dropped us at the hotel. As soon as they had gone, I went round to the British embassy. This was supposed to be a covert operation. 'Listen,' I said, 'there's no way we're staying here. We're compromised, and we're moving – now. I'll let you know when we find somewhere else.' Someone at a pretty high level had leaked the information that we were coming.

Not having spent much time in the capital before, I was taking in the surroundings and marking points. As you drive into Bogotá, there's a surface impression of normality. Then, gradually, you begin to see the poverty-stricken and murderous reality underneath. The central section, the square mile or so that's minutely controlled by the police, is relatively safe and secure, much like any Western European capital. Stray outside this core, though, and things go to pieces fast. Bandit-taxis prowl, ready to take you somewhere you never wanted to go, strip you of everything you own, and sometimes slit your throat. Almost anywhere you walk is unsafe. Street mugging is rife. Cartel henchmen infest the population, at every level of their lives. Pigs' heads stare down on all this from the *corazones* kiosks on the street-corners, offering Colombia's greatest delicacy: strips of fried pig's heart. Or, if that doesn't tickle your fancy, there was always *chiquino* – a kind of roasted giant rat. Every night, the military police set up vehicle checkpoints to intercept the small-fry cocaine runners; these do little to stem the flow of drugs but much to ensure plenty of night-time gunfights.

For all this murder and mayhem, or more likely because of it, Bogotá's a real party town. No one ever seems to go to sleep: they stay up all night drinking, shouting, robbing and killing. Standing on the balcony of our hotel that first night back, with Matt, I remember listening to the rip of automatic weapons, watching the tracer going up into the sky, and concluding that we might as well be in the Lebanon.

At Police Headquarters we soon discovered that the Colombians, as we had been warned, didn't want us to look at their operational establishments. But once the signallers had laid out the kit we'd brought in, and shown them what it could do, they began to change their minds. We pointed out that the new gear had to be specially calibrated in its operational location, and all personnel using it would need training, which meant travelling to all the bases where it would be used.

Finally, after much manoeuvring, they agreed to take us to all the main camps and some of the outposts. This would take a few days to set up. What, I wondered, could we do profitably in the meantime? By now, I was getting on well with the Colombian liaison officer, a lieutenant by the name of Raoul. 'Much happening in Bogotá at the moment?' I asked him casually.

'Plenty, Señor Hunter,' he replied, flashing his perfect teeth. 'There's always plenty happening in Bogotá.'

'Great. How about Matt and I coming out on some of your patrols while we're waiting to go?' He looked at us doubtfully. I nudged him a bit harder. 'We won't interfere. Strictly for purposes of observation. Yes?'

'All right,' he said at last. 'I'll see what I can do.'

Two days later, I was on my own in the police office where we kept our equipment, working on a document, when Raoul hurried in looking furtive. He wasn't smiling any more.

'There's a patrol going out now,' he told me. 'Do you want to come?' I reached one of the scaleys (signallers) on the phone, told him to tell Matt I'd gone out on patrol, grabbed my long and my belt-kit and jumped in the jeep.

It was dark by now. We were the lead vehicle in a convoy of three. From 13A Street, things got steadily worse as we kept driving east out of the city. The solid buildings became shanties, which deteriorated from dilapidated brick through wriggly tin to cardboard and even newspaper kennels. The whole place stank to high heaven of rotting vegetables, urine and festering shit. Everywhere there seemed to be pimps, pushers and people ready to do anything at all for a score.

'Where are we going?' I asked Raoul. 'Anywhere in particular?'

'We think there's something going on just up here,' he replied, pointing ahead. 'We're going to meet up with another patrol and do a raid.'

'What? You mean you're just going to drive straight up on to the target?'

'Yes,' he said, teeth flashing. 'That's right. Of course! We will drive straight up.'

He couldn't see anything wrong with that. We came to a halt. There was a man in the gutter at our feet. He had been shot. From the look and the smell of him he had been dead for at least two days. A little further along the street there was a woman. By her side was a six- or seven-year-old girl. They had both been stabbed to death, and recently – the blood on the ground all around them was still wet. One breast was hanging out of the mother's flimsy cotton dress. Her stomach, thighs and various other parts of her had been slashed by the killer. She was soaked in blood.

I looked around. I could sense all these people scurrying about in the shadows, watching us. They slid away before us, their eyes peering out from chinks in the piles of filth. Their fear and hatred felt like a physical weight on the back of my neck. As we ploughed ever

220

further on into this sewer, I could feel the hairs standing up on my forearms. Armed or not, I didn't want to stop again: this was no place to be. This place was much, much more frightening than the Creggan or the Bogside.

Raoul announced we were near our target. We were clear of the shanties by now, in a kind of half-overgrown wasteland. The road had turned into a beaten earth track. In a little while we stopped in a small clearing by the side of the trail. There was an isolated house standing off to one side. This, said Raoul, was where they had discovered a cartel hideout.

A detachment of men was already on the scene. As we rolled up, I could hear thumping and banging from inside the house, as though a massive brawl were taking place. Suddenly, the fighting inside stopped. It was followed by a long burst of automatic gunfire. I took cover behind a broken fence. There was a second volley of shots. A man burst out of the front door and came running straight down the road at me. I put the Armalite on him and took up the first pressure. Almost at once I eased back the trigger – I could see that he was unarmed, trying to put his hands up. He had a look on his face like he'd just met his own ghost. He was about to: several of the policemen opened up on him at the same time and he went face down, dead, into the dust. Blood spread out across his back.

I waited. There was no more firing. In a minute or two, a generator started up in the house and the lights came on. Good one, I thought. Stroll on in and start the generator. Talk about asking for it. I was thinking the cartel boys might easily have left us a nice little booby-trap. It wouldn't be the first time they had caught the police that way. But there was no explosion. I went forward into the house.

Inside it was dim, almost dark. Tiny light-bulbs the size of large peanuts fizzed and crackled overhead. A middle-aged man was lying face up in the corner of the main room. He had been shot once through the head. Another round had severed a main artery in his right leg. There was blood all around his body, black and shining in the dismal light. Next door, in a smaller room, was a second man. He, too, had been shot: there were entrance wounds in his back, and more blood seeping out from under his body. He was lying on his side with his arms stretched out. They'd put an extra round, from close range, through the back of his head, to make sure he was dead. You could see where the muzzle-flash had burned his hair and scalp.

Everywhere I looked there was money. It was all in American dollars, mostly fifty- and hundred-dollar bills. There were great towers of it, piled up high – money skyscrapers. Cardboard boxes were strewn carelessly about, and these, too, were overflowing with dollars, loose not stacked, mostly smaller denomination bills. There was no sign of any cocaine.

A smart-looking vehicle rolled up outside, followed by another: the senior police officers were arriving now that the action was done. I watched them take charge of the cash. They noticed me, and had a quick, venomous conversation with Raoul, glancing across at me with a look on their faces I didn't like. It was clear I was about as welcome as a leper. They've come for a pay-off, I thought, only something's gone wrong. Either that or they've double-crossed the cartel.

You could see why they didn't want witnesses.

Raoul came over and grabbed me by the arm. 'Come on, Señor,' he said. 'You're not supposed to be here. You'd better vanish now.' We got into the jeep and roared back off into the darkness and the unbeckoning slums.

Back at the hotel, I asked Raoul about the money. There had been a lot, far more than you would expect to find in a shack in that sort of run-down area. It looked to me as if there had been a big pay-off out in the jungle somewhere, and this was the temporary counting-house before the cash was moved on. The standard operating procedure was to count the sum, log it, then take it to be used against the cartels. Somehow, I had the strange feeling that wasn't going to happen. Raoul looked at me with a sad little smile on his face. 'Money, Señor?' he said quietly. 'What money?'

We reached Pablo Escobar's vast ranch and zoo complex on the Medellin peninsula right after the initial attack. Although they had failed to catch – or kill – him, the attack was considered a great success. Escobar himself had run off into the jungle, minus his trousers and shirt in his panic, leaving his animal – and human – menageries behind to face the music.

With his limitless money, he had created probably the largest and best-stocked zoo in South America. There were rhino, hippos, all kinds of exotic bird-life, monkeys and almost everything else roaming free across the huge estate, even big cats. Giant, gaudily painted fibre-glass models of dinosaurs reared up here and there in the luxuriant grounds. The ranch itself was like an old US cavalry fort, made mostly of hardwood, with watch-towers for the permanent guard force set at every corner. A massive white-painted satellite dish poked its antenna skyward at the rear of the place, by the Olympic-sized swimming pool.

In the outbuildings, we discovered dozens of expensive adult toys: all kinds of motorbikes and motorized tricycles, go-karts, cars and jeeps – if it was wheeled and had an engine, Escobar had at least one of it. In one garage, set slightly apart from the rest, we found a rusted antique limousine, its flaring wings and running-boards peppered with what looked like bullet holes. It was Escobar's proudest boast that this old wreck had once been Al Capone's personal vehicle. It's important to have a positive role-model in your life.

We went inside the main house. An old black servant who hadn't bothered running away because his legs didn't work too well any more started telling us lurid tales of the sex and drugs parties Escobar held there. He led us through into Escobar's tennis court of a bed-room. In the middle of the room was a huge black leather and steel chair, with a long narrow seat, and a high padded back. On it were various shackles and attachment points. Our fugitive liked bondage games: dangling down on either side of the seat was a pair of stirrups. 'Escobar's Love Chair,' the old man said. 'He put his women in it, then he do what he want with them.'

'Hope he paid them well,' I muttered. It looked like they earned every penny. Apart from the chair, which was probably too heavy to move without specialized lifting gear, the inside of the house had already been stripped almost bare – by the police, the locals or both: as usual, no one could say. We spent two weeks in and around the Escobar ranch complex, interviewing the men there as the signallers

223

set up and trained them in the new communications gear. I needed to talk to as many men as I possibly could to help me get a clear idea of where the force stood, in terms of its training, morale and operational capability.

At the end of the two weeks, some senior officers turned up and announced there was to be a new raid. The idea was to meet up with some people they described as *comancheros*, which translated as bandits, who would take us to a cartel house out in the rainforest that was packed, they said, with money and drugs. I could go with them if I wanted to.

The officer in charge was a major, in his thirties, with receding hair and a thin mouth. 'How can you be sure you can trust these people?' I asked him for interest's sake. 'What if they're in league with the cartel, and want to lead you into an ambush?' This caused much amusement all round. Impossible, they assured me. These stupid *drogistas* didn't have the wit for that.

We had trained the men, but the senior officers were still a problem. This was a pity, because the men were now taking on that unmistakable look of professional soldiers. It was the old story: 'lions led by donkeys'. But although I'd been advised against getting into any contacts, I was ready to go out on any mission they asked us to: it was the best way of fulfilling the assessment brief. We grabbed our Armalites and ops waistcoats, and went bouncing off with a patrol of about two dozen men along a thin metalled road that disappeared into the bush. After ten or fifteen spine-breaking miles, we pulled into an isolated one-pump filling-station.

The Colombians jumped out, lit their eternal cigarettes, and asked the attendant where the building was that they thought might be the cartel hideout. The attendant acted as though the police asked him this kind of question several times a day. 'Five or ten miles that way.' He shrugged, pointing down the road. I couldn't see a telephone anywhere around but it would have been surprising if he didn't have one. And if he didn't have a phone, he would have had a two-way radio. These little kiosks, in some cases selling no more than a few packets of cigarettes and some bottled water, were everywhere in the bush. Just when you were sure you were miles from the nearest

Colombia. The good guys wear white hats

Matt and me on a Colombian police Huey. Would you mug these guys?

What we came to do – seek and destroy

Bagged for burning

Cartel airstrip. Coming in for the attack

On the ground. Feeling lucky?

Above Who moves, dies

Below Pablo Escobar's ranch. Making myself at home

The Washington Post

WEDNESDAY, MARCH 3, 1993

©THE WACO TRIBUNE-HERALD

...ureau of Alcohol, Tobacco and Firearms agents don bulletproof vests yesterday at command center on the campus of Texas State Technical College in Waco.

After Broadcast, Agents Await Cult's Next Move

By Mary Jordan

Waco: the ATF on the front page of the *Washington Post*

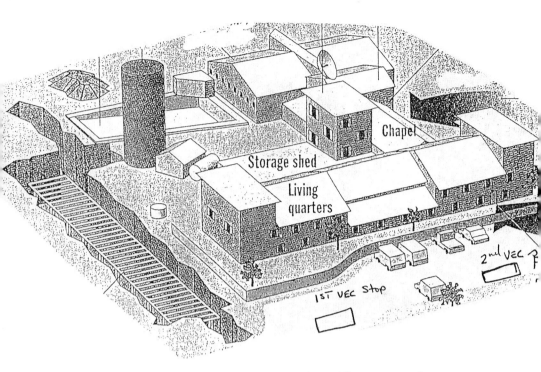

FBI assault sketch of the Branch Davidian compound

Opposite above Part of what we came to protect

Opposite below Heart of Darkness. Sierra Leone rebels

Above Me and the team – Chris Ryan in the shades

Below The Gulf. The men of Bravo Two Zero died here;
I needed to see it for myself

civilization, there at a crossroads in the jungle would be some old boy flogging bits and pieces to non-existent customers. It was a simple system, cheap to operate, and it worked extremely well: these men were lookouts, bankrolled by the local cartel boss. The areas around important refining bases or hideouts were saturated with them and they were an important part of the cartel security system. As we drove off, you could bet your life's savings our friend was out at the back on the two-way radio, warning the *narcos* to expect a little visit.

We still had a long way to go before the officers got a professional grip.

We trundled on a bit further, until suddenly three men stepped out of the jungle on to the road in front of us. The Colombians stayed in their vehicles, fingering their weapons. Matt and I jumped off and stood ready in cover at the side. The strangers told the police there were eight to ten men at the hideout, which they explained helpfully was just up ahead, in the hills to our right. Their readiness to volunteer this information struck me as extremely suspicious. People didn't inform on the cartels. If they did, the penalty was a 'Colombian necktie': they cut your throat, pulled your tongue out through the slit and left you by the side of the road as a warning.

'What are you going to do now?' I asked the major.

'Lead us in, of course,' he replied blithely.

'No CTR first, no OPs?'

'No, no,' he waved his hands. 'No need for all that – we'll go straight in.'

We turned right and ground slowly up an overgrown track only just wide enough for the vehicles, in first gear, with high ground dominating us on the right, and dense jungle all around. I told the driver to stop. Enough was enough. Going in like this, without planning, making enough noise to wake the dead and in ideal ambush conditions, we were asking to get jumped.

'Where is the hideout now?' I asked. I was thinking I'd skirmish up to the position and get in ahead of the pack – even a few minutes' recce on the target might make the difference between life and death. One of the three men who had stopped us said he would guide me in on foot. The major offered me six men, while Matt stayed with the convoy. Keeping a close eye on our guide and my new section, we broke track and began to climb steeply through the steaming low-canopy jungle. All the time, to our left, we could hear the roar of the police vehicles grinding slowly up over the broken ground. Then, through the foliage, we caught sight of a brand-new building in the middle of a small clearing. It was well built for this remote spot, made of wood, with a new corrugated-iron roof; there were some small outbuildings scattered around it. Except for the sound of chopping somewhere off in the distance, all was quiet.

We stole silently up to the edge of the clearing. Suddenly, with a great roar of noise, the police rolled up. The entire patrol got out and charged in through the building's front door — all of them at once, like the Keystone Cops. I led my section round to the back of the clearing. Here, the land fell sharply away, down the bank of a re-entrant towards a small river. As we came round the corner of the main hut I saw three men. They were hesitating on the lip of this slope, trying to decide whether or not to make a run for it. They were unarmed. We arrested them and led them back to the front of the house. It was clear they were minnows, low-grade workers. But that didn't stop the major. He began to question them with the back of his hand. Quite quickly they told us that 'five or six' of their bosses had run away when they heard the noise of the approaching vehicles.

'They can't have gone very far,' I said. 'Let's get after them. Hot pursuit.'

The younger policemen muttered their agreement. One raised his rifle.

'No, no,' said the major airily, 'there's no time. We will return now.' He waved everyone back into the vehicles. The thin smile on his face made me suspect that our dashing leader had been on the end of a little pay-off.

On the way back to Bogotá, Matt and I quietly quizzed the junior officers and men: were these operational methods typical?

'Yes,' they replied. 'Always the same.' If they suggested any tactics other than charging in with guns blazing, they were either ridiculed or accused of cowardice.

*

We picked up our weapons and ran to the waiting Hueys, a dozen men to each one. Tucked in close behind one another, the helis took off, dropped their noses, and snaked out low over the jungle, weaving constantly in case of ground fire. Climbing steeply to get out of small-arms range we turned south. The Hueys had 7.62 mm M-60D machine-guns mounted on pintles in their port-side doors, one to each helicopter. A thin layer of high cloud blocked the sun and as we climbed it grew bitterly cold. I shivered inside my DPM combat gear. It was our third week in Colombia. We were way down in the south of the country now, with a different regional command group. Our mission was to seek and destroy the local cartel's main airstrip and processing centre. Acting on information received, we were hoping to catch them with their next shipment ready to go.

After twenty minutes airborne, we came on a small coca plantation, several acres across, with a small hut at its heart: the captain in charge told one of his men to note it for future attention. The coca bushes were planted in neat rows, a few feet apart, in land that had been slashed and burned out of the jungle. This little farm was a good sign: it meant we were probably getting near one of the cartel's main operational nodes. Sure enough, we saw a second, larger, coca plantation below us almost at once.

We plunged down to tree-top height. The captain turned in his seat and waved at me. 'Danger area,' he said.

I nodded enthusiastically. 'Great.' I locked and loaded. I had that tight feeling you get when there's the chance of a contact, half fear, half anticipation.

A broad river appeared below us, gleaming like a mirror in the light. The pilot dropped the helicopter right down on to it. Now we were below tree-top height, flying very fast and very low, skimming the surface of the water. There was a massive sensation of ground-rush, the brilliant green walls of the jungle flashing past in a blur on either side. The thump and clatter of the Huey grew louder still, echoing back up off the river, the machine bucking and yawing in the low-level turbulence.

We shot out over a small mud village. The captain shouted something I couldn't hear. He pointed at the ground. We looped into a tight turn, and set down hard on a scrubby little football pitch. You can go just about anywhere in Colombia and never be more than a click from a kick-about pitch. The policemen bundled out, trotted over to a nearby hut and squeezed inside. I took a good look around, then followed them. Obviously we weren't going to be staying long: the pilot was still turning and burning. When I reached the door of the shack I found the men arguing over a map. Gradually the locals from the village wandered up, in singletons and small groups, to have a look at the strangers who had landed from the sky.

'Is it usual for helicopters to come this way?' I asked the captain.

'Oh, no,' he assured me. 'It's very unusual.'

Christ, I thought, another sneak attack. After about ten minutes of map-wrangling we took off, flying back up the river we had just been following. Then the pilot turned the machine back on to its original heading, coming back down over the water for the second time. This was bad operational practice and, with the map business, it meant only one thing: we were lost. We started circling. 'It's here some-where,' the captain shouted. It was his job to pin down the location before we got airborne. He hadn't bothered doing his staff-work.

But I still had the feeling this was going to be our lucky day.

We were dead low, clipping the tops of the trees. I wasn't the only one there with that feeling in my gut: the door-gunner cocked and made ready. I grinned at the policeman opposite. Like me, I could tell he wanted to get out there and do the job. Then, suddenly, there was the airfield, right below us, a scrubby rectangle blown out of the virgin jungle. Someone shouted, 'Armed men! On the ground.' The captain looked at us, giving us the thumbs down. Oh, no, I thought, you're not backing out of this one now. I tapped the stock of the Armalite with the heel of my palm, giving him some teeth and point-ing down at the strip. 'Let's go get them,' I shouted. He looked at the door-gunner. The gunner waggled the barrel of the M-60 up and down and nodded vigorously. He, too, was raring to go.

The Huey bucked and lurched. I wondered if we had been hit. There had been no thumps, but I was acutely conscious of the fuel-cells under the floor of the cabin: 844 litres of high-octane aviation fuel. 'Incoming!' the pilot screamed. Through the door I could see bright orange tracer floating up at us from the edges of the trees. Everyone went very quiet. I tapped the gunner on the shoulder and pointed at the flashes. '*Si*,' he said. We were within range. He squinted briefly along his sights. The gun roared as he opened up.

I couldn't hear or see the captain giving any commands. 'Down!' I signalled to the pilot. 'Get us down! Lower!' He pushed on the Huey's collective and we screamed in along the edge of the field. Our gunner hosed down the tree line, M-60 hammering. Glancing back out of the door, I saw the second gunship swoop in behind us, spraying the other side of the strip. There was a hot smell of cordite, and big brass cartridge cases flying everywhere. Fumes whipped around the cabin and back out into the slipstream.

I could feel my heart pumping hard and my blood running. There was the deafening noise of the M-60 and the rotors, the smell of hot engine-oil and gunsmoke. Everything was bright and pin-sharp.

We peeled off out of the attack, but our own pilot turned the wrong way, putting us directly into the path of any ricochets from the following Huey, and stopping our own gun from bearing on the target. I shouted at him and pointed, but he looked blank. We turned sharply at the end of the strip and came back in for a second pass. I couldn't see any return fire from the ground now. We shot back along the runway again, then banged down hard at its northernmost end. In a second we were all out and down, firing into the trees where we had last seen the muzzle-flashes. There was no return fire. After one short burst of three I quit firing to save ammo.

We started pepper-potting: one man forward, down, observe and fire, next man forward, down, observe and fire, the first on his feet again making a short zigzag dash forward. Matt's group in the second Huey had landed right behind us. The police started running along a narrow track to our left, spearing its way into the dense jungle. There was only enough room for them to run in single file. Against all my instincts and training, I followed. There wasn't much choice. At once we came under fire from the trees to our left. I could hear rounds slapping and whacking into the surrounding bush, the heavier thud of the tree-strikes.

I had closed right up on the leaders of our group. I got down on one knee and waited. A burst of fire came in close to my position, the bullets whistling through the undergrowth, the air pressure parting the leaves, and buzzing past like huge wasps. Another burst rapped into the trees just above my head: *Thwock! Thwock! Thwock!* The fat punching sound in the dense, moist wood was exactly like that of a round going into a human body. One bullet came right out of the other side of an atap palm directly in front of me: a huge chunk splintered out towards my face. I ducked aside. There was the high-pitched *ping!* of a ricochet, and I saw yellow-orange muzzle-flash in among the dark green. I could tell where that one had come from. I swivelled slightly, took aim at the blue haze in the bush, and blasted back, firing controlled double-taps, moving the Armalite in a slow arc to cover the location.

At my back, Matt was firing at the same spot. There was a high-pitched scream as someone made a hit. At that it was up and on. The jungle ahead of us suddenly opened up: I saw a clearing with some buildings dead in the centre. The policemen swept up and around these shacks, then stopped.

'Clear through, clear through,' I yelled in Spanish. 'Follow on and fire!' The men had regrouped at the far edge of the clearing. They stood there, looking pleased with themselves, instead of going in pursuit. As far as they were concerned, the job was done. I thought we had just started. I could still hear the distant sounds of cartel gunmen crashing off into the jungle. 'They're running away,' I said. 'Let's get after them and finish the job.'

'No, no,' called the captain, lighting a cigarette. 'They've gone now.'

I looked around. All over the clearing and in atap-covered lean-tos around the central hut there were big fifty-gallon oil drums, filled with a mixture of fermenting coca leaves and petrol. The smell was putrid, rank and disgusting in the hot air. Boxes and crates of chemicals, sulphuric acid, acetone and the rest, all stacked ready for use, lay next to what looked like a huge washing-machine. Some of the police had started searching, and there was a sudden shout. They had found three drugs workers cowering under the beds in a long wooden accommodation hut. They dragged these men out by the scruff of the neck and began to interrogate them, shouting in their faces and slapping them.

The rest of us got busy destroying the processing plant. There was too much equipment and cocaine paste to ship out on the helicopters, so we made a big pile of it, doused it in fuel, and burned it. Next we carried all the chemicals into the huts, threw in anything else lying around that looked like it might be useful, and set fire to them. There were cracks and whizzes as it went up, and sharp snaps from the blazing wood. Columns of oily smoke billowed up into the air. We backed off and stood for a while, watching the firework display. Some of these labs, the really big ones, can produce as much as $1 billion a month in refined cocaine. This outfit wasn't quite in that league, but it was a start, the best drugs-enforcement effort I'd seen yet.

The captain came up and told us we were going off to hit another, even bigger, drugs camp: they had extracted its location from the prisoners. I decided there wasn't all that much wrong with our leader's commitment, it was just the lazy, haphazard way he went about things. We mounted up in the Hueys again.

With directions from the captured men, we were over the next target in no time. From the air, we saw that the strip was pockmarked with deep holes, as though it had been deliberately cratered. The Huey shimmied in, lifted its nose and we jumped off its skids from the hover. Fanning out, we skirmished around the main house. A woman with a small child on her hip came out, waving her arm and shouting abuse. The police charged past her and arrested a man inside.

After slapping this man across the face a few times, they rushed off across the airfield like a pack of dogs. The prisoner had told them something. Watching the tree line, I followed them across. Hidden in the tall growth were four huge metal barrels lined up in a row. They were filled to the brim with semi-refined coca paste. Bingo! We had found one of the major shipment points for the local operation. Alongside these barrels were dozens of wooden planks, which at first was a bit puzzling. Then I realized they went over the craters in the runway, so that the shipment planes could land. The craters were deliberate, designed to make us think that the strip was disused.

We were inspecting these finds when I heard two shots from the

231

other end of the field. Two or three of the policemen had remained down there with the prisoner. It might be that they were trying to scare more information out of him. Or it might be something else. We made a new bonfire out of everything we could find, including the planks, set it alight, and went back to join the rest of the team.

The prisoner was on his knees. They had his hands tied behind his back, and they were really laying into him, slapping, punching and kicking. When they saw us, they stopped, stood him up and dusted him off. Things seemed to calm down a bit.

There was another shout, this time from the nearby riverbank. Someone had found a second cache of semi-processed cocaine, about eight drums of it, hidden near a small creek leading down into the river. Following this inlet back towards the camp, we found two rubber boats with powerful outboards carefully hidden in among the undergrowth: getaway craft. From the air, we had missed them. We poured petrol over them and left them blazing.

When I got back, the police were jumpy, scared-looking. The prisoner had been talking. He was white and his mouth was running blood. 'This is a very bad place,' said the captain encouragingly. 'Many narco-terrorists here.'

The Hueys, which had been standing off at a safe distance, came whopping back in for the pick-up. 'This is a big find,' I said. 'Why not use it? They'll be back to see what the damage is. Leave an OP in for a few days – say, three or four men. Let them watch what hap-pens. If they do come back we'll extract the OP covertly, come back in with the Hueys, only this time we'll land clear and work our way in. Surround the bastards. Then we'll catch them all, just when they think they've got rid of us.' The captain smiled back at me, shaking his head.

As we finished talking, there was a loud bang from the rainforest and I turned with the Armalite up. Low-velocity, I thought. Pistol round. Four policemen came out of the trees and started climbing into the helis. Last I'd heard, the man we'd caught was coming back to base with us for further questioning. 'Where's the prisoner?' I asked.

'He was small fry,' replied the captain. 'They've let him go.'

That night, as every night, we listened to the World Service news. The ground war had begun. There was no news about the rest of Bravo Two-Zero.

We did the rounds of a few more camps but without getting into any more contacts. The signallers had installed all the comms gear we had brought along. It was working, and I felt we had enough material to write a full assessment report for Hereford. It was time to go home. We arranged our flight out, and headed back for Bogotá.

Feeling we knew the city well enough now to socialize a bit, Matt and I went out for a drink that first evening back from the bush. Walking around Bogotá at night is a quick way of getting your urban warfare tactics up to scratch, even in the centre where it's supposed to be safe. We'd gone about a hundred metres from the hotel door when we hit trouble. We saw the muggers long before they thought we had. One man stepped out of a doorway up ahead, saw us coming and stepped back into the shadows. The other came at us on a diagonal from across the street. I glanced sideways at Matt, and raised one eyebrow. He made the slightest tilt of his head. We walked on as though we hadn't spotted them, watching them all the time, taking a detached professional interest in how they meant to go about attacking us.

We had to be sure they weren't carrying firearms. Even though our pistols were licensed by the Colombian police for our personal protection, a firefight was bound to cause a diplomatic incident. If they were armed, we had agreed we'd be better off just chucking our wallets on the ground and forgetting about it. But if they weren't carrying guns . . .

They were close, now, one on either side of the pavement directly ahead of us. There was no sign of any guns. But I caught a gleam in the street-lights, something metallic. We had to assume they were both carrying knives.

As we came within five or six metres of them, we increased speed, taking long strides for the last few steps. Never give a mugger time to take the initiative. We hit them without speaking or breaking stride. Matt took the one on the left. I went for the one on the street side. I aimed a side-kick at his balls, missed, and caught him high up on one thigh. He rocked backwards slightly under the impact. I saw a mixed look of horror and surprise appear on his face, and drove my fist straight into it. He staggered back a step or two, turned on one heel, and ran off into the night – along with another two men who were obviously back-up.

Leaving their pal to face the music.

I looked round. The mugger stood there swaying slightly, looking very shocked: *gringo* businessmen out on the town weren't supposed to fight back, they were meant to cave in at the first sign of trouble and hand over their Rolexes. Those were the rules of his game – but Matt and I weren't playing to them. Judging by the expression he was wearing, our friend was pretty upset about it. I stepped up and hit him hard on the ear. He flew sideways across the pavement. His head bounced back off the wall with a sharp *toc!* As he fell, Matt caught him by his shirt-front, drew back his fist and thumped him again. We dropped him in the gutter.

'Shall we go for that drink now?' I said.

'Why not?' replied Matt. 'I reckon we've earned it.'

Chapter Twenty-six

By now the Gulf War was into its end-game. I still had no clear idea whether any of the Bravo or Alpha patrols had survived.

Then, by chance, just as we were about to fly out, the team coming in to provide further training arrived. They told us about Will, A squadron's missing sergeant-major. The squadron had been patrolling in Pinkies when they ran into a massive Iraqi force, the best part of an armoured brigade. In the firefight Will had been shot through the thigh. Faced by overwhelming numbers, the patrol had withdrawn. Will was bleeding so badly he couldn't be moved. They offered him the option of being shot, which luckily he declined – they all thought he would die anyway. So, at his own request, they stuffed him full of morphine and left him there, propped up behind a GPMG with a box of ammo. By some miracle the Iraqis, when they finally got to him, took him prisoner instead of shooting him on the spot. By some further miracle, there was a London-trained Iraqi Army surgeon in the attacking unit, who insisted on operating on Will right there and then, locking off the artery, putting in a drip, and stopping the Iraqi grunts from smacking him around too much. This prompt and expert action certainly saved Will's life. Matt thought his best mate had been dead for four weeks – but he had made it.

As for Bravo Two-Zero, the news was good and bad. Andy McNab had survived, Dinger was still alive, and three more. But Bob Consiglio, Steve Lane and Vince Phillips were dead. Like the rest of that patrol, these were all men I had trained with, fought with, and knew as friends. As I listened to the sorry tale unfold, I felt the same overwhelming sense of guilt I'd experienced on first learning they were missing. I felt responsible for what had happened, and that feeling would haunt me always. But nothing I said or did or felt was going to bring them back.

I got back to the UK to find I had just missed their funerals. This sickened me almost as much as the fact of their having died.

Tracy was waiting to pick me up at the airport. Technically, although she had no idea where I'd been, the mere fact that she was at Heathrow to meet me constituted a breach of security. But that didn't stop me hugging her. I was so glad to see her I could hardly speak.

Matt and I were supposed to make an initial report on the Colombia trip to the ops office clerk who had threatened me with platform four. Instead, we reported directly to the CO. We put it to him that what the police needed most urgently was their own *independent* command, right up to the highest levels of tasking and co-ordination. Also, their officers had to undergo exactly the same initial training as the men, and extra leadership training too. He listened, took detailed notes, and asked us to submit our written reports in due course. He also thanked us for doing the job. He was one of the best COs I had ever had the privilege to work under, professional and astute. Which was absolutely no consolation when we had to go straight out and pay our respects to the Gulf War dead.

The Regiment's dead are buried in a dedicated plot at one end of St Martin's, the regimental church. This cemetery is one of the few places on earth where I can stop and take time to think. From that spot, I can see the school I attended and the playing fields I ran around in; the river I fished as a boy lies beyond the school. The whole area is rich in personal associations for me.

Although he'd served his time with the Regiment there was no place for my Dad in this cemetery. I went to each of the graves in turn. At this stage there were only wooden name plaques. Here lay the dead men of Bravo Two-Zero, and all the other men lost to the Regiment in recent years.

Tracy and I stood in front of Bob Consiglio's grave. He had been

236

killed on Bravo Two-Zero, dying of gunshot wounds after his stand-alone battle against vastly superior forces. Like this gravestone, the regimental clock would now have his name on it. His mother had left an unopened can of Guinness on the freshly dug mound. It was his favourite drink. I knelt down, cracked it open and poured the black liquid down through the earth. I reckoned where Bob was he'd be needing a drink by now. I reached over and touched the spot where I thought his head would be. I do this every time, when I'm paying my last respects to a dead mate – it's a kind of superstition. But I've done it too many times, now, more than I care to remember.

I hadn't known Bob all that long, months rather than years, but for some reason his death had got to me. I tried to think of things we'd done together, the places we'd been, the people we'd met, the good times we'd been through. I remembered giving him a bollocking once. As I knelt there remembering, I found myself talking to him, as if he were there with me, instead of lying dead in the ground. It could so easily have been me down there, I thought, instead of him. When nothing more came to mind I got to my feet and said quietly, 'See you around, mate.'

The first thing the Gulf survivors said to me when I met up with them after those desolate funerals was: 'Where the fuck were you when we needed you?' That made me feel a whole lot better about things. I spent many, many hours listening to all the stories, most of them sad and bad. With three men dead, B squadron's morale was the lowest I had ever known: they felt they'd let themselves down, while D and A squadrons had pulled off some successful – and therefore largely unheard-of – missions. Their self-criticism was wrong, in my opinion, and I told them so.

The various versions of the Bravo Two-Zero mission were fascinating, all completely different, each an entirely personal account of 'the truth'.

A few days later, the whole Regiment went into closed session, in a kind of Chinese parliament, to examine mistakes made in the Gulf War and lessons learned. This is one of the best things about the SAS: everyone, no matter what their rank or seniority, can have an input on these occasions. I stood up. My point was simply that the command structure of B squadron had failed, placing missions in jeopardy, because Matt and I, the squadron's most senior NCOs, hadn't been allowed to go and do our job. Why was that?

To his credit, the colonel acknowledged publicly in reply that it had been a mistake to send us to Colombia and not the Gulf.

'It was seen as a two-squadron commitment,' he explained. 'I mean A and D squadrons, as you know. But once B squadron started getting sucked in as well, the focus should, with hindsight, have switched to the Gulf as the major theatre. Colombia was still an important issue – who knows how many policemen's lives will be saved because of the report you were able to provide? Or kids? Yes, with hindsight, it could have waited – but at what cost? The entire squadron command should have gone, there's absolutely no doubt about that. You and Matt should have been there. At the time I can only say that things rolled extremely quickly. But there you are. We've learned.'

I'd learned my own lesson from what had taken place. I knew now that when I wanted to get my way, when it was vital to do so, there was no use going at it like a bull at a gate. Next time, I would have to play politics.

I spent a happy two weeks on leave, with Natalie and Tracy, and visiting Stuart and Susan Henderson in Oxford. This seemed to be the only place I could wind down and switch off anything to do with the Regiment.

Then it was back to Colombia again, as always in tandem with Matt. Our brief now was to implement the recommendations of our own latest report. This would be my third trip, and this time I was determined to make effective, radical changes in the running of the unit. Luckily, I now had the power to implement them. The colonel of the Regiment was backing us, and the FCO was behind him. So one of the first things I did when I got back to Bogotá was get the Colombian colonel in charge of the training school sacked. For as long as I had worked with him this man had been unfailingly obstructive. He had done his best to foul up our training routines, and his own refusal to train had encouraged his junior officers in the belief that they, too, were above learning how to lead an attack. With him out of the way, though, and a replacement in command, things improved fast. We saw a difference in the culture of the force almost at once. To reinforce this change, while I worked at headquarters on strategy and long-term planning, Matt took charge of the training camp, working with the new CO, making sure he understood what was needed and setting up the structure to implement it.

From this time on, every recruit, including all the officer candidates, left the hands of the SAS with a thorough grasp of the basics: small arms, vehicle checkpoints, convoy and helicopter drills, hot pursuits, clearing areas and making them secure, dismantling booby-traps, camp attacks, putting in covert and reactive OPs, demolitions, close-target reconnaissance drills, and the rest. By the end of four months down there, it was clear that the police were getting the hang of it: there was a new pride in their step. Right up and down the command structure, a coherent force was coming together. That intake was the best batch we had ever trained, and we, in our turn, could be proud of them. At last, the Colombians were taking seriously the war against the drugs industry: all our recommendations had been acted on. Our staff sergeants, especially Matt, had done a superb job on training the raw officer recruits — that in itself was probably the most crucial improvement in the culture of the force.

By setting up a well-trained, effective and corruption-free Colombian drugs enforcement unit, the SAS has had some influence in checking the global trade in drugs. They are now a thoroughly professional, efficient fighting force, with a first class OC, which is having significant success in containing, if not entirely defeating, the cartels.

There are those who like to say that the police have been *too* successful, in recent years, that routing the home-grown cartel bosses like Escobar, who was shot dead in a police ambush, has merely meant the fragmentation of the Colombian trade and the arrival of fresh gangster blood, mainly in the form of the Russian mafia. All I can say to this kind of criticism is that a small drop of contamination is easier to stamp on than a big drop. The main thing is to keep stamping. I was glad to have been involved: I was sure that, however indirectly, the

Regiment's creation of a force in its own image had saved lives, maybe many hundreds of lives. For me, even though it had kept me out of the war in the Gulf, there was some satisfaction in being a small part of a major job the Regiment had done well.

I was away for four months on that last trip to Colombia. The transport dropped me off at the back of Hereford cathedral. I looked up and saw Tracy walking towards me through the snow lying thick on Cathedral Green, her face glowing rosy pink. For a moment, we didn't say anything, we just looked at one another and then smiled. Then I took her in my arms and we were together again. Coming home can be the happiest thing.

Chapter Twenty-seven

I was taking some time off at home one evening after the assessment trip, when my pager went off. It was Chris Ryan. 'The ops OC's after you,' he said. 'Have you seen him?'

'No? What's on?'

'It looks like the Waite option's on. And you're doing it.'

We were on Standby squadron, so I knew exactly what 'the Waite option' meant. My face dropped. Tracy was in the room. 'What's the matter?' she asked. Although I had once played a sea-anemone in a school play, and had to wear long purple fronds and wave them about over my head, I'm not really given to drama. But I put down the phone, turned to her and said, 'You're looking at a dead man.'

A plan to get Terry Waite and the other hostages out of Lebanon had been put together. As leader designate of the operation, I knew more about the intelligence picture in Beirut than the rest of Free-fall Troop. And as a result of this knowledge I was under no illusions: if we went into Beirut, it was unlikely we would come out. During the brief it had been blindingly clear to everyone in the room that, unless we were tremendously fortunate, this was a non-viable mission, also known as suicide. But, then, that's what the SAS is for – it's what all Special Forces are for. There's no one else to do this kind of job, and occasionally they're going to throw you a curve ball. Be under no illusions about this if it's ever in your mind to go for Selection.

Next on the line was the OC himself. 'Ah, Hunter, there you are. Come and talk to me first thing in the morning, will you?'

So it was true, then, I thought, and not just Chris winding me up.

Best make a last will and testament, something I should have done before.

I told Tracy I thought they wanted us to go in after the British and American hostages in Beirut. She stared at me for about five seconds then burst into tears. You didn't need a special intelligence brief to get the big picture. All I had running through my own head as I tried to comfort her was Desert One, the catastrophic attempt by US Special Forces to rescue their hostages from Iran, which had resulted in abject failure and eight men dead. Like that, this was a mission impossible.

I stayed up late, pushing paperwork around, trying to get some of my affairs in order. Like me, Tracy couldn't sleep. In the end, we walked over to her parents' house and stayed up all night drinking coffee with them.

I walked into camp the next morning like a man on his way to get measured for his coffin. The OC had a list of names on his desk. 'These are the people available. Anyone you'd like to leave out?'

I scanned the list. I saw Chris Ryan's name there, and hesitated for a moment. I was sure he had had a much harder time of it out in the Gulf than he liked to admit, even to himself. But, then, look what he'd achieved: probably the greatest Escape and Evasion in the history of the Regiment. 'No, they look fine,' I told him. 'I'll take all of them.' We walked across to Intelligence together for the brief.

'Morning all,' began the Int officer breezily as we sat down. 'Now then, first things first. The country brief.' He pulled down a map. 'Zaïre.'

'*What?*' I almost burst out laughing.

'Zaïre. You know, turbulent country in Central Africa. Anything wrong?'

'Hang on,' I said. 'I just need five minutes.' I went outside, took a few deep breaths, rang Tracy on the mobile, told her I'd probably remain alive for the foreseeable future and would she mind telling her mum and dad the good news?

Ryan had got it wrong. Never trust the rumour mill.

I went back into the brief. Like most people in the Regiment, I was aware that things were getting out of hand in Zaïre – not surprisingly, after years of systematic plundering of the country's resources and revenues by 'President for Life' Mobutu Sese Seko and his cronies. The Int officer said the breakdown of law and order in Zaïre had reached the point where an evacuation of the remaining British embassy staff in Kinshasa looked like it would be necessary. My job was to fly to the capital with an eight-man team, protect the embassy and its staff, devise an evacuation plan and, if necessary, execute it.

There was an Augusta 109 helicopter standing by on the pad outside, and we got on it. In London, an MI6 desk officer gave us an even more up-to-date and thorough intelligence brief, and we were invited to put questions to an embassy staff-member who had just come out of Zaïre.

The Int man had told me that the embassy was in the middle floor of a block of flats in the city centre. 'It's in a block of flats, then, is it?' I asked the embassy wallah.

'No,' he replied sharply. 'It is not. It was until a year ago. Now, though, it's in a brand-new purpose-built complex on the edge of the Congo river.' He gave me an idea of what the complex was like, sketching out a plan view in pencil, which enabled me to put together there and then a rough plan of action. I submitted this, along with a request for the various items of equipment, vehicles and the weaponry I thought we would need. I asked for a new type of lightweight boat that I knew had just come into service with the SBS. The embassy stood right on the river, and the river was the international border. Once we were across that, we would be safe. If push came to shove, my plan was simple: everyone on the boats, across the river into Brazzaville, the capital of the Congo, on the opposite bank. In that kind of theatre, where there was a complete breakdown in law and order, the simpler the plan the more chance we had of it working.

I had a think next about the matter of our small arms. Most of the younger guys I was taking knew and liked the Sig P226 9 mm pistol better than the Browning, which I preferred, so I settled for the Sig. I wanted to take the G3 rifle, with its 7.62 mm round for stopping power but, for some reason no one would explain to me, this request was refused. I was told we had to take the 5.56 mm Colt Commando. 'What about the new inflatable boats?' I asked.

'Refused, not available,' was the short reply.

243

Eight strong, we were going in to protect the new complex, built at a cost of many millions of pounds, from the rioting hordes. Eight men. The French were sending in one and a half battalions, plus specialist infantry support in the form of a French Foreign Legion parachute battalion, on immediate readiness to go: about two thousand men in all. The eight of us had no back-up whatsoever. We *were* the specialist infantry support – but Whitehall had forgotten to send the battalion of regular infantry.

We stood by, we stood to, we stood down. We got the movement order and travelled up to RAF Lyneham; we came back again to Hereford. If this happened once, it happened a dozen times. All the time, the FCO dithered. It seemed that the minister, Linda Chalker, and behind her Douglas Hurd, who were the people with the ultimate responsibility, couldn't make up their minds about sending us in. Their overriding priority appeared to be not, 'Let's get in there and have some kind of presence just in case,' but, 'We mustn't be seen to overreact.'

While all this shilly-shallying went on, several French citizens and some French troops were killed in the escalating rioting. Many European families lost their homes, their possessions and even the clothes off their backs. As for the Zaïrian Army, not only was this force out of control on the streets but its troops were the very people doing most of the looting and the killing. Still we went back and forth to RAF Lyneham, like yo-yos on the end of the FCO's string. Two weeks later, we finally boarded the aircraft.

We flew out in a C-130. As we taxied at Kinshasa, I got everyone together at the back of the aircraft before we lowered the ramp. 'Let's get the weapons out, loaded and locked,' I said. 'We don't know what we'll be walking into on the outside.' We kept our longs – Colt Commandos – out of sight. This was a country in melt-down: I was expecting trouble, straight off the bat. I had the feeling I wasn't going to be disappointed.

There were two vehicles waiting for us on the tarmac, one with a member of the embassy staff in it, who was about twenty-five, called Callum. The other contained a Belgian-born local 'fixer' the ambassador had taken on to help out, and a MILO, who was a major in the

British Army. The first thing the MILO said to me was, 'You can put your weapons away. You won't be needing them here.'

I glanced over his shoulder. About fifty metres away a detachment of Zaïrian troops was manning a quadruple-barrelled Triple-A gun, by the look of it a Russian-supplied ZSU-24. This gun-crew looked drunk or doped or both. They were waving its barrels about all over the airfield, shouting and brandishing bottles of beer. Small knots of starved-looking people were shuffling about, some circling nearer to where we were standing, all of them interested in our kit. And our vehicles. I looked back at the MILO.

'I'll decide what needs to be done here,' I said evenly.

I turned to the blokes. 'All-round defence,' I told them. 'Weapons out of sight in the bags, but no one's to approach the aircraft.'

'No need for all that,' the MILO insisted.

I ignored him. We unloaded all the kit in the sweltering heat and humidity – the boats, razor-wire, rations, steel pickets, tools, ammunition, tons and tons of stuff.

Once the C-130 had lifted off again, we set out for the embassy. As we got going, the drunks on the gun brought its barrels round to bear on our little convoy. 'Standby,' I said to the guys. 'If there's the slightest sign they're going to open fire, we de-bus and go for it. OK?' They nodded. 'If you want to stay alive,' I told the Belgian fixer and Callum, 'please do exactly as we tell you.' I stared the MILO down. 'That includes you,' I said. As we drove past the gun position, they trained its barrels right on us and followed us round. We could see the piles of empty beer bottles littered all around them on the ground. Like the rest of my team I had my hands on the long, keeping it hidden but ready to shove it through the window at a moment's notice and put down return fire.

Driving into the city we saw burned-out cars and buses abandoned everywhere, looted businesses, shops standing open and ransacked, hundreds of people milling about aimlessly, some of them chanting and waving weapons, mostly sticks and clubs. It was generalized mayhem. The months of violence in the bush, mostly perpetrated by the Army (which, like most other public institutions, hadn't been paid for months on end), had sent thousands of people streaming into

Kinshasa at the very time when hardly any food was reaching the city from the countryside they had deserted. A very bad form of Catch-22.

At the embassy I asked the MILO to give us a quick situation report, then show us round so we could get the lie of the land. It was an impressive site – brand-new, as the man had said, enclosed by a high wall topped with floodlights. One side, however, was exposed – the side nearest the town that included the ambassador's residence. This was set slightly apart from the embassy proper, and protected only by a low picket fence. We would definitely have to strengthen that.

I had been told that the only water we would have down there would be what was in the swimming pool, and I wasn't looking forward to drinking all that chlorine. But this turned out to be more false information. In fact, there was a large freshwater tank right inside the compound, which also boasted its own electricity generators. If it came down to lasting out a siege, we were quite well off. I asked to meet all the embassy staff, including the local night-watchmen employed there, and the ambassador himself, to find out exactly who it was we were supposed to be protecting, and how many they were: never trust an intelligence brief. Thankfully, the ambassador, Sir Roger Westbrook, was a good man, with a very large built-in bullshit detector. We got a rapport going between us straight away. 'Look,' I said, 'obviously the embassy runs its business and routines as you wish. We don't want to interfere in any way with that. But if you could just get your people together and tell them that if we have to evacuate they must do exactly – *exactly* – what we tell them it would be a great help.'

'Consider it done,' he replied.

'Do you have any objections to anything we'd like to do to improve your security?' I asked.

'No. The only thing is, I'd like to keep it as low-profile as possible.'

'You don't want to look like you're sitting in a fort?'

'Exactly.' He nodded.

'OK. We'll keep it as low-key as we can.'

I split my tiny force into two teams of four, one to each of the neighbouring two-storey complexes we had been allocated. I took charge of one team. We had an officer with us, a young captain called James, not long into his three-year Regiment attachment, and I asked him to take charge of the other team. I worked out a basic day-on, day-off duty roster. One team was always responsible for embassy defence, one team for VIP protection. Then I sat down and devised the different 'actions on' that might be necessary, depending on the given scenario: stand-to positions in case of attack, fall-back rendezvous, final defensive positions, rules of engagement, evacuation procedures, and so on. We went through all of these together, all eight of us, in fine detail. I chose not to use the embassy as a final defensive position, because it was too easy to besiege. There was a big metal strongroom in the main embassy building we could shut ourselves inside as a last resort, but once we had slammed the door on the howling mob we would be trapped in what was effectively a giant vault, whose air would eventually run out and become a giant tomb. I decided to use one of the accommodation blocks instead: it had better escape routes, better firing vantages and it was closer to the river. This would be our 'keep', or final defensive position, if we could not get to the Congo.

I worked out a large number of evacuation plans, taking every different chain of events into account that any of us could come up with. Then we established our defensive positions inside the block. I asked the Belgian fixer and his team of embassy workers to saw down one or two of the trees in the compound to give us improved arcs of fire. We had two Gemini inflatable boats on trailers, with Mariner outboards, which we stowed ready for instant action in a secure place under the keep close to the river. Then we put steel pickets strung with barbed wire right round the embassy walls. I decided the ambassador's residence was beyond defending, so we would have to write that off. While we got on with all this, the MILO was faffing around sticking his oar in and being a pain. As best we could, we worked around him.

When all the immediate stuff was taken care of, I went next door to talk to the Americans, whose embassy adjoined ours. Their diplomatic compound was being guarded by a large group of US Special Operations Forces. I talked over the situation with my opposite number, the leader of the US team, and we agreed on mutual support when and if the time came to clear out. In terms of numbers, it was very much to our advantage to co-operate with the Americans, who had upwards of three hundred men ready to fight in warships offshore, besides the strong force they had in their compound. We also agreed to leave small removable areas in the barbed wire on the walls between our embassies, with ladders standing by so that people would be able to cross readily from one compound into the next, according to the direction of the initial threat.

The Americans had a proper evacuation organized. One of the warships was an amphibious assault ship: its helicopters would come in and lift out all their nationals, Saigon-style, but better organized, with luck. Their offer of co-operation did not, though, extend to airlifting all us Brits out as well, which was fair enough. They had their own priorities.

This left us one option: to cross the mighty Congo in our little rubber boats. And it was mighty. The River Congo, at the back of the complex, was five hundred metres wide, and much too swift to swim against. One kilometre downstream there was a set of killer rapids. The two inflatable Geminis we had were too small to get everyone out and across the river all at the same time. But there was no way we could make a return trip, which meant we had to get another boat from somewhere. There was an abandoned Swedish medical centre further along the bank; on my initial recce, I had noticed an inflatable boat in a garage. Since this particular medical team had long since gone back to Europe, they weren't going to be needing it in the foreseeable future. I took two of the guys, Mark and Tim, out for a stroll one evening, just after dusk, and we borrowed it.

Day by day the situation outside the walls looked – and sounded – as if it was getting worse. When we had been in Zaïre for about a week, the French diplomatic mission cleared out, lock, stock and barrel, leaving their embassy closed and unoccupied. They had decided that the risks in staying were too great, outweighing the gains. Our own remaining staff began to burn some of the less important paperwork. We had built a two-roll razor-wire and picket fence between the main building and the ambassador's house, with a lockable gate in it. I wanted to let Roger Westbrook continue working in there so that he could get on with his job in an environment that was as normal as possible, but one of my team stayed with him at all times. He had a panic-button already installed in the house, which would help get reinforcements to him fast in time of dire emergency. The only problem we had was in being so undermanned.

I gave my team strict orders to shoot anyone attempting to get into the embassy from the Congo side, especially any of the Zaïrian troops we could see stationed at an outpost about five hundred metres along the bank. I knew for a fact that these troops had orders to shoot anyone trying to get out of the country. Part of my main evacuation plan was to kill these Zaïrian troops, pre-emptively, if we needed to quit in a hurry. I made sure everyone on the team understood they must also kill the Congolese border troops, on the opposite bank, should they open fire on us as we went in.

Having just got hold of the situation, I discovered that the MILO was sending independent security reports back to Whitehall, without first referring to the ambassador or myself. Only one person there was supposed to be reporting on the security situation in country and that was Roger Westbrook, acting on my advice. I had a chat with him about the MILO's behaviour. He called the major in and told him in no uncertain terms that his job was solely to advise on military matters as requested. It was not to make and send off a stream of rogue threat assessments.

Under normal circumstances, once a Special Forces team had arrived on the spot, the MILO was surplus to requirements and the FCO would call him back. In this case, because all movement was difficult and dangerous, he had had to stay. This should not really have caused any problems. But the major couldn't accept the reality. Matters came to a head when he got into an embassy vehicle one day and drove off. I had made it clear that all vehicle usage had to be authorized by me personally, for obvious reasons.

When the MILO got back, late in the evening, he told us he had been playing golf at a country club on the edge of town. I asked him what he would have done if the Zaïrians had taken him hostage, or what we would have done if we had had to get the staff out. He turned and walked away without so much as a word.

His antagonism was getting out of hand. I set up a meeting, asking Captain James to sit in. When the MILO arrived, I said, 'Let's get one thing clear, shall we? You are not in command here. You are under our command.' His face told us plainly how much he hated this. 'Your job here is finished,' I continued, 'and you do not leave this compound without our permission. I need you to accept my authority and these conditions.'

The major did not reply. I seem to have this effect on majors.

He had left me with little alternative. I went in to see Roger Westbrook for the second time. 'Let's get him out,' I said. 'You're not happy with him, I'm not happy with him, he's got no function here. He's putting himself, and therefore the rest of us, at risk. We've got enough potential problems without having to dig him out of a hole. What do you think?'

'How are we going to get him out?' asked the ambassador.

'We'll escort him down to the ferry,' I replied. 'It's still working, occasionally. He can fly home from Brazzaville.'

Two days later, the major got his orders by telex from London – and out he went.

With the violence getting steadily closer to the embassy, we began to empty the main communications vaults of documentation and burn it. Brilliant, I thought, Three million hungry people in a place the size of Hereford and eight of us to defend the embassy. It looked like the cooking-pot option was high on the cards for us. We'd have to evacuate soon, but even with the extra boat I still wasn't happy about the river-crossing. We discussed joint evacuation and defence plans with other embassies, but if the crunch came we were prepared to stand alone.

There were still plenty of British citizens hanging on in Zaïre who had long since been warned to leave, but who had chosen to stay to protect their interests. You could bet your boots they would be clamouring at the gates when the crunch came. Whenever I met these people, I told them as politely as I could that we were not there to protect them: our priority was the ambassador and his staff, and that they could not rely on us for help if the situation became critical. I always advised them that they should get out while the going was good, and while the ferry was still working. Few took this advice.

Meanwhile, time was slipping by. The posting had been scheduled to last no more than two weeks. We had already been there a month, and Zaïre was no place to be if you like to sleep easy in your bed at night. Like everyone else in the embassy, I had a feeling of deep foreboding. You felt that anything could happen, at any time – and probably would. The mounting stress and tension took people in different ways. In my case, I couldn't bring myself to call Tracy, or indeed anyone at home, although it was occasionally possible to do so. Later, I couldn't explain this to her. I just had the superstitious idea that if I did contact her and tell her I was OK, everything would suddenly go off.

All the time we were in Zaïre, we had trouble from the FCO, and even from our own command. One minute we were responsible to Hereford, the next minute to London. There was no sense of any hands-on management. The FCO officials who were supposedly in charge seemed pathologically complacent, ignoring any and every report we sent as though their careers depended on it. When the rioting came close and tension was high, we would wait hours for a reply to even the most urgent message from the ambassador himself. Even though they came through routinely, twice a day, communications from the UK were vague, which contributed strongly to our feeling of isolation.

So it came as something of a shock when Chris Ryan told me I had an exclusive message waiting. Exclusive messages in a situation like that usually mean someone close to you has died. I immediately thought about Natalie and Tracy. It was a one-line telex: 'Regret to inform you your friend Stuart Henderson has died.'

Stuart, who had guided me into the world of business when I had been trying to save my marriage, had gracefully accepted my return to the Regiment, and remained a friend ever after. I had been over to see him just before leaving for Zaïre. His appearance had worried me then: he had looked drawn and tired. Leaving that day, I had turned to him and said, 'You take care of yourself now? Will you promise me that?' He had nodded and smiled, as if what I had said was in the nature of a joke. But it was no joke. And I had lost another friend.

Now I rang Tracy. She told me Stuart had died of a heart-attack, on a business trip in the United States. He was forty-five, which is no age. I shut away the thought of this new death to deal with at another time.

Tracy dealt with it by going to see Sue in Oxford. When she got back a girlfriend called her: 'Did you know that the squadron is deploying to try to get Gary's team out? Nothing's been heard from them.' The routine embassy message hadn't got through to Hereford. It was a long twenty-four hours before Tracy was told we were OK.

Before the trouble broke out, Callum, the second secretary who had come out to meet us at the airport, had lived outside the embassy on the edge of the city. His house had long since been ransacked. But, he now told us, he had left some official documents there, as well as a small amount of personal stuff. If the papers were still in the house, we needed to get them back. He could pick up his own stuff at the same time.

I had been wanting to get out into that particular area of Kinshasa, which was known to be volatile, to make my own up-to-date assessment of the threat there and in the rest of the city. We set off in the Range Rover and another vehicle, two up in each car, with Callum directing us up front in the lead car. The streets of the city were filled with crowds of desperate people, prowling for anything they could find to loot. We had our ops waistcoats on, with our longs ready on the seats beside us. 'If it all goes wrong,' I said, 'we drive away at speed. If they come after us, fire a warning shot or two over their heads. If that doesn't stop them coming, shoot to kill.'

We went at noon. Sometimes the rioting died down a bit in the heat and humidity of midday. Not this time. As we closed on the bungalow we heard yelling and chanting, spiked with the sound of glass smashing. Not good. We parked up outside the house, facing back the way we had come. The driver and front-seat man got out and stood behind the vehicle doors, ready to put down protective fire. The rest of us went inside.

Callum's villa was a complete shambles, stripped bare of its contents and fittings, right down to the lights. All the windows were smashed in. But there, scattered across the floor, were the missing documents, lying in a heap with his photographs and various other personal possessions. Bizarrely, a pair of his trousers was in the middle of the room, one of the few useful items that hadn't been taken. He grabbed them, stuffed all the papers and personal gear down the trouser legs, and tied the whole lot up into a bundle. In my earpiece, I heard that a large mob was closing on the bungalow.

We'd been spotted.

'Right,' I said. 'We've got what we came for. Let's go.'

But as we turned to leave, Callum started going on about his dog. He had left it behind in the house when the rioters came. It was running about in the back garden, whining. He said he couldn't just leave it there. It had to come with us. 'We don't have time to rescue your dog,' I told him. 'We've got to get ourselves out. Now!' I took his arm, but he pulled away from me and ran outside. 'Grab him!' I shouted. Someone got hold of him and brought him back. Outside, the sound of chanting was getting louder and louder. There was the sound of another window smashing close by. 'Callum,' I said, 'get in the vehicle, now!'

'My dog! My dog!' he wailed.

The back door of the bungalow was hanging off its hinges. Through the opening, I saw a scabby little mutt sniffing about in the muck. I pointed. 'Is that your dog?' I asked.

'Yes,' he said. 'That's it.' Telling the lads outside I was about to fire, I raised the Colt Commando and put a single round through the animal's head. 'There,' I said. 'You don't need to worry about him any more. Now get in the car.'

There was a huge ugly crowd outside the house, chanting, calling and waving bottles and sticks. Everything about their faces and movements told me they were watching for their chance to rush us. We climbed into the lead Range Rover. Chris told me that when I had fired, they had fallen back a few feet. But now, as we got in, they shuffled forward again, egging each other on. They looked angry, and very, very hungry. As we drove off, they ran after us, flinging stones and shouting abuse.

On the way back to the embassy, Callum suddenly yelled, '*You shot my dog!*' The shock had delayed his reaction.

I turned to him. 'Look,' I said, 'I'm sorry, I really am. I had a dog of my own once. But we were in big trouble back there. I couldn't take the risk.'

Callum had another dog inside the embassy compound, a blind one. He was a real animal-lover. I had that shot the same day. I'd ban all diplomats from keeping pets. They're more trouble than they're worth. The pets, that is.

On our return Chris Ryan was edgy and upset, which was unlike him. I went to see him, to find out what was up. We shouldn't have been out there today, he said. There was no point. All we got was a pair of trousers.

'It wasn't just the trousers, Chris. We went for the docs, and to get better information. If we're stuck in here all the time, we've no idea of what's going on. We know a lot more now and so does the ambassador.'

He was quiet for a while.

'It was necessary, Chris.'

'OK, yes, OK. I'm still edgy from the Gulf.'

'No worries.' But I *was* worried. I'd have to keep an eye on him.

I still felt we didn't have enough boats so I took my team down to the nearby marina, which was still under protection. There was a nice nine metre moored up there, with big twin outboards hanging off it. I requisitioned it in the name of the Queen – mooring it with the Americans, who would bring it round for us if need be.

Next day, Roger Westbrook had an audience with the Zaïrian prime minister. We drove up to his compound in the Jaguar and the Range Rover. I was acting as close protection officer (CPO) for the ambassador himself, with Tim and Mark making up the rest of the bodyguard (BG). We carried Colt Commandos, loaded and locked, and the pistols. We kept the longs out of sight, in bags on the seats; the pistols we had holstered, as always. We had full communications on us and all the medical kit: in this environment I was taking no chances.

Driving through the streets of the capital, we saw groups of mutinous, drunken soldiers roaming around, stopping people at gunpoint, robbing, beating and even killing them. Shots rang out as we passed the market area. We reached the prime minister's compound. At first, as the great iron gates swung shut behind us, I felt a wave of relief. Normally, once you're inside a diplomatic enclave you can assume it's safe. But this country was one of the world's most corrupt police states. I took one look around me and saw it wasn't even remotely safe. The prime minister's personal bodyguards were lounging about in the shade, wearing dark sunglasses and looking for all the world like tin-pot thugs for some superannuated Third-World dictator. That's because they *were* tin-pot thugs for a superannuated Third-World dictator. As we drove in, they got to their feet. It was like a scene from that film *The Comedians*. What wasn't so funny was that they had their weapons up – and pointed at us. Not surprisingly, I was unhappy about this. They might not intend to kill us, but the way they were handling those AK-47s there was every chance that one of them would loose off an ND (negligent discharge), which would kill equally as well as a deliberately aimed shot.

'Be aware, sir,' I warned, putting myself between him and the idiots. 'Do exactly as I say.'

One of the goons detached himself from the group and came swaggering forward. He was a big man, acting the part of an even bigger one. Approaching at an angle so he could cut us off, he kept the muzzle of his rifle trained on us as we walked. My priority now was to get the ambassador inside the building, fast: if he wasn't safe inside with the prime minister, then there was no hope for us, we'd better turn round and go back. The rest of the guards were watching and shouting encouragement to their pal. I was right up on Roger's left shoulder, with my body between him and them; Chris Ryan was on his right.

This meeting had been arranged a while ago, and confirmed that same morning. There was no call for any of this tough-guy act. I could feel myself starting to get annoyed.

As we came up to the main entrance of the mansion, the big body-guard stepped in front of us, blocking our path. Keeping the rifle trained on my gut, he gave me the hard-man stare. We stopped. I stared back at him. His eyeballs were bloodshot and there was a flat, drunken, stupid look in his eyes. He stood there, daring us to move. I thought, there's no way I'm going to reason with him.

I drew my pistol fast, flicked it round in my hand, and struck him as hard as I could on the breast-bone with the butt. He staggered back a pace. I stepped in after him and hit him again, then a third time. The gun-butt made a dull, thick sound on his sternum. His eyes opened wide with shock. He stepped back about five paces and I moved with him, the pistol rammed down hard into his chest, its muzzle pointing right up his nose, forcing him back further and further away from the ambassador.

From the corner of my eye, I could see Chris hurrying Roger towards the doorway. I flicked the pistol back round in my hand and stuck it in the goon's face. Now he would know what it felt like to be staring down the barrel of a live weapon.

'Keep your distance,' I told him. 'Step back, and stay away!'

His weapon drooped. Nobody dared argue with the presidential guard. They were Mobutu's chosen, his special boys: the whole country lived in fear of them. But here was a white man who had raised a hand against him. As the goon stood there, open-mouthed, I caught up with Roger and Chris, took the ambassador's arm and stepped into the mansion with him. I glanced across at Chris. He looked composed and well on top.

There were more armed guards in the large vestibule, but they looked sober and a lot more disciplined than the rabble outside. We went up the stairs to the prime minister's office. 'Do you want me to stay with you?' I asked Roger. In his place, I'd have wanted some-body with me at all times.

'I bloody do,' he replied, with a wry smile. 'But I think I'd better go in alone, don't you? The meeting was supposed to be in private.'

'Fair enough,' I said. 'We're right outside the door if you need us.'

On the way back out we had no trouble at all.

★

During all this the ambassador still had his duties to perform, as well as he could under the circumstances, ranging from further visits and meetings to entertaining in his residence. When we had the chance we sat for hours with him, discussing all sorts of subjects and sipping Earl Grey tea. He was a cultured man who valued what we had to say. I learned a lot about the world and its ways from our conversations.

Roger had a long-standing injury to his knee, which needed further medical attention, and finally London made the decision to pull him out. It seemed to us on the ground that we should just pull out with him. We had been there six weeks. Except for the fact that we were safeguarding British Crown property, which wasn't really an SAS task, no one was achieving anything. Almost all regular embassy business had been suspended. We BG'd Roger out to the airfield, chartered a DC-3 from a South African, and I sent a two-man team with him to Brazzaville until he was on board the flight to the UK. I was glad to get him out of there in one piece, but sad to see him go.

They sent a woman down to replace Roger Westbrook, a first secretary.

Things were bad again the next morning: a big mob came down to the gates. Whenever this happened we crashed out and 'manned the barricades', which meant we went to the perimeter fences, showed the crowd we were armed and pointed at the signs reading: 'Anyone entering these premises without permission will be shot.' We were long past the stage of keeping a low profile.

Chris Ryan became edgy again, showing signs of post-traumatic stress. I'd worried whether he had been ready for this trip, and had asked him privately what he thought before including him. He had said he was over it. But as time went on, with no sign of the tension lessening in Kinshasa, he started snapping a bit, in a way that was quite out of character. I had ignored this, hoping to give him enough space and time to sort himself out. But now he was worrying me. I thought he needed out.

As luck would have it, he was due to go to Buckingham Palace to get his Military Medal for bravery from the Queen. At the same time, I wanted to reduce the numbers in the embassy still further by sending home the young female communications officer. I discussed this with the incoming first secretary and with Captain James, and we agreed that the best thing was for Chris to escort her home.

No sooner had those two gone than the FCO, having left us to stew for nine weeks, at last decided to pull us out, replacing us with an eight-man Royal Military Police team to protect the embassy buildings from damage. The physical protection of our embassies and consulates throughout the world is one of the Military Police's special-ized tasks. As soon as they had taken over, we would go back.

'That's fine,' I sent back to the FCO and Hereford, 'but if the crunch comes during the changeover, we haven't got space on the boats to evacuate any extra people. So only send people in as we get them out.' As always, the FCO ignored this message, and sent out four Military Police on the next flight. We had a few days of danger-ous overlap before the final order to evacuate came through.

We still weren't quite out of the woods: no sooner had our old Dakota taken off than the port engine started to cough and splutter. Inspecting it out of the window, I could see that it was long past its sell-by date, and in need of immediate retirement: it was starting then stopping again, and there was a big plume of oily black smoke pour-ing out of it. The starboard engine didn't look all that healthy either. As it lost airspeed, the ancient aircraft began weaving and wallowing in the sky.

Marvellous, I thought. We survive ten weeks of Zaïre, only to die in a flying antique. Miraculously, the pilot nursed this crate on to the deck across the river in Brazzaville – but only just.

We got everyone on the scheduled flight home out of Brazzaville the next day without any more drama, apart from the usual menacing demands for money from the Congolese customs officers. It wasn't until I saw the bright blue Mediterranean under our wings a few hours later that I felt the immense weight of Zaïre lift away from me. Until that moment, I hadn't understood how great that pressure had been.

Later the FCO asked me to give a presentation in London about my experience of their management in Zaïre. This was a turn-up for the books – and I jumped at the chance. I gave them chapter and verse of where they were going wrong, concentrating especially on the deaf-ear syndrome we'd been at the end of for so long. My remarks didn't please some of the mandarins, but I could see that I was getting through. Then I made my report to Hereford. In the wake of these briefings, the whole FCO/SAS relationship changed. The Regiment's senior management told their FCO counterparts in no uncertain terms that if they wanted to use the SAS for any more work of the kind we'd just done in Zaïre, then they must listen to, and immediately act on, our local advice. Otherwise they could find someone else to guard their diplomats. Life in the SAS is far from being all action. The Regiment does a lot of low-key work of the kind we'd done in Zaïre, protecting the interests of the British government as and when required. It helps to have proper support. The SAS had moved with the times, becoming a modern, professional and adaptable organization. Other organizations needed to move with it.

I went back to Hereford. It was time to deal with Stuart's death. Tracy had been to the funeral and done all she could, and now I went to see Sue. Tears in my eyes, I knelt by the grave of a close friend, touched the ground where his head would be, and said farewell.

It was time to hand over the troop, which I'd been leading for two years, and move on to Training Wing, which is one of those jobs you have to do at a certain point in the Regiment to get promotion.

The troop decided to give me a farewell send-off in a restaurant in downtown Hereford. We had about reached the end of the speeches, official and off-the-cuff, when the manager asked if we would mind two more people joining us in our privately booked room. They wanted to have dinner but the restaurant was full. 'Let them come,' I told him. 'The more the merrier.' Two men came in, sat down, and ordered their dinner. There was nothing particularly remarkable about them, so we got on with the festivities. But I did notice them noticing us a bit too much. After a little while they sent a bottle of champagne over to our table. We were quite happy to receive free champagne, especially in our by now pretty inebriated state. But it seemed a bit strange, on reflection, champagne from strangers – so we sent them a bottle of bubbly back.

They sent over a second bottle.

At this, I nudged Andy McNab, who was sitting next to me. He got up and wandered over to their table.

'Hi, guys,' he said. 'Thanks for the champagne. What's the score?'

'Well,' they replied, 'obviously we sussed who you were. We just wanted to buy you boys some champagne. Gulf War and all that.'

'What do you do?' Andy asked, giving them the look.

'Oh, we're *Sun* reporters,' one replied.

Andy took a big mental step backwards at this. His face hardened. Totally unfazed, they grinned at him. 'It's all right,' said one. 'We're not here to stitch you guys up – honest. We're here to cover the murder – you know, the body found under the floorboards in Gloucester the other day?'

Bastards, we thought. They bloody *are* here for us. This drink-up will be all over the *Sun* tomorrow morning – 'SAS in drunken orgy'. And we'll be identified. But we were wrong. The *Sun* reporters were as good as their word. Nothing happened.

I'd come to the end of one of the best jobs I'd ever had in the Regiment. During the time I'd been running the troop we had been on operations almost continuously. Anything new, I felt, was going to be an anti-climax. Running stores and training, though it's one of those necessary stepping-stones, had to be a big come-down. This was not helped by the banter, which was of the 'Hello, Blanket-stacker' type once the news got out. But there were compensations: in theory, although there were still two eight-week jungle trips to be run annually, the Training Wing job should mean I'd get more time at home, and be able to lead a more normal kind of life with Natalie and with Tracy, for the first time ever.

Training Wing is usually a two-year tour of duty, but after about eight months in the job I was called in by the adjutant. He told me I was being promoted to sergeant-major as of then, and posted second-in-command of the Counter-revolutionary Warfare (CRW) department.

This was the job I'd always wanted. CRW is one of the most prestigious jobs in the Regiment, with the responsibility for national VIP protection and counter-terrorism. But while I was really happy about the new job, Tracy was less so. She asked if this would mean me being away more. 'No, no,' I assured her, 'nothing like that. If anything, I'll be around more. No more eight-week jungle trips.'

Twelve hours later, I was on a plane bound for Waco, Texas.

Chapter Twenty-eight

David Koresh, self-styled Messiah and leader of a religious cult known as the Branch Davidians, was the kind of person I would normally go a long way to avoid. Now, like many misguided people before me, I was half-way across the world, trying to get as close to him as possible. Only in my case it was a matter of duty.

Koresh and ninety-five followers, forty-six of them children, had been holed up in their Mount Carmel ranch complex, just outside Waco, Texas, since 28 February 1993. On that day the US government's Bureau of Alcohol, Tobacco and Firearms (ATF) launched a raid to inspect the cult's stockpiles of weaponry. Documents in the ATF's possession showed that Koresh had spent almost $200,000 on weapons and ammunition in the eighteen months to February. A United Parcel Service driver said he had delivered two cases of hand grenades to 'Ranch Apocalypse', as Koresh styled the place, as well as large quantities of gunpowder, all of which was in clear breach of Federal firearms legislation. Koresh, though, had refused point-blank to let the ATF men anywhere near the ranch complex so that they could verify what the cult held.

As they went in, the ATF assault force had come under massive fire, much of it from heavy automatic weapons, including .50-calibre Brownings and M-60 machine-guns

The ensuing gun-battle lasted for an hour, the longest firefight in US law enforcement history. Four of the Federal agents were shot dead, and sixteen wounded. Six of the cult members were killed, and Koresh himself was hit.

Barry Coles, the squadron OC, was with me on the flight. We were half expecting the siege to be over by the time we got there. To keep up with developments we tuned into latest news bulletins at Dulles International, where we refuelled, and then at Dallas, Texas. There were plenty of them: the Waco siege had gripped not just America but the whole world.

The security agencies of friendly Western nations have long-standing reciprocal agreements whereby they can attend one another's major terrorist incidents to observe, to learn and, when requested, to give advice. On taking over responsibility for CRW, I had systematically set about beefing up the Regiment's contacts with all Western security and Special Forces agencies. Wherever possible, I made it my business to get to know their leadership personally. When a major incident took place, I wanted to be there and learn from it. We arrived in Waco on 3 March, three days after that first abortive assault.

We had come willing to watch and learn. We would leave wishing we had been able to advise.

Waco is a small, sleepy town lying about a hundred miles south of Dallas, on the banks of the River Brazos, known by the first Spanish settlers as 'the arms of God' because they thought it so beautiful. This is cowboy and Indian country, home to the Texas Ranger Museum and Hall of Fame, a land of flat prairies patrolled by circling buzzards.

Waco doesn't run to much in the way of accommodation, and when we got there the town was already filled to the gills with Federal and State agents, scores of media people, and a clutch of Biblical scholars brought in to decipher the arcane, Apocalyptic ramblings of David Koresh. Finally we found a room in a motel about thirty kilometres away from the scene of the action.

As a result of the ATF's perceived failure, the FBI's élite Hostage Rescue Team (HRT), had taken over responsibility for the crisis. Under US law, no military forces are allowed to deploy within three miles of the American coast, which is why the FBI was in control and not US Special Forces.

It is fair to say that the HRT, roughly equivalent to the SO19 branch of the Metropolitan Police, is generally deployed as an aggressive force, mostly concerned with bank robberies, kidnaps and the like, where hostages have been taken. With the HRT came the FBI's hostage negotiation team, whose priority, of course, was to negotiate a peaceful surrender.

By the time we arrived the HRT had set up three forward operating bases (FOBs) around the complex: Sierra-1, Sierra-1 Alpha, and Sierra 2. The negotiation team, meanwhile, set up shop in a hangar on a USAF base some eight kilometres away. The physical distance between the two teams, I quickly discovered, was symbolic: their agendas were entirely different.

This was not a standard hostage situation. No one was sure whether Koresh was delusional, living in a parallel universe of his own creation, or whether he was just a manipulative con-man. Certainly, he was resourceful, cunning, and exerted an iron grip on his followers: as in most cults, they had surrendered all their personal possessions and wealth to their leader. And as again was often the case, their leader used food as a weapon to keep his acolytes in line, threatening members who deviated in the slightest way with the prospect of starvation. If that didn't work, the recalcitrant were taken to a utility area known as the 'spanking room', where they were held down and beaten on the backside by a chosen disciple (form an orderly queue) with a wooden oar inscribed, 'IT IS WRITTEN'.

For light entertainment, Koresh had a rock band in the place, the Mighty Men, of which he, of course, was the leading light. And while every other male in the place was kept celibate in the downstairs rooms, Koresh used their wives and daughters for his sexual pleasure on the floor above. In theory, people could leave the compound whenever they pleased. In practice, Koresh and his trusted lieutenants made sure they didn't.

On the inside, as I saw it, David Koresh was a living god; on the outside, he would be sent directly to jail for the murder of Federal agents. What was in surrender for him? The Branch Davidians had their own water, food and plenty of ammunition. And they were prepared for the Apocalypse – Koresh preached it on a daily basis. The Sixth Book of Revelation was his favourite reading matter.

It might, I thought, be a long siege.

The morning after our arrival, we drove out to the site. The FBI negotiators were getting first bite at resolving the situation. The Mount Carmel compound loomed up out of the bleak, flat Texas landscape, a set of wooden-frame buildings with long two- and three-storey pitched-roof blocks arranged loosely around a tall rectangular central tower, a bit like an overgrown watch-tower. Beneath the tower was a bunker, where weapons and ammunition were kept.

As far as the eye could see, there were shiny aluminium mobile homes, driven up and parked anywhere and everywhere in the surrounding scrub by hopeful gawpers; there were at least three dozen TV satellite uplink trunks, 500 journalists and TV crew, plus catering trucks that had arrived to feed them. We drove in through the outer press cordon. This area was a massive circus. One man was selling T-shirts bearing the hastily printed legend: 'WACO – We Ain't Coming Out.'

The first thing Barry Coles and I noticed was the confusion between the various agencies. This was especially marked in the stand-off between the negotiation team and the HRT proper. In the UK, the various agencies, which include the Cabinet Office, the FCO, the SIS, MI5, the Special Forces Directorate, and the emergency services, are closely integrated. This is because we stage regular 'remounts', or combined exercises, which deliberately test the command and control system to its limits. In the US, we discovered, co-operation between the various governmental bodies was at best patchy, and there was far more inter-agency rivalry. In theory, the local FBI agent in charge (AIC) had overall command.

In a windowless room at the back of the hangar we were introduced to a stocky, muscular man called Bill, who had had an idea: Koresh liked the sound of his own voice; he believed he had a mission to convert. As we waited, he struck a deal with Koresh whereby for every two minutes' air time Koresh got to rant on the local radio station, two children were released from the ranch. It worked. A number of small children duly came out. For the negotiators, this was a good start. But the sight of these little tots, who came into the hangar where we were sitting and spoke to their mothers on the phone, brought home as sharply as it could to every one of us there just how important it was to get the rest of the kids out. All of them.

Hoping to build on this initial success, Bill next offered Koresh air time on a national channel, in return for more releases, including the remaining children. Again, Koresh agreed, and Bill had one of his team get the cult-leader dictate the agreement, word by word, over the telephone. The broadcast went out. Steve Schneider, Koresh's deputy, called to say the children all had their coats on and their bags packed, and were standing in the main hallway waiting to go. The FBI sent in the buses. Koresh reneged on his word. Not a single person was released.

'God told me to wait,' Koresh claimed.

At this point, the HRT proper became involved. So far they had failed to establish a perimeter around the ranch. This was now rectified, and the complex surrounded. Tanks and APCs rolled up. The senior HRT commander made an initial recce, driving right round the complex looking for the best places to position them. He decided on two locations, the first at Sierra-2, to the north of the complex, and the second to the south-west at Sierra-1 Alpha. In this kind of situation, the SAS team on site would immediately devise a set of detailed plans, the 'actions on', aimed at covering every conceivable crisis contingency. These were written down and agreed by the commanders with responsibility on the spot. The FBI had no such contingency plans. Instead, just to be going on with, an HRT leader sent in a tank to crush one of the Davidian guard-posts.

This aggressive action infuriated the negotiation team. They felt aggression at this early stage only made the cult members draw closer together, and become more volatile. The gap between the two sides widened.

Koresh stopped talking. A day later, the HRT offered him six gallons of milk in return for the release of two kids. The Messiah's reply was, 'Kiss my ass.' The HRT sent in the milk anyway. They had implanted tiny listening devices inside every carton, and each of the Styrofoam cups that went in with it. The bugs worked. One ended up in Koresh's own room. Now we could hear what was being said on the inside.

Time was passing. In this kind of crisis, there's what's known as the 'ten-day rule': if you haven't resolved matters within ten days, you're in deep, deep trouble. The longer your tactical forces sit around burning adrenaline with nothing to do but eat pizza and kick their heels, the less chance there is that any action will be successful. On day ten, at my suggestion, the AIC switched off the electricity supply to the compound. That night, the temperature fell to 20° Fahrenheit (-6°C) 'What about the kids?' someone asked. The next day the AIC switched it back on. They were sending confused messages.

Then the negotiators asked Koresh to make a home movie, which he did, milking the opportunity by parading a succession of good-looking, intelligent children to camera, exploiting their innocence, while giving away nothing useful about himself. One thing we noticed, though, from the video: the children had clean hair, so the cult members weren't worried about water.

On day thirteen, Janet Reno was appointed US attorney-general, taking over as head of the Justice Department, which oversees the FBI, and inheriting a poisoned chalice. It struck me that Koresh was holding the negotiators hostage: they were stuck there for ever, cut off even from the HRT, while he dictated events. And, like the HRT, as every day went by, they grew more frustrated and demoralized.

For the next few days, the HRT and the negotiators took it in turns to break the deadlock, the HRT by using Psyops – in this case the aggressive use of incredibly loud, weird music – the negotiators by staging a face-to-face between Steve Schneider, the Koresh trusty, and two of their own leaders. Nothing worked – Koresh played louder, weirder music back.

Then, on 21 March, in a surprise move, seven more adults left Ranch Apocalypse of their own volition. The negotiators saw this as a breakthrough, a sign that the cult members wanted to deal. But on that same day the AIC sent in the tanks to crush the cars and motorbikes parked in front of the ranch. The remaining Davidians – and the hostage negotiation team – were furious.

At last, twenty-three days into the siege, the negotiators admitted defeat, and wrote a report counselling the use of tear gas. Reno, a long-standing champion of children's rights, thought this too aggressive, that it might lead to children suffering permanent damage. For five days, the FBI wrestled with the attorney-general. Finally, on

16 April, and apparently persuaded by someone inside the FBI that the kids were suffering physical and sexual abuse, she approved the 568-page assault plan.

In essence, the plan was simple. I saw a summary not long before it went ahead. Just before dawn on the given day, three combat engineer vehicles (CEVs) – battering rams mounted on tank hulls – would break through the walls of the complex simultaneously at three separate points. Over the next forty-eight hours, they would insert the CS gas. And the Branch Davidians would meekly come out.

Despite its enormous length, the assault plan was full of holes. What would happen if Koresh started to kill his followers? What would be their emergency response? Supposing they didn't come out? We were forty days plus into a siege here: these were determined people. What if they had gas masks, and sat tight?

Then there was the question of fire. The complex was built of tinder-dry pinewood, plasterboard and tar-paper. Since we had been there, I had become uncomfortably aware of the strong winds that prevailed across the open plain. If a fire started, the FBI could have a major problem on their hands. Was there a fire-protection plan in the document?

Understandably civilian fire services will refuse to go in if there's a chance of getting shot, so, as a specialist unit, you have to work out some way of dealing with the fire yourself. Since taking over the CT team, I had bought our own special breathing apparatus and made sure everyone in the assault team was trained in using it.

How were they going to clear the ranch of booby-traps and bombs if they did go in? How would they get their bomb-disposal team in?

To be fair to the FBI, the chain of command was by now extremely muddled. The politicians wanted minimum force. Fair enough. But for a Special Forces team there comes a point at which you have to say, 'This is the minimum force we will need to win. If you won't allow us to use that level of force, then we can't help you.'

Hereford asked for my operational assessment. I told them that while the FBI had this plan it was anyone's guess as to when they might use it. The ops desk decided that if there was no sign of any immediate action there was no point my staying in Waco. I was told to return.

I had been back in the UK only a few days when I got a fast-ball: 'Get back on the plane to Waco.' It was a Sunday night. The assault was scheduled to go in over the next forty-eight hours.

It went in earlier than we had expected, at 6 a.m. the next morning, on Monday 18 April, while I was still on my way to the scene. There was a strong prairie wind blowing when the State Troopers went round the homes in the locality of Ranch Apocalypse, warning people to 'expect some noise'. The HRT negotiators called through their loudspeakers one last time for Koresh and his disciples to surrender peacefully. When there was no response, they called the ranch and told Koresh exactly where the tear gas was going to come in so that they could move all the children out of harm's way. The effects of tear gas on small children are not predictable.

Koresh – or one of his followers – ripped the phone out of the wall and threw it out of the front door. At that the HRT sent in the CEVs. The big steel rams went through the wooden walls as if they weren't there and the gas went in. No one ran out. The FBI had ignored a local Waco weather advisory that morning, warning of a 30 m.p.h. wind. This blew up before the assault went in – and propelled the gas straight back out of the building.

The Branch Davidians started shooting at the CEVs from the windows, sending sparks up in showers from the steel hulls. Koresh had placed bales of hay in many of the rooms, and fire broke out. Within a minute it had taken firm hold. It raced through the building, driving the cult members before it. A man appeared on the roof, clothes blazing. Rolling in pain, he fell to the ground, where he was dragged to an armoured vehicle. Orange flames shot up everywhere into the sky, topped with huge columns of black smoke. The building was rocked by explosions. And still no one came out.

The assault team tried to get gas into the underground bunker under the central tower, to stop anyone barricading themselves inside. They failed. All the women and children in there died.

Only nine of the ninety-five people inside the compound when

269

the attack went in survived the blaze. All the children died. It took a week for the wreckage to cool down.

Later I spoke to a number of the FBI assaulters. None of the local civilian fire services was alerted before the final assault. Six minutes after the fire had started, the Waco firefighters arrived on the scene, but the AIC kept them back in case of shooting.

A short time later, the big Congressional (and media) debrief got under way in Washington.

Fingers were pointed at the FBI. Why, after a siege lasting fifty-one days, had they finally decided on the assault? Had there ever been any real negotiations between the two sides, and if not, why not? (There clearly had been.) Why hadn't anyone tried to speak to Koresh in his own language, the language of the Book of Revelation, and in particular the passage about the Seven Seals, which he apparently knew by heart? What truth was there in the FBI's claim that an agent had seen a cult member deliberately starting the fire? (This was proven, at least to my satisfaction, by the overhead infra-red video evidence taken from a helicopter.) Was there any substance at all to FBI claims of child abuse inside the ranch, claims that had been instrumental in getting Janet Reno's approval to go in with the gas and the CEVs? (Most likely not.)

It's easy to accuse with hindsight. It's a lot less simple to see what else the FBI could have done. Four agents had been shot dead by the men inside. They couldn't just walk away from that.

Chapter Twenty-nine

Back in Hereford, my promotion to Warrant Officer, First Class, was confirmed and I received my Royal Warrant. Not many soldiers achieve this promotion; normally the colonel of the Regiment presents you with it on parade. Mine arrived in the internal mail. Not a problem; I'd received medals this way before, as had lots of others. The warrant is normally on watermarked parchment paper with coloured stencilling, hand-written details and the Royal Seal. It is signed by the Secretary of State for Defence in person. It's something to be proud of, to have framed and to be placed on the wall. Rifkind was now the Secretary. Mine was on parchment paper, but all the details were typed. Even Rifkind's signature was photocopied; he was too busy to sign it. Stuff him and his warrant – I sent it back in disgust.

I was watching television at home one evening. Tracy had left, apparently for good, fed up with never seeing me and with my attitude, which was the same as my father's had been: the Regiment always came first. Just as I was getting up to make some coffee, the programme was interrupted by a sudden newsflash: the announcer said that a CH-47 *en route* from Northern Ireland to Scotland had crashed on a Scottish mountain. That was it – the bare event, no details of any deaths or injuries. But straight away I had a bad feeling which by now I recognized all too well: the feeling that someone I knew and cared about had been killed.

Only a few days previously I had been back in Northern Ireland, spending some time with Ian Phoenix and his wife, Sue. He was due over in the UK for a top-level security meeting. Sue was coming across on her own by ferry, Ian planned to join her later. They were going to holiday in the West Country and Wales, staying at my place for a few days.

I rang Sue. 'Is the boy there?' I asked.

'Yes,' she replied, sounding tense and distracted. 'I'll get him.'

Thank fuck, I thought. Thank fuck for that. But then I heard Sue shouting for her son, to come on the line. 'No, no,' I said, when she returned. 'I meant Ian. Is Ian there?'

'No,' Sue replied. After a long pause, she added, 'He was on that helicopter. No one knows what's happened yet.'

'I'll get off the phone,' I said. 'But, Sue, if you hear anything, will you let me know?'

'Of course,' she said, sadly. 'Of course I will.'

But as I put the phone down I already knew. The Phoenix was dead.

Ian had left me a message on my answer-machine the day before the flight saying that he and Sue would be down to visit after the meetings in Scotland (a message I still have). At his funeral, I walked with him for the last time, proud to be one of the bearers who carried him down the long gravel drive from his door to the waiting hearse. That evening, Sue and I stood by the embers of the fire she had built in their back garden, with a glass of champagne, looking out over the sea to the Mull of Kintyre where he had died. We both looked skyward. It was a clear, starlit night. As we watched, a bright object trailed across the heavens towards Scotland and the Mull. I held Sue a little tighter and said, 'That's the Phoenix on his Pegasus.'

'Yes, it is,' said Sue. We raised our glasses, and drank a toast to him.

It wasn't until October 1995 that I finally said goodbye to Ian, when I visited the crash site with Sue. She showed me the exact place where he had been killed. I knelt down, touched the ground where he had lain and said goodbye.

After Tracy left – and Ian died – I was badly upset for the best part of a year. I couldn't sleep, I kept telling myself I should have had a better attitude, it was all my fault, and all that. But when it came right down to it I simply missed her. Natalie and my long-standing friends were supportive, devising things to cheer me up, but I needed something to occupy my mind.

Reflecting on what had happened over in Waco, and concerned that I might one day find myself in a similar position, negotiating for people's lives, I asked for, and was offered, a place on the Metropolitan Police negotiator's course, at the Police Training College at Hendon, in West London.

A major part of my job as second-in-command of CRW was to be the interface between the police and the CT team so it made sense if I understood police procedure and thinking, especially in a siege where hostages had been taken and where their lives might be in the balance. I completed the course successfully, and enjoyed every minute of it. The excellent training I was given at Hendon came in useful much sooner than anyone could have imagined, in West Africa.

In November 1994, two British VSO workers were taken hostage in the former British colony of Sierra Leone. By 9 February 1995, a total of seventeen foreign nationals had been snatched and were being held in the remote, dense bush of north-central Sierra Leone by the rebel Revolutionary United Front (RUF), under the leadership of Foday Sankoh, a former Sierra Leone Army corporal who had mounted a coup against the government.

Among the mainly German, Swiss and British hostages were seven Catholic nuns, six Italians and a Brazilian. Most of the male hostages had been working for Sierra Rutile, Sicromco, or one of the other large mining companies. For some months the International Committee for the Red Cross (ICRC) had been trying to negotiate the release of these hostages, but its task was being made difficult by Sankoh never having explained why he had taken these hostages in the first place, or what he expected to achieve from their continued detention. Also he was difficult to contact, always on the move, and he did not, in any event, seem to want to strike any deal.

Since a number of the hostages were British nationals, the British High Commission in the capital, Freetown, was automatically

273

involved in efforts to support them and effect their release. As part of these efforts the FCO decided to send a specialist four-man Metropolitan Police hostage-negotiating team to Sierra Leone, not necessarily to take over direct negotiations with the rebels but to see what it could do to help the ICRC team with that responsibility. The FCO also decided that a two-man SAS team should go to Sierra Leone to carry out feasibility studies for a possible military option. The police negotiators and, if the rebels succeeded in winning power, the British High Commission would also benefit from the extra protection.

The Directorate of Special Forces (DSF) in London sent the request through to Hereford, where I was asked to head the op. I chose a man called 'Dave' to go in with me.

The police negotiating team was a very professional group. They were staying in a hotel, rather than in the consulate, so they were seen by the rebels as neutral. Given that one of our tasks was to protect the team, I suggested to the FCO that Dave and I move in with them. This was vetoed by the FCO. We were told to stay in the High Commission 'because it would save money'.

I pointed out that, while it might be cheaper, it made no kind of operational sense. The FCO replied that I was being 'alarmist'. Ian Cluney, the High Commissioner, supported me. Telexes flew. With breakfast thrown in, the rooms in the hotel in question cost ten pounds a night each – twenty pounds a night for the entire SAS presence. Too much, said the FCO.

Ian Cluney was a switched-on man who used us constantly to provide military analysis and to advise the police team on crisis-management options. But some of the junior officials didn't want to know. If a British citizen came into the Commission in need of help, their attitude seemed to be that he or she was a nuisance, to be resisted and, if possible, ignored.

Dave and I needed transport to carry out our reconnaissance missions. They gave us the two oldest vehicles they had, with no radios fitted and dodgy brakes. Meanwhile, the junior officials had appropriated the new Land Rover Discoverys to go shopping and see their mates.

I called a meeting to put them in the picture: we were there on official business; our recce and protection tasking had priority over their shopping: therefore, the two best radio-equipped Land Rovers would be left on permanent standby for our exclusive use so that we could go straight to the assistance of the police team if they called for help. Not a popular move but then we weren't there to be popular.

As I was doing a recce near the main Army command centre later that day I suddenly heard a sound that stopped me dead in my tracks. *Whop, whop, whop, whop, whop* . . . Only one thing made that sound. I slowed to a crawl, gripping the steering-wheel in dread. It couldn't be. Looking up, I saw a Hind D helicopter gunship, nose down in the attack mode, thundering towards me. I pulled off the road and jumped from the vehicle. As I did so the Hind flew overhead and landed in the Sierra Leone Army camp. For a few long seconds, I thought I was in the grip of a waking nightmare, a post-traumatic flashback. I got down by the side of the wheel and sat there, head in my hands, seeing the man buried alive in the earth, the horror on the face of Sméagol, the shattered body of the Sparrow, hearing the roar of the rotor-blades and the cannon, the smash of the rockets hammering down.

I had no idea how long it was before I came back to myself, how long it was before I drove off. But every time I saw that thing out there I had the same total recall.

With the rebels mainly in the north and east the British commission wasn't under any immediate threat, but Freetown was in chaos as a result of the civil war. Many of its citizens had fled into the bush. They feared their own police and Army as much as any rebel incursion. There was a total breakdown of normal life. Both sides were killing, raping and mutilating innocent civilians. There was very little food. Small groups of famished looters roamed around, scavenging scraps from the rubbish. It was like Kinshasa, only on a smaller scale.

Complicating matters further was the presence of a mercenary force hired through a UK security company by one of the rutile mining firms with a view to liberating its employees by means of armed response. There were ex-Regiment men I recognized in this force, ex-Paras, and various others, all living in a complex on the edge of town. They had a barge filled with weapons anchored offshore, ready for the great hostage rescue operation. It was like something out of Frederick Forsyth, and just as dodgy.

There was also the best part of an ex-Gurkha battalion in Sierra Leone, working for the government, and they, too, were apparently preparing to go after Foday Sankoh, guns blazing, in the meantime sending out the odd patrol to keep the major roads open to traffic. The OC of this force was a man I'll call Rees. One day, Rees went off into the jungle with the Gurkhas and a senior member of Sierra Leone's government. I never did find out what they were trying to do, but they strayed up near to where the Catholic sisters were being held.

They got bumped by a large force of rebels. Rees and the diplomat were shot and went down. A British captain named Catesby was wounded as he tried to rescue Rees, and captured with him. Two Gurkha troopers were killed as, with great courage, they ran in to rescue their officers. Worse was to come. The force was beaten back by the overwhelming rebel firepower, leaving the prisoners stranded. Rees, who had been shot in the leg and the gut, was tortured. The rebels cut off his ears, disembowelled him while he was still alive, and then beheaded him. His head was paraded round the nearby villages as a totem – and a warning – for a few weeks. Captain Catesby's body was never found.

I would advise anyone against working as a mercenary soldier in West or Central Africa.

Although there was the need to gather intelligence, my main concern, aside from getting the hostages out, was to make sure nobody else was taken. I would only let the police team go up-country if I thought it absolutely vital to the negotiations. Then word came in that there was a chance of picking up some useful information on the hostages' whereabouts from a source in Bo, a town to the south-east of Freetown. It was too good a chance to miss: I agreed to escort the police and the MILO out there.

Some of the things I had already seen in Sierra Leone made me feel sick to the core. Sankoh's preferred method of operation was to attack a defenceless village, loot, pillage, burn and rape, torture captives who hadn't managed to run away in time, and round up all the children.

Children were of great military importance to the RUF leader: he used them as beaters. When he was launching an attack on the Army, he sent the children out ahead, armed only with sticks, to beat the undergrowth – on pain of death. The well-armed RUF men hung back behind the kids until they ran into opposition. If the Army opened fire, the rebels usually ran. If they didn't, the rebels went in past the kids and pressed home their attack. Children as young as six or seven were forced to 'fight' in this way. Sometimes, these little kids were given arms and, without any hope, traumatized by seeing their parents cut down, came to enjoy killing as much as the men who had pressed them into it in the first place.

Worse still was to come in Bo.

We flew across country in a chartered Russian Antonov, landing on a dirt strip used by the local mining company before the trouble started. The town, when we got to it, was a total shambles: all around the streets lay the hulks of APCs shattered by rebel rockets; most of the houses were shot through with shells and bullet-holes or simply flattened. But the worst thing was the bodies. Everywhere you looked, there were piles of dead people. Wild dogs swarmed over the heaps, tearing the flesh off the corpses in great chunks. In a few cases the dead had been hurriedly buried in shallow graves, but even these corpses weren't safe, the animals digging down frantically through the red earth to get at them. Small gangs of regular Army troops were in the town, threatening the few people left in it. The police team asked some of them if they could tell us anything about recent rebel activity, or the whereabouts and condition of the hostages. The locals were all too afraid to talk. Soon we understood why.

In the centre of the town, we came on a regular Army unit with a rebel they had just captured. Some of the soldiers were holding beer bottles. They had him on his knees, in the middle of the road, with his hands tied behind his back, kicking him and slapping him to make him talk. The man looked groggy from the beating they had given him. Except for a pair of ragged blue underpants he was naked. A small crowd of people was watching in a circle.

277

One of the soldiers had a machete. He caught hold of the prisoner's right ear, stretched it taut, and sliced it off. The rebel fell forward, shrieking. Rolling in the dust, he caught my eye. At once I was back in Afghanistan and saw the Russian staring up at me. I stepped back and looked away, with the same overwhelming feeling of powerlessness. There was no way we could stop what was happening. The soldiers were mean from drink and they outnumbered us twenty to one. If we tried to stop them, we would be into a major firefight.

They dragged the man back to his knees. He was babbling and wailing incoherently. Blood was gushing down the side of his neck and on to his shoulder. The severed ear lay on the ground in front of him, more food for the dogs. We had an interpreter with us, who said the man was giving out details of the rebel strongholds.

It was too late.

The soldier with the machete moved round, brought it up a second time, and slowly cut off the rebel's other ear. Then he grabbed the man's hair and forced his head right back. Taking great care to avoid the major arteries, he started to cut the man's throat. The rebel made a soft desperate choking sound. Tears rolled down his cheeks, mingling with the blood. I saw Sméagol again, with his thin face and his wicked knife. The soldier kept sawing. With the same cruel calculation, he increased the pressure on the blade so that it bit its way ever deeper into the flesh. At last, the blade sliced through one of the major arteries. A great gush of blood came out, spraying across the earth. The rebel slumped forward, twitched once, and died, his eyes fixed wide open, in an expression of eternal horror.

Here, in Sierra Leone, I had found a new heart of darkness.

From the soldiers, we learned that Foday Sankoh had split the hostages into two main groups: the Catholic nuns were in the group right up in the north-central part of the country; the rest were in the north-east, close to the border with Guinea. Sankoh had the camps organized something along the lines of an early British hill-fort, with layers of outworks defending an inner camp. This report confirmed the initial SAS recce: any military option was out – the hostages would be killed long before we could fight to the heart of the camp.

Negotiations with Sankoh over the hostages ebbed and flowed as the weeks went by. They were continually being compromised by the Italian chargé d'affaires. Because the six Catholic sisters were Italian nationals, this diplomat was privy to all our confidential intelligence briefs, including any direct radio conversations with Sankoh himself. Instead of keeping these discussions confidential, the chargé d'affaires was broadcasting them directly to the world's media in an attempt to take personal credit for the negotiations. We pointed out that Sankoh's reaction to this might be violent – he was at best an unpredictable character. When the diplomat persisted in leaking, we stopped him coming to the briefs. But at least Sankoh was talking, a breakthrough in itself. The prospects for release were beginning to look a little rosier.

Dave and I began scouting around the countryside around Freetown, looking for suitable places to land a C-130. On one of these trips out we heard of a French couple who had been cut off along the coast. They had two children and, with rebel activity in their neighbourhood, they were understandably desperate to get out: what Sankoh's men would do to them didn't bear thinking about. Although we had been briefed against taking such action, we couldn't just leave them there, so we took the Land Rovers and our weapons, drove through the rebel lines, found the stranded family and brought them back to Freetown. This was in no way heroic, we just felt we had to get it done, if only because we were there and we could.

About two days later, following negotiations in which I acted as number three man in the police negotiation team, Sankoh decided to let the nuns go. But he wanted the release to take place immediately, sooner than the Red Cross could arrange it. The Anglican bishop of Bo therefore volunteered to travel up to the release site near Sankoh's northernmost camp and bring the sisters out. The team wanted to go up-country by helicopter with him. I decided that it was too dangerous, with the rebels on the outskirts of the city, and if things could go wrong they would: the last time we had been up in Bo, the pilot, even though we had chartered the flight specially, had tried to leave us on the airstrip until he made a few extra dollars moving some locals. I had to put my gun in his face to make him change his mind.

As it was I had not needed to waste a bullet: a few days later the Antonov crashed killing everyone on board. (And a few days after that the Russian Hind D pilot was assassinated in the camp.)

But the Sisters came out safely. The Met team and I sat down with them to learn all we could about Sankoh's mind-set. Despite the humiliations and terror they had been through, the nuns were articulate – and goodness personified. I can only describe them as angels who had been in hell.

Sankoh now agreed to release the remaining hostages. We decided that releasing them into Liberia was out of the question. Charles Taylor's rebel National Patriotic Front for Liberia (NPFL) was active there, a group that was as bad if not worse than the RUF. Which left Guinea. A few days later, all the hostages were driven into that country and handed over to the ICRC.

I suggested to Hereford and to the police that Dave and I sit in on the main hostage debrief, find out how it had all happened, learn from the mistakes made, and so be in a better position to offer our own nationals informed security advice in similar situations. Hereford agreed. The police were more than happy. But the FCO told us there was no threat and to return. It was all about money.

When I came back from Sierra Leone, my spell as second-in-command of CRW was up, and I had to hand over. This brought home something I'd known for some time: my active days were over. From now on, only admin and training jobs would be open to me.

I decided to leave.

I informed the adjutant, who told the CO, a man I had known when he was my first troop officer. When the time came for me to leave, the CO was too busy to see me. I wasn't even dined out as was usual. I'd spent nearly twenty years in the SAS, leaving as a warrant officer, first class (WO1), and – nothing. Not even a thank-you. I'd expected to be shown a little more respect than that.

Since first setting out from home all those years ago to join the SAS, I had changed in ways I would never at the time have believed possible. And the Regiment had changed with me, shedding its dinosaur minority and, seen or unseen, moving to centre-stage in many of the world's most important events.

In my time, I had been part of a new wave that had stopped the Regiment promoting people into dead men's shoes. With others, I had tried to drive the SAS on to still greater professionalism, and encouraged it to embrace the new technology. It had changed from a low-tech, rather inward-looking, insular unit to something very much the opposite of that. It is impossible to spend the best part of twenty years in a unit as small as the SAS and not feel that you've had some positive influence on that process, especially if you've risen to senior rank.

I left the Regiment in better shape than it was in when I had joined it. It had been through a cultural, operational and technical revolution. It still wasn't perfect.

But it was the best in the world.

Chapter Thirty

―――――――――

I didn't look back, even though I could feel its stare over my right shoulder. There it stood, the clock-tower, brooding over the Regiment's dead, the long roll-call of men who had died on active service carved into its base. It had used up all its chances to add my name to the list. I walked out through the high-security barriers around the camp and away for the last time.

I had escaped. If anything, I felt respect from my old enemy, and it was a mutual respect. Many was the time I'd cursed that clock, as another friend's name was added to the list. Often, in theatres as far apart as Ulster and Afghanistan, I had thought it would be my turn. The Remembrance Day poppies looked beautiful and proud, yet somehow forlorn. They spoke of death.

I had walked through these same gates in August 1977 as a hopeful recruit, eager to do Selection. Now, nineteen and a half years on, at the top of the Regimental tree, I was leaving. I had won. I had beaten the clock.

The clock has stood marking the dead for as long as I can remember, a memorial to many a brave man.

It honours them all.

Epilogue

It was my first freelance job.

Before leaving the Regiment, I had worked with a certain Far Eastern power, training their Special Forces in marine counter-terrorism (MCT). Now, this country's government invited me back to advise on a large joint MCT exercise with other ASEAN pact members.

It was an attack on an oil rig out in the South China Sea, that for this exercise had been taken over by terrorists. I was in the cabin of the command helicopter, a UH-1H of the type I had grown to know and love in Colombia. As dawn was breaking we took off from the base. The four assault helicopters lifted clear of the runway first, eight MCT specialists in each, followed by the two sniper helicopters that would stand off on either side of the rig and provide covering fire as the assault went in. We took off last, with our gunship escort right behind us. Turning out to sea, we assembled at a prearranged rendezvous for the attack proper, dropping right down, hugging the surface of the sea to get below radar cover.

We closed on the rig. It was a clear morning, the flying fish scoring brief furrows across the millpond surface of the sea as they, too, became briefly airborne and then splashed down behind us.

We were standing off about two hundred metres from the main attack formation. Up front, the officer commanding the exercise was watching, and controlling, the flow of events. I was observing him. Something was worrying me: we were way too low. His job was to take an overview: there was no way we could see what was going on unless we gained height. Looking past the loadie and the radio operators, I tried to make out the commander's face. He was talking agitatedly to the pilot, telling him to get the Huey up, which got my vote. I leaned forward, watching our downdraught kick up the surface of the sea, a matter of inches away. I was in the rear right-hand well of the Huey's cabin, with my interpreter/driver directly behind me. There were two other men in the seats on the left-hand side opposite. Their faces were pinched and set, like my own. We were way, way too low.

The Huey bucked then, its nose coming right up. The tail rotor smacked down into the sea with a massive jolt. The engines screamed, the whole airframe shuddered. There was an ear-splitting *crack!* from behind as the tail section broke off. The impact threw me hard up against the Perspex window to my right. I remembered that if you whacked this window it was supposed to fall out: it was a safety feature. With the heel of my hand, I gave it everything I'd got. Nothing happened.

Everything was shaking, the whole machine was coming apart. Already, we were sinking. Spray was everywhere around us in a great cloud. There was a series of massive thuds as the rotor blades crunched into the sea, and then a roaring, grinding noise as the engine started chewing itself apart. We lurched to the right, capsized, and there was grey-green water right beside my face. I was wearing coveralls over my civilian clothes, and light shoes. Both the aircraft's main doors were open. Nobody was wearing a safety harness. None of us was wearing a life-vest. I wasn't carrying a knife.

Sea-water poured into the cabin in a great rush, immediately covering my knees. It was filthy, full of oil from the rig and freezing cold. The cargo netting that had been piled on the floor started to move, catching me in its folds. I felt the edge of fear. I struggled out of my seat, trying to fight my way clear of the clinging nylon. The more I fought, the more it seemed to clutch and drag me back.

The helicopter lurched again, the floor tilting upward at a 45-degree angle. Hauling myself up, I came out of the edge of the net and saw the loadie scrambling through the left-hand door ahead of me.

'Watch out – the blades are still turning!' I yelled.

The whole cabin stank of engine oil. The pilot was still in his seat, fiddling with the controls. We were all shut up in our own little private hells. I was climbing, but the water was up to my chest and still rising. I had to get out. The Huey was sinking fast. At that moment I saw the door by the commander open, and he dived out. The Huey was still vibrating horribly, the engines still trying to turn the broken blades.

There was a sickening roll, followed by another surge of oily water. The door I was aiming for was directly above my head, now, at an angle of 90 degrees to the sea: the sky looked so blue and close and yet impossibly far away. I pulled myself up the net towards it, the water following me and sucking me back. Just then, the sky disappeared and the whole weight of the cargo net fell back on me in a huge lump.

The Huey had flipped on to its back.

Now I felt something like panic. The cargo net ensnared me again. I went in the same direction I'd been moving in before. This was a mistake. I realized I was confused and struck out with all my strength the other way. The net plucked at me, clawing and suffocating. I felt something around my legs, dragging me down. I tried to shake it off and failed. I couldn't get out. Something was wrapped around my ankles, drowning me; I had to get free of it. I took a deep breath, and went down.

My hands met human hair. It was the interpreter. He had his hands wrapped tightly around my ankle, he was drowning, and he was taking me down with him. I grabbed his hair in a big fistful, and yanked up hard, at the same time shoving the netting away from us with great heaves of my free arm.

The helicopter wallowed, threatening to roll again, and then settled. Sea-water closed over my head. I had my eyes open, I was swimming. I could see bubbles, there was cargo netting all around me. I was pushing and heaving at it, determined to get free. I was holding something – what was it? There was a patch of light above me. I struck out frantically for the light with my legs and my free arm. My feet hit something solid – the roof. I kicked off against it as hard as I could. Suddenly I was clear of the entangling net. Reaching out, I felt a thick metal rail and grabbed hold. It was the skid. Only it was below me, not above. The Huey was sinking. Something flashed through my head: *I must get clear of the skid*. I had to breathe, my lungs were burning with the lack of air. I looked up and saw the surface of the water, waves lapping above my face. I felt a surge of hope. Pulling hard on the hair in my right hand, I struck out for the last time. I saw more light, it was all around, and then my hand broke the surface. Suddenly I was clear, gasping in air, right by one of the skids. The interpreter came up next to me with a great *whoosh!* shooting clear of the water and then bobbing back under. I hauled him up and we struggled there, treading water, whooping air. I saw boats closing towards us. Then I saw the pilot, still wearing his helmet, trying to shout and swallowing water at the same time. A helicopter came overhead, blinding us with its spray, and then pulled off.

The boats came up to us and hauled us aboard.

I had spent years dancing with death in the SAS, and here I was, still trying to cheat it.

As I lay there in the boat, coughing water, the soothsayer's prophecy came back to me. It was getting very near the deadline he'd set, on that bleak mountain with Bilbo back in Afghanistan. Soon, perhaps, the clock that ticks for all of us would beat me after all.